**THIRD EDITION**

K

# OUTCOMES
## ELEMENTARY

**Hugh Dellar**
**Andrew Walkley**

Australia · Brazil · Canada · Mexico · Singapore · United Kingdom · United States

**Contents** 3

| GRAMMAR | VOCABULARY | READING | LISTENING |
|---|---|---|---|
| • Present perfect questions (*been*, *tried*)<br>• Present perfect positive and negative | • Visiting places<br>• Words with different meanings | • A blog post about bucket lists | • A conversation between a local person and two tourists<br>• A radio show about experiences of getting help |
| • Explaining quantity<br>• *Me too*, *me neither* and auxiliaries | • In a restaurant<br>• Food | • An article about public health in Finland | • Two tourists order food in a restaurant<br>• Three conversations connected to food |
| • *Too much*, *too many* and *not enough*<br>• Superlatives | • Travel and tickets<br>• Guided tours | • An article about solutions to traffic problems | • A conversation in a train station ticket office<br>• Extracts from a guided tour |
| • *Should / Shouldn't*<br>• *Because*, *so*, *before* and *after* | • Health problems<br>• In the news<br>• Feelings | • Articles from local newspapers | • Five conversations about health problems<br>• A podcast about being happy |
| • *Be going to* and *might*<br>• Present perfect and *how long* | • Weather<br>• Animals | • A blog post giving strong opinions about where to live | • Three conversations where people make plans<br>• Three conversations about pets and animals |
| • *It's* + adjective + *to* + verb<br>• *Will / Won't* for predictions | • Describing films, plays and musicals<br>• Life in different places | • An article about people who have moved to different countries | • Two conversations about a film and a musical<br>• A news report |
| • *Be thinking of*<br>• Descriptive adverbs | • Choosing a phone<br>• What technology does<br>• Technology going wrong | • A newsletter describing three types of technology | • Two conversations where people ask for advice about buying things<br>• Four people answering questions about technology |
| • *Will / Won't* for promises<br>• Past continuous | • Love and relationships<br>• Promises | • Four poems about promises | • Four conversations about relationships<br>• Three people describe experiences of love at first sight |

**VOCABULARY REFERENCE page 191**   **INFORMATION FILES page 199**   **AUDIO SCRIPTS page 203**

# 1 People and places

**IN THIS UNIT, YOU:**

- have a conversation about yourself when you arrive in a place
- talk about what's good / bad about the place you're from
- talk about the jobs people in your class do

## SPEAKING

**1  Work in pairs. Discuss the questions.**

1  Look at the photo. Where are the people – in a café / on holiday / at home / at work / somewhere else?

2  Do the people know each other?

3  Do you like talking to people you don't know?

4  Do you know other people in your class?

**2  Look at these sentences. Which do you say when you first talk to someone you don't know?**

1  Hi. How are you?

2  Hi. I'm **Chet**. How are you?

3  Hi. I'm **Chet**. Nice to meet you.

4  Hi. Where do you work?

5  I'm **Chet**. I'm from **Thailand**.

6  I'm **Chet**. What's your name.

7  It's hot today, isn't it?

8  Are you enjoying **your trip**?

**3  Talk to different people in the class. Use sentences from Exercise 2. Change the words in purple.**

**4  Work in pairs. Say the names of other people in the class.**

*A: The man next to me is Chet, then the woman next to him is Andrea then you have Jan. I don't know the next woman.*

*B: I think her name is Maria.*

Travellers eat together in a hostel in Patagonia, Chile.

MENU
Sopa de
Verdura

Pure con el
Pollo + Rico

Espuma de
Limón

ANTARES x10

**1A**

# Where are you from?

**IN THIS LESSON, YOU:**
- have a conversation about yourself when you arrive in a place
- talk about where you're from and where places are
- practise listening to people talk about where they're from
- use the verb *be* to talk about yourself and others

## SPEAKING

1 ▶ **Work in pairs. Listen to the conversation between a taxi driver in Paris and a tourist. Then say it.**

A: Hi. How are you?
B: Good, thanks.
A: Where are you from?
B: **Spain**.
A: Oh, nice. Where exactly?
B: **Tarragona**. Do you know it?
A: No. Where is that?
B: It's in the **north-east**.
A: OK. Is it nice?
B: **Yeah**. I **like** it. It's **on the coast**.
A: Is this your first time in **Paris**?
B: No. It's my second time.
A: Well, welcome back!

2 **Change the words in purple. Use a dictionary if you need to. Then practise your new conversation with your partner. Exchange roles and repeat.**

## VOCABULARY Where?

**V** See Vocabulary reference 1A.

3 **Match the words in bold with the photos (a–i).**

1 I'm from Salvador in Brazil. It's **on the coast**.
2 I'm from Jinan **in the east** of China.
3 I'm from a place in the **north-west** of Italy. It's not far from Turin.
4 I'm from a little place **in the countryside**.
5 My mum is from Ghana in west **Africa**. She's from the capital, Accra.
6 My grandparents are from a little place **in the mountains**.
7 I'm from Japan. I'm from a quiet, little place on the south **island**, Kyushu.
8 They're from the west coast. It's a **rich** part of the country.
9 A lot of people from other **parts of Asia** visit Bali.

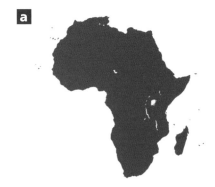

**4** 🄿 ▶ **Listen to the words from Exercise 3 and practise saying them on their own and in a phrase. Which words / phrases do you find hard to say? Practise saying them again.**

**5** **Work in pairs. Think of one or two places for different words in bold in Exercise 3.**

*Barcelona is on the coast. Rio de Janeiro is on the coast.*

*New York is in the east of the US. Kenya is in east Africa.*

## LISTENING

**6** ▶ **Listen to a conversation between a taxi driver (Gede) and a tourist (Nancy). Which of these places are they from?**

| | | | | |
|---|---|---|---|---|
| Bali | Denpasar | Koonara | Kuala Lumpur | Malaysia |
| the North | the South | Sydney | Thailand | the UK |

**7** ▶ **Listen again. Are the statements true (T) or false (F)?**

1  It's Nancy's first visit.
2  Nancy is tired after her flight.
3  Nancy's parents are from Kuala Lumpur.
4  Nancy is from a big city.
5  Nancy is a student.
6  Nancy doesn't like quiet places.

**8** **Work in pairs. Tell your partner about you and people you know. Use these words and patterns. Change the words in purple.**

1  I'm from **Turkey**, but I live in **Germany**.
2  I'm Spanish, but I was born in **Peru**.
3  My **dad** was born in **Liverpool**.
4  I was born in **Rome**, but I moved here when I was **two**.
5  My **sister** lives in **Chile**.

## DEVELOPING CONVERSATIONS

### Where exactly?

When people say where they live or where they're from, we sometimes ask *Where exactly?* to get more information – especially if you know the place.

*A: Where are you from?*

*B: I'm from Mexico.*

*A: Oh, OK. **Where exactly?***

*B: Chihuahua. Do you know it?*

**9** **Work in pairs. Have conversations using these ideas. Ask: *Where exactly?***

1  Argentina / Córdoba

   *A: Where are you from?*

   *B: Argentina.*

   *A: Where exactly?*

   *B: Córdoba. Do you know it?*

2  New Zealand / Wellington
3  Turkey / İzmir
4  the south of Italy / Bari
5  here / the north of the city

**10** **Work with a new partner. Have the conversations from Exercise 9 again and continue.**

*A: Córdoba. Do you know it?*

*B: Yes! My wife is from there. / Yes! It's really nice. / No. Where is that? / No. I only know Buenos Aires.*

## GRAMMAR

### Present simple *be*

In the present simple, *be* has three forms: **am** (short form *'m*), **are** (*'re*) and **is** (*'s*).

*I**'m** from Australia.*
*You**'re** / We**'re** / They**'re** late.*
*He**'s** / She**'s** / It**'s** / That**'s** American.*

We make a negative by adding **not** (**n't**).
*I**'m not** from here.*
*Bali **isn't** very big.*

To make questions, use *be* + subject (**Am I** / **Are you** / **Is it**, etc.).
***Are you** from here?*
*Where **is that**?*

**11** **Write complete sentences using the correct form of *be*.**

1  My name / Taylor.

   *My name is Taylor.*

2  I / not / good at English.
3  you / from Paris?
4  My grandmother / very old. She / 92.
5  She / from the South. It / not / a rich part of the country.
6  Mario / my boyfriend. We / not / married.
7  This / my first time here. it / always so hot?
8  How old / you? you / still at school?

**12** **Write sentences about you and your family with the verb *be*. How many different sentences can you write? Then work in groups. Compare your ideas.**

🄶 See Grammar reference 1A. ›››

## CONVERSATION PRACTICE

**13** 🄼 **Work in pairs. Roleplay conversations between a taxi driver and a tourist. Start the conversation like this and continue. Take turns to start.**

*A: Hi. Let me take your bag.*

*B: Thanks.*

*A: My name is _____ .*

*B: Hi. I'm _____ .*

# A nice place to live

## SPEAKING

**1** Work in pairs. Tell your partner:

1 your favourite place in the world.
2 your favourite place in your country.
3 your favourite place near where you live.

## VOCABULARY Describing places

**2** Work in pairs. Check you understand the words in bold. Use a dictionary if you need to.

1 It's nice to walk in the city because there are a lot of **lovely** parks and **trees**.
2 A **river** goes through the town, but people don't swim in it because the water is **dirty**.
3 It's on the coast, so I often go to the beach and swim in the **sea**. It's lovely and warm.
4 There's a new part of the city with a lot of tall, modern **buildings**.
5 It's quite **boring** because there's nowhere to go out at night.
6 A lot of **tourists** come here. We have a lot of famous old buildings.
7 It's quite **noisy** at night – restaurants and bars close late and there's a lot of traffic.
8 The beaches are quite dirty. There's a lot of **rubbish** on them.
9 There's a beautiful **bridge** over the river where tourists like to take photos.

**3** Which of the words in Exercise 2 describe your favourite places from Exercise 1?

## READING

**4** Work in pairs. What do you see in the photos on page 11? Where do you think the places are?

**5** Read how people introduce themselves on an online course on page 11. Match the people with the photos (a–d).

**6** Work in pairs. Read again. For each sentence, choose Jeff (J), William (W), Rocío (R) or Barbora (B).

1 Who lives in a city near nice countryside?
2 Who was born in a different place to where they live?
3 Who gets a lot of tourists in their city?
4 Who likes living in a quiet place?
5 Who likes going out to local bars and restaurants?
6 Who lives in a place which is never cold?
7 Who thinks their place is a bit boring?
8 Who swims outside in winter?

**7** **M** Work in groups. Say which place you like most / least and why.

## GRAMMAR

*There is / There are*

We use *there + be +* noun to explain what things a place has / doesn't have.

*There + is +* singular noun
**There's a** big supermarket.
**There isn't any** rubbish.
**Is there** a cinema near here?

*There + are +* plural noun
**There are** mountain**s** and a lot of quiet place**s**.
**There aren't** any big shop**s** or noisy bar**s**.
**Are there any** place**s** to go out at night?

**8** Look at the examples in the Grammar box. Complete the sentences with the correct form of *there is / there are*.

1 _____ an airport near here. You need to take the train.
2 _____ a university in your town?
3 _____ enough places for kids to play. _____ a park, but it's very small.
4 _____ a famous restaurant near here. It's very expensive!
5 _____ some beautiful buildings in the old part of the city.
6 _____ some nice little places to eat next to the river.
7 _____ a lot of rubbish on the streets near my house.
8 _____ any schools in the village. We go to the next town.

**9** Work in pairs. Complete the sentences with your own ideas about where your school is.

1 There's a good _____ near here.
2 There aren't any good _____ .
3 There aren't enough _____ .
4 I'm happy there isn't _____ here.
5 It's bad that _____ a lot of _____ here.
6 It's great that there _____ .

**G** See Grammar reference 1B.

**10** Work in groups. Compare your sentences from Exercise 9. Do you agree?

## SPEAKING

**11** Think about your answers to these questions. Write some notes. Use a dictionary if you need to.

1 What are the good / bad things about the place you are from or the place you live?
2 Which places in your country are very good / bad to live in? Why?

**12** Work in pairs. Discuss the questions in Exercise 11.

# READING

Hi, everyone! I'm Jeff, your teacher. Welcome to the course. Can you all say something about where you live? So, for example:

I live in a little place called New Romney on the south coast. I'm from London, but I moved here because my wife is from here and it's cheaper to live. The town has one main road with some small shops and restaurants. There's a big supermarket where people from other villages come to do shopping. But for me, there aren't enough things to do here. There's a beach, but I don't like swimming in the sea – it's too cold and a bit dirty.

Hi! I'm William. I'm a student in Cuiabá. I was born here. People from outside Brazil often don't know Cuiabá, but it's quite big. It's famous for its food and culture. Now, there are quite a lot of tall buildings and there's a big modern stadium, but I like the old parts of the city and all the parks and trees. Cuiabá is the capital of the Mato Grosso region, which has lots of beautiful rivers and forests. It's very hot here all year and it rains a lot from October to April.

Hi, I'm Rocío. I live in a little village in the north-east of Spain called Arnedillo. I went to university in Zaragoza but I prefer it here. There aren't any big shops or noisy bars. People from other parts of Spain and Europe visit here because there are beautiful mountains and quiet places to relax. Arnedillo is also famous for natural hot water and I sometimes go in the river in the winter when it's 0 degrees outside.

Hi. I'm Barbora. I'm from Prague, the beautiful capital of the Czech Republic. I live in the centre, not far from the famous Charles Bridge. People from all over the world come here. My parents are sometimes unhappy because they say there's rubbish from the tourists and it's noisy at night because places close late. But I don't agree with them – I don't think it's dirty and it's good to have lots of places to meet friends at night.

# What do you do?

**IN THIS LESSON, YOU:**
- talk about the jobs people in your class do
- say what you like / don't like about jobs
- practise listening to people asking about what other people do
- ask and answer questions about your normal life now

A shop in Chennai, south India.

## VOCABULARY Work

V See Vocabulary reference 1C.

1 **Work in groups. How many jobs can you write in English in one minute?**

2 **Work in pairs. Match the descriptions (1–6) with the jobs (a–f).**

1 I work in a local school – ten minutes from my home. I love it. It's **hard work**. The children are noisy sometimes, but it's great when they learn new things.

2 I work in a big clothes shop in town. I'm interested in **fashion** and I enjoy helping **customers**. But the money's not very good – I need to **earn** more.

3 I work in lots of different places. I enjoy meeting people and **showing** them our beautiful country, but I work **long hours**. I sometimes travel with a group for one week and I work from seven in the morning till ten at night.

4 I work in the centre of town. I enjoy the job **most of the time**. It's nice when I can help people, but sometimes it's **dangerous** and you see sad things.

5 I work in a small company that makes computers. I answer emails. It's a job – it's not very interesting but the money's OK. My **boss** is nice and I like **the other people** at work.

6 I **look after** my baby and two-year-old boy. It's hard work because I'm **alone** with them most of the time and don't have any help.

a  a parent
b  a teacher
c  a tour guide
d  an office worker
e  a police officer
f  a shop assistant

3 **Work in groups. Say which is better.**

1 a job that is always boring or a job that is sometimes dangerous

2 having a good boss or being the boss

3 working in the same place or travelling a lot for work

4 being an office worker or looking after little kids at home

5 working alone or working with lots of other people

6 working long hours and earning a lot or having more free time and earning less

## LISTENING

4 FS ▶ *Do you* can sound different in slow and fast speech. Listen to five questions said twice. Which is faster: a or b?

5 ▶ **Listen to four conversations about jobs. What job does each person do?**

1  Jana
2  Lewis
3  Marta
4  Marc

6 ▶ **Listen again. Are the statements true (T) or false (F)?**

1 Jana works in a hospital in Warsaw.
2 She doesn't enjoy it.
3 Lewis teaches English in a school in Bristol.
4 He enjoys his job all of the time.
5 Marta works in an office in Cali.
6 She doesn't work long hours.
7 Marc doesn't like his job now.
8 Marc is a police officer.

**7** Work in pairs. Ask and answer these questions. Use the ideas in Exercise 2.

1 What do you do?

2 Where do you work?

3 Do you enjoy it?

*A: What do you do?*

*B: I'm a guide.*

*A: Oh, yes? Where do you work?*

*B: Lots of places. I travel with people and show them different places.*

*A: Do you enjoy it?*

*B: Yes, most of the time. I like meeting new people, but sometimes I work very long hours.*

## GRAMMAR

### Present simple

Use the present simple to talk about people's normal life now – their home, their job, their likes, their habits.
*I **work** in Cali.*
*She **works** in an office.*

We make the negative using *don't / doesn't* + verb.
*I **don't speak** French.*
*He **doesn't like** his job now.*

For questions, use *do / does* + subject + verb.
*Where **do you work**?*
***Does your town have** any museums?*

**8** Look at the examples in the Grammar box. How are the forms different for talking about *he / she / it*?

**9** Complete the text with the present simple form of the verbs in brackets.

My wife ¹_____ (work) for a local newspaper. I ²_____ (not see) her a lot because she ³_____ (do) very long hours. She ⁴_____ (get up) early and she sometimes works all night. When she ⁵_____ (have) free time, we ⁶_____ (not go) out because she only ⁷_____ (want) to sleep! But she ⁸_____ (not want) a different job because her job ⁹_____ (be) very interesting and she ¹⁰_____ (like) it a lot.

**10** Write about three people you know, answering the questions in Exercise 7. Then tell a partner.

*My friend Juan is a shop assistant. He works in a bookshop. He doesn't like it. He says it's boring and he doesn't earn enough money.*

**11** Put the words in the correct order to make questions.

1 A: What / do / do / you / in / your free time ?

B: I look after my dog, I watch videos. I sometimes read.

2 A: Who / with / you / do / live ?

B: I live alone.

3 A: How / come / do / to class / you ?

B: I drive here.

4 A: What time / you / do / get up ?

B: At half past seven.

5 A: When / to bed / you / go / do ?

B: At about 12 o'clock most nights.

6 A: How many / languages / you / speak / do ?

B: Two – French and Arabic.

**12** Work in pairs. Ask and answer the questions in Exercise 11.

**G** See Grammar reference 1C.                            ⟫⟫

## SPEAKING TASK

**13** **M** You're going to find out information about the people in your class. Follow the instructions:

1 Work in pairs. Decide what question(s) you need to ask to find out the information for a–f.

a How many people are from the same place?

*Where are you from?*

b Who lives close to each other now?

c Do most people like where they live?

d Does anyone do the same job or work together?

e Do most people enjoy their job?

f Does anyone want a different / new job?

2 Ask your questions to people in the class.

3 With your partner, compare what you learned about the other people in the class. Can you answer questions a–f?

## ■ MY OUTCOMES ■

**Work in pairs. Discuss the questions.**

1 What did you enjoy talking about in class?

2 What words and phrases about people and places did you learn?

3 What part of this unit was easy / difficult for you?

4 How much time do you have to practise English this week?

# 2
# Daily life

**IN THIS UNIT, YOU:**

- plan where and when to meet
- talk about what you do in your free time
- explain how much time you spend doing things

## SPEAKING

**1** **Work in pairs. Discuss the questions.**

1 Look at the photo. What are the people doing?

2 What are two things you like doing with friends in your free time – and two things you like doing on your own? Use a dictionary if you need to.

**2** **Tell your partner which sentences are true for you.**

1 Reading is boring.

2 Watching TV is interesting.

3 Going to concerts is expensive.

4 Shopping is great.

5 I'm good at dancing.

6 I'm not very good at sports.

**3** **Change one part of each sentence in Exercise 2 to make six sentences that are true for you.**

*Reading is great. / Cooking is boring.*

**4** **Work with a new partner. Share your ideas. Does your partner agree?**

Many people like having picnics in the parks of Ankara, Turkey.

# Do you want to come?

## SPEAKING

1 ▶ **Work in pairs. Listen to the conversation. Then say it.**

A: Do you like **sports**?

B: Yeah, I do.

A: Oh, great. Do you want to **play basketball** tonight?

B: OK. What time?

A: Is **seven** OK?

B: Yeah, fine. Where do you want to meet?

A: **In the park near the station**.

B: OK. See you later.

2 **Change the words in purple. Use a dictionary if you need to. Then practise your new conversation with your partner. Exchange roles and repeat.**

## LISTENING

3 **Look at the people in the pictures. What activities do you think they like / don't like?**

4 ▶ **Listen to the two people talking about what they do in their free time. Complete the table with DL (= doesn't like), OK (= thinks it's OK) and L (= loves).**

| | Woman | Man |
|---|---|---|
| doing sports | 1 L | 2 DL |
| walking | 3 OK | DL |
| playing video games | 4 DL | 5 L |
| going to the cinema | L | 6 L |

5 **Work in pairs. Ask each other *Do you like …?* questions. Reply with *I love it*; *It's OK*; or *No, not really*.**

A: Do you like reading?

B: Yes, I do. I love it. What about you?

A: I love it too. Do you like cooking?

B: It's OK, but I'm not very good at it. What about you?

## GRAMMAR

### Verb patterns (-ing or infinitive with to)

a After some verbs, we use the -ing form.

I really <u>enjoy</u> **playing** tennis.

b After some verbs, we use the infinitive with to.

Do you <u>want</u> **to see** I Want You Back?

6 **Look at the Grammar box. Which of these sentences are the same as pattern a? Which are the same as pattern b?**

1 He really <u>likes</u> <u>swimming</u>. a

2 I <u>need</u> to <u>go</u> now. b

3 I <u>love</u> <u>working</u> from home. a

4 I want to <u>learn</u> to drive. b

5 Try to <u>use</u> the words you <u>learn</u>. b

6 I hate <u>living</u> in the city. a

7 **Write complete sentences using the notes.**

1 My daughter / want / get / a new phone.

2 you / like / dance?

3 I / try / study English / every day.

4 I / not / enjoy / shop.

5 We / need / buy / some things later.

6 I / really hate / cook.

8 **Complete the sentences to make them true for you.**

1 I love *Playing football*

2 I don't really like *to cook*.

3 This week I need *to take rest*

4 I want to learn _____ .

5 I don't really enjoy _____ .

**G** See Grammar reference 2A.

## DEVELOPING CONVERSATIONS

### Making plans

We can make future plans using the present simple.

A: **Do** you **want** to go shopping on Saturday?

B: OK. What time?

A: **Is** ten OK?

B: Yeah, fine. Where **do** you **want** to meet?

A: Outside the book shop on Main Street.

B: Great. See you then.

**9** Match these questions with the pairs of possible answers in 1–5.

Do you like going to the cinema?
Do you want to see the new *Avatar* film on Sunday?
What time does the film end?
What time do you want to meet?
Where?

1 A: *What time do you want to meet?*
  B: Is four good? / Is seven OK? The film starts at eight.

2 A: *What time does the film end?*
  B: I'm not sure. About seven, I think. / About 11:30.
  It's a long film.

3 A: *Do you like going to the cinema*
  B: OK, that sounds nice. / Sorry, I'm busy then.
  *4*

4 A: *Do you want to see the new Avatar film on sunday* *3*
  B: Yes, it's OK. / No, not really.

5 A: ~~Were~~ *Where*
  B: Outside the train station. / Outside the cinema.

**10** ▶ Listen to two conversations where Declan makes plans with his friends. Choose the correct words to complete the notes.

| **25**<br>SAT | ▮ Watch ¹*match* / film with Cara<br>▮ Meet outside ²café / *North Street station* at<br> ³four / *five* o'clock |
| **26**<br>SUN | ▮ Lunch with Tina<br>▮ ⁴French / *Italian* restaurant<br>▮ Meet ⁵*one* / two o'clock outside the<br> ⁶*station* / restaurant |

**11** Work in pairs. Which of the two days in the conversations do you think sounds best – Saturday or Sunday? Why?

## CONVERSATION PRACTICE

**12** Decide two things you want to do at the weekend (on Friday night, Saturday or Sunday). Decide where you want to meet and when.

**13** M Work in pairs. Roleplay conversations about making plans. Agree to do something together at the weekend.

Friends meet in a café on a cold day in London, UK.

# I usually finish at five

**IN THIS LESSON, YOU:**
- talk about what you do in your free time
- discuss daily activities
- explain how often you do things
- read an article about how people spend their free time

## VOCABULARY Daily activities

**V** See Vocabulary reference 2B.

1 **When do people usually do the activities below? Put them in the three groups in the table.**

| check your phone | do homework | do some exercise |
| get home from work | go to bed | go to the supermarket |
| have a coffee | have a little sleep | have a shower |
| leave work | prepare dinner | tidy your flat / house |

| in the morning | in the afternoon | in the evening |
| --- | --- | --- |
|  |  |  |

2 **Work in pairs. Compare your answers. Do you agree?**

## GRAMMAR

### Adverbs of frequency

We use some adverbs to show how often we do something. We usually use them before the main verb in a sentence.

I **always** have a shower in the morning.

I **usually** go to bed at midnight.

3 **Complete the table with these adverbs.**

| always | never | often | sometimes |

| | |
| --- | --- |
| 100% | 1_____ |
| | usually |
| | 2_____ |
| | 3_____ |
| | not often |
| 0% | 4_____ |

4 **Tick (✓) the sentences that are true for you. Change the adverbs in the other sentences to make them true for you.**
1 I always check my phone in the morning.
2 I sometimes have a little sleep after lunch.
3 I never have a coffee in the evening.
4 I don't often read the news.
5 I often listen to music when I go to bed.
6 I sometimes go to rock concerts.
7 I always do my homework for my English class.
8 I usually go swimming at the weekend.

5 **Work in groups. Take turns to say your sentences. Who is the most similar to you?**

6 **Write four true sentences using these phrases and an adverb. Then say them to a partner.**
1 cook dinner for friends
2 use English outside class
3 go to the cinema
4 work at the weekend

**G** See Grammar reference 2B.

## READING

7 **M** **Read the article on page 19 about how four people spend their free time. Then work in pairs. Discuss these questions.**
1 Who is most similar to you? Why?
2 Who do you think is the happiest person? Why?

8 **Read again. Answer the questions.**
1 Who plays a sport?
2 Who spends a lot of money?
3 Who is usually tired at the weekend?
4 Who likes watching TV?
5 Who enjoys being outside?
6 Who has a busy social life?
7 Who goes to bed quite early?
8 Who has friends who like different things?

9 **Complete the sentences with the prepositions in bold in the article.**
1 I always go running _____ Sunday mornings.
2 I don't usually work _____ Fridays. It's great. I get up _____ 9 or 10.
3 I sometimes have a little sleep _____ the afternoon.
4 We don't usually do much _____ the weekend.
5 The film starts _____ 8 and ends _____ 10:30.
6 I'm usually very tired _____ the morning. I need to have a coffee!

## SPEAKING

10 **Work in groups. Discuss the questions.**
1 What do you usually do on Friday nights?
2 What do you usually do on Saturdays?
3 What do you usually do on Sundays?
4 Do you go out in the evening during the week? When? What do you do?

Playing basketball in the park in Bologna, Italy.

# TELL US ABOUT YOUR
# FREE TIME

Many of us spend most of our time working or studying. Then there's sleeping, eating and sitting on buses or trains! So how much free time do our readers around the world have? And what do they do in it? Here's what they told us:

### → ERASMO, **MEXICO**

I do something most nights. **On** Mondays and Wednesdays, I go to my English class, and on Tuesdays, I usually go to the cinema with friends, because the tickets are cheap then. On Thursdays, I always go to the gym. I usually go out dancing on Saturday nights. I often get home **at** four or five in the morning, so on Sundays, I sleep! I sometimes get up at three **in** the afternoon.

### → LENA, **SWITZERLAND**

Free time? I don't have any free time because I have my own business. I sometimes go to rock concerts, but not very often – maybe once or twice a year – and I sometimes go shopping at the weekend. I like buying nice things with the money I make. I have an expensive new car and a very big TV. I like watching sport.

### → IBRAHIM, **EGYPT**

I'm a student and I'm lucky because I have a lot of free time. I try to do some exercise most days. I often go running in the morning and on Tuesdays and Thursdays I play basketball in the park. I usually prepare dinner for my family. I like cooking and everyone says I'm good at it. My friends often play video games, but I don't like them. In the evening, I usually tidy my room, answer emails and then read.

### → MALEE, **THAILAND**

I don't go out much during the week. I usually study for two hours in the evening. I never watch TV, really. I usually play the piano every day. It helps me relax. Then I go to bed at nine or ten and listen to music. **At** the weekend, I go out with my family to a park or to the countryside, and we go for a walk. I sometimes go to a shopping centre with friends, but I don't usually buy much!

**Unit 2** Daily life **19**

## 2C

# A lot of homework!

## SPEAKING

**1 Work in pairs. Discuss the questions.**

1 Do you like doing courses in your free time?

2 Is this your first English course?

3 Do you like:

  a doing homework?

  b watching films or TV shows in English?

  c listening to songs in English?

  d reading in English?

  e finding new words in a dictionary?

  f practising your pronunciation?

## VOCABULARY In the classroom

**V See Vocabulary reference 2C.**

**2 Match the first part of the phrases with the second part. Match 1–4 with a–d and 5–8 with e–h.**

| | | | |
|---|---|---|---|
| 1 | write | a | to the front / in and sit down 4 |
| 2 | **turn off** | b | your phones / the light 2 |
| 3 | take | c | in **pencil** / it in your **notebook** 1 |
| 4 | come | d | a break / **notes** 3 |
| 5 | check | e | your **scissors** / a **rubber** 6 |
| 6 | use | f | the answers / the **meaning** in your dictionary 5 |
| 7 | **bring** | g | and find a new partner / and move around the room 8 |
| 8 | **stand up** | h | a pen tomorrow / it here 7 |

**3 P ▶ Listen to the words in bold from Exercise 2 and practise saying them on their own and in a phrase. Which words / phrases do you find hard to say? Practise saying them again.**

**4 Work in pairs. Take turns to practise.**

**Student A:** Don't look at Exercise 2.

**Student B:** Say a verb from Exercise 2, e.g. *write*.

**Student A:** Say a phrase, e.g. *write in pencil*.

## LISTENING

**5 ▶ Listen to three conversations in an English class. Which conversation (1–3) happens:**

  a at the beginning of the class? 3

  b in the middle of the class? 1

  c at the end of the class? 2

**6 FS ▶ In fast speech, the word *is* sometimes sounds like /ɪz/, but often we use the contracted form *'s* and you just hear /z/ or /s/. Listen to eight sentences from the conversations. Which include *is* / *'s*?**

**7 ▶ Listen again. Are the statements true (T) or false (F)?**

1 Kasia has money for two coffees. T

2 The break is 25 minutes long. F

3 They need to do two exercises for homework and learn some words. T

4 Simon wants a lot of homework. F

5 Simon sits next to Kasia. T

6 Kasia gives him her dictionary. F

**8 Work in pairs. Discuss the questions.**

1 Do you think Kasia and Simon are good or bad students? Why?

2 Do you like the way Matty teaches? Why? / Why not?

3 How often:

  a are you late?

  b do you forget things?

  c do you do homework?

## GRAMMAR

### Countable and uncountable nouns

**Countable nouns** have both singular and plural forms, e.g. *pencil / pencils* and *book / books*.

Before singular countable nouns, we usually use *a / an*. *Do you have **a pencil**?*

Before plural countable nouns, we can use *some, a lot of, many* and *any*. *I try to watch **some films** in English.*

**Uncountable nouns** have no plural form, e.g. *food, help* and *music*.
Before uncountable nouns, we can use *some, a lot of, much* and *any*. We don't use *a / an*. *I have **a lot of work** to do.* *I don't have **much free time**.*

**9 Write down all the countable and all the uncountable nouns you see in these sentences.**

1 Do you have an **exam today**? C

2 Do you need any **help**? U

3 I need some **paper to take some notes**. U

4 There's a lot of **rubbish in the street**. U

5 I want to be a **teacher**. C

6 There's some **very nice countryside near here**. U

7 We don't have much **time. We need to be quick**. U

8 We don't have many **tourists here**. C

9 There are a lot of **parks in my town**. C

10 Do we have any **homework for tomorrow**? U

**10** Work in pairs. Look at Exercise 9 again. For each sentence, change the words in purple to use a different noun.

**11** Write questions to ask other students. Use these ideas. Then work in groups. Ask and answer your questions.

1  Do you have a / an _apple_ ?
2  Do you have any _time_ ?
3  Do you have many _jobs_ ?

**G** See Grammar reference 2C.

## SPEAKING TASK

**12** You're going to find out about the daily / weekly activities of people in your class. Work in pairs. Write four questions to ask about study habits and free-time activities.

*How much time do you spend doing homework?*

*How much time do you spend watching TV?*

**13** **M** Talk to other students in the class. Ask your questions and give answers. Use these phrases to help you answer.

*(Quite) a lot – maybe two or three hours a day.*

*Some, but not a lot – maybe fifteen minutes a day.*

*Not a lot – maybe an hour a week.*

*Not really any.*

**14** Work in pairs again. Tell your partner what you remember. What is the most popular activity?

## MY OUTCOMES

**Work in pairs. Discuss the questions.**

1  Which reading or listening texts were most interesting? Why?
2  What can you now say about free-time activities?
3  How much language in this unit was new for you?
4  What can you do at home to practise language from this unit?

# Completing forms

**IN THIS LESSON, YOU:**
- complete an online application form
- learn questions that ask for information about people
- talk about things from different countries
- explain your reasons for taking a course

## SPEAKING

**1** Match the questions (1–7) with the answers (a–g).

1 What's your first name?
2 What's your surname?
3 Do you have a middle name?
4 Where are you from?
5 Where do you live?
6 What's your phone number?
7 When were you born?

a Yeah, I do. It's Sebastian, but I don't really use it. **3**
b 1987. October the fourth. **7**
c Abbott. **2**
d In Dublin. 25 Cook Street. **5**
e David. **1**
f Canada. I'm Canadian. **4**
g It's 07791–73–119. **6**

**2** Work in pairs. Take turns to ask and answer the questions in Exercise 1.

## WRITING

**3** Complete the application form for an online language school with these words.

| | | |
|---|---|---|
| Address | Date of birth | Email address |
| First name(s) | Nationality | Surname |
| Telephone number | Title | |

## USEFUL LANGUAGE

### Countries and nationalities

We use both noun and adjective forms to talk about which country we're from.

*I'm from* **France**. (France is the country. It's a noun.)

*I'm* **French**. (French is the nationality. It's an adjective.)

We also use these nationality adjectives to describe food, people, etc.

*I love* **Mexican** *food.*

*I live with two* **Australian** *women and a* **Polish** *man.*

**4** Complete the table.

| Country | Nationality |
|---|---|
| Brazil | ¹Brazilon |
| ²Egypt | Egyptian |
| ³Italiy | Italian |
| Japan | ⁴Japanes |
| ⁵Maxico | Mexican |
| ⁶Oman | Omani |
| Peru | ⁷_____ |
| Poland | ⁸Polash |
| ⁹Spain | Spanish |
| ¹⁰_____ | Thai |
| Turkey | ¹¹_____ |
| ¹²_____ | Vietnamese |

## THE FINSBURY SCHOOL:
### Helping the world learn languages

¹ Sushame Abbott
² First name David Sebastian
³ Title  Mr ☑  Mrs ☐  Ms ☐  Miss ☐
   Other ☐
⁴ Nationality Canadian
⁵ Date of birth 4 October 1987
⁶ Address 25 Cook Street, Dublin, Ireland
Telephone number 07779173119
Email address davidabbott87@email.com

Reason you want to do this course:

I travel to Zurich, Switzerland a lot for work. They speak German there. I love meeting new people too. German can help me do this.

**5** Work in pairs. Discuss what you can see in the photos.

*A: Is that a Spanish beach?*
*B: No. I think it might be in Brazil.*

**6** Work in groups. Discuss the questions.

1 Can you think of famous people from each of the countries in Exercise 4?

2 Do you have friends from any of these countries? If yes, who?

3 What do you know about the different kinds of food from each country?

4 Do you know any other famous things from each country?

## Writing sentences

Sentences start with a capital letter and end with a full stop (.) or another punctuation mark (! or ?).

Sentences in English often follow a subject–verb–object pattern. The verb matches the subject.

*They speak German there.* (*They* = subject, *speak* = verb, *German* = object)

**7** Put the words in brackets in the correct place in the sentence. Use a capital letter if necessary.

1 I the language. (love)

2 partner is from Canada. (my)

3 I want to visit next year. (New Zealand)

4 I want to read in English. (books)

5 need English for my job. (i)

6 I want to a good job. (get)

**8** Write four true sentences about yourself. Use these ideas.

- Something you love
- Where you / your partner is from
- Something you want to do
- Something you need

## PRACTICE

**9** Complete the application form for an online English course with your own information.

Surname: Alrashed

First name(s): Faisal

Title:  Mr ☑  Mrs ❑  Ms ❑  Miss ❑

Other ❑

Nationality: Saudi

Date of birth: 5/10/2001   01

Address: saudi, Dammam

Telephone number: +966 560651818

Email address: faesl.2001@gmail.com

Reason you want to do this course: study English

~~becose~~ I want to ~~looking~~ for a job, because ~~of~~ all jobs in my contry need English. country

**10** 🅼 Work in pairs. Read your partner's form. Do they do the following? Tell your partner.

- Is the information in the right place?
- Is the spelling correct – including capital letters?
- Do the sentences in the last section follow the subject–verb–object pattern?
- Are there full stops in the right places?

**11** With your partner, compare your forms. How similar are your reasons for wanting to do an English course?

## VIDEO Out and about

1 Work in groups. What's your hometown like?

### Understanding accents

Some accents use a /z/ sound instead of a /ð/ sound, so *then* /ðen/ may sound more like *zen* /zen/.

2 Watch four people answer the same question. Then work in pairs. How much can you remember about they said? Which place sounds most similar to where you live?

3 Watch again. Match two sentences with each speaker.

a There are lots of different things to do there.

b It's near the mountains.

c It's a nice size – not too big and not too small.

d It's cold in the winter and hot in the summer.

e I live in the capital.

f It's a small city, but I really like it.

g I'm from a village.

h I go to college there – and I really love my college.

4 Work in groups. Discuss the questions.

1 Are there lots of different things to do where you live?

2 What's your favourite thing to do where you live?

3 Do you ever go to the mountains? What do you do there?

4 What's good about living in the capital of your country?

5 What's good about living in a village?

## VIDEO Developing conversations

5 You're going to watch two people arranging to go out. Watch and take notes on what they say.

6 Work in pairs. Compare what you understood. Watch again if you need to.

7 FS Watch again. Complete the sentences with two words in each gap.

1 Do you _____ go for a run at the weekend?

2 I really enjoy it, but I'm not _____ .

3 I like _____ late on Sundays.

4 _____ the café inside the park?

5 We could _____ a coffee after our run.

6 I _____ with my whole family.

7 Do you _____ on Saturday?

8 So you can go to _____ , then.

## CONVERSATION PRACTICE

8 Work in pairs. You're going to practise a conversation.

1 Choose a Conversation practice from either Lesson 1A or Lesson 2A.

2 Look at the language in that lesson.

3 Check the meaning of anything you don't remember with your partner.

4 Have the conversation. Try to do it better than the last time you did it.

# Grammar and Vocabulary

## GRAMMAR

**1 Choose the correct option to complete the sentences.**

1 A: Where *are* / *is* he from?
   B: France.

2 A: Do you want *to go* / *going* to the cinema later?
   B: OK. What time?

3 A: Do you have *a* / *any* paper?
   B: Yes, but I don't have *a* / *any* pen.

4 A: *Are* / *Is* you OK?
   B: Yes, I'm fine thanks.

5 A: Do you like *play* / *playing* tennis?
   B: Yes, I *love* / *loves* it.

6 A: *Does* / *Is* your town big?
   B: Not really. There *is* / *are* only about 10,000 people.

7 A: What *you do* / *do you do* at the weekend?
   B: I usually stay at home. I *don't* / *I'm not* earn much money.

8 A: *Do* / *Does* your son like basketball?
   B: He *love* / *loves* watching, but he doesn't play very *often* / *sometimes*.

**2 Write full questions to complete the conversation. Use the words in brackets.**

A: ¹_____ ? (what / do)
B: I'm a doctor.
A: ²_____ ? (where / work)
B: At a hospital in the north of Rome.
A: ³_____ ? (enjoy / it)
B: Yes. It's a great job.

**3 Put the words in brackets in the correct place in the sentences.**

1 I need do some shopping. (to)
2 I play computer games. (never)
3 Sorry, I understand. What does *receptionist* mean? (don't)
4 I don't know English. (much)
5 Is a palace near the river. It's beautiful. (there)
6 She speaks English very well, but she's from the UK. (not)

**4 ▶ Listen and write the six sentences you hear. Include these words.**

1 you / money
2 need / help
3 time / want
4 there / places to visit
5 I / need / homework
6 gets up / six / work / seven

## VOCABULARY

**5 Match the two parts of the phrases.**

1 check
2 have
3 turn off
4 do
5 leave
6 go
7 bring
8 look after

a my homework / some exercise
b work / at six in the morning
c to bed / shopping
d it here / your books tomorrow
e my baby / my grandmother
f a shower / a little sleep
g the meaning in a dictionary / your answers
h your phone / the TV

**6 Decide if these words and phrases are about places, work or everyday activities. There are four items in each group.**

| boss | building | countryside | customers |
|------|----------|-------------|-----------|
| earn | island | long hours | mountains |
| prepare dinner | sit down | stand up | tidy my flat |

**7 Choose the correct option to complete the sentences.**

1 I live in a small town on the *countryside* / *coast*.
2 It's not a very nice area. It's really *dirty* / *clean*.
3 I want you to listen and *bring* / *take* notes.
4 It's a difficult job. It's very *easy* / *dangerous*.
5 There's a lot of traffic. It's very *noisy* / *quiet* sometimes.
6 I usually *leave* / *get* home from work at six in the evening.
7 A *river* / *building* goes through the town. I swim there in the summer.
8 Come with me. I want to *take* / *show* you something.

**8 Complete the text with these words.**

| boring | east | fashion | lovely |
|--------|------|---------|--------|
| other | part | rubbish | trees |

I work in a very nice ¹_____ of the city. It's in the ²_____ and it's a really ³_____ area. There are lots of beautiful buildings and ⁴_____ there. It's very clean. I never see any ⁵_____ in the street. I work in ⁶_____ and I really like my job. The ⁷_____ people in my office are great – they're all really nice. The money's good and the work is never ⁸_____ .

# 3 Home

## IN THIS UNIT, YOU:

- ask and answer questions about local shops and other places

- talk about home and what you like / don't like about it

- ask someone for help with a problem in a shared house

## SPEAKING

**1 Work in pairs. Look at the photo and read about it. Discuss the questions.**

1 Would you buy a house here for 1 euro? Why? / Why not?

2 Why do you think the houses are so cheap?

3 Are there any places like this in your country? Where?

**2 Work with a new partner. Which of these things is important to you for a place to live?**

a It has a big kitchen.

b Everyone has their own bedroom.

c It has an outside space.

d It's very near some shops. I can walk there.

e It has good transport – train, metro, bus – to go to different places.

f It's in the countryside.

g It has a place for my bike / car.

**3 With your partner, say one more thing that is important to you.**

The government of Gangi, a small village in Sicily, sold this house for just one euro.

## 3A

# Is there one near here?

**IN THIS LESSON, YOU:**
- ask and answer questions about local shops and other places
- practise listening to people asking and saying where things are
- explain exactly what you want to get or do
- explain exactly where things are

## SPEAKING

1 ▶ Work in pairs. Listen to the conversation between two people in the street. Then say it.

A: I want to **buy some gifts for my family**. Is there a **market** near here?

B: There's one on New Street.

A: OK. Where's that?

B: So this is High Street. Go to the end and turn left. That's New Street. The **market** is **opposite the station**.

A: OK. Thank you.

2 **Change the words in purple. Use a dictionary if you need to. Then practise your new conversation with your partner. Exchange roles and repeat.**

## VOCABULARY Places for things you need

3 Match the places (1–6) with reasons you go there (a–f).

1 I'm looking for a **bookshop**.

2 Is there a **chemist** near here?

3 It's a big **department store**.

4 I need to go to the **library**.

5 Is there a **post office** near here?

6 There's a **sports centre** near here.

a I need some **shorts**. / I want to buy some gifts.

b I don't have anything to read. / I want to get a **birthday card**.

c I need a **quiet place** to study. / I need a book for school.

d I need to do some exercise. / I'd like to go **swimming**.

e I want to send someone a gift. / I need to **change some money**.

f I **forgot** my toothbrush. / I have a headache.

4 🅿 ▶ **Listen to the words from Exercise 3 and practise saying them on their own and in a phrase. Which words / phrases do you find hard to say? Practise saying them again.**

5 Work in groups. Do the following:

1 Say how often you go to each place in Exercise 3.

2 Say what you usually buy or do in each place.

3 Say a time when you forgot something.

## LISTENING

6 ▶ Listen to three people ask about places. Where do they want to go?

7 ▶ Listen again. How do you get to the three places? Choose the correct option to complete the sentences.

**Conversation 1**

1 It's in the street behind. Go out of the building and turn right / _left_.

2 It's next to a _food shop_ / bookshop.

**Conversation 2**

3 You need to take a number _15_ / 50 bus.

4 Go to the end of the road and turn _right_ / left. The stop is in front of a pool / _school_.

**Conversation 3**

5 Jeffer's is on _High_ / Eighth Street in the _centre_ / south of the city.

6 It's next to a shop which sells clothes / _is closed_.

## DEVELOPING CONVERSATIONS

### Asking for information

When we ask people about places, we often explain why we want to go there. They can then give us other ideas.

A: _Is there a bookshop near here?_ **I forgot my book and I don't have anything to read.**

B: **No, sorry, but maybe try** Jeffer's. It's a department store.

8 **Work in pairs. Look at the reasons to go to places in Exercise 3. Where can you go for these things near your school?**

9 **Work with a new partner. Take turns to ask _Is there a(n) … near here?_ and explain why. Answer with places you know.**

A: _Is there a bookshop near here? I want to buy a birthday card._

B: _Yeah, there's one on Second Avenue. / No, but try Antonio's. It's a newspaper shop. I think they sell cards._

## GRAMMAR

### Prepositions of place

We use these prepositions and phrases with prepositions to describe where things are:

_at   behind   between   in   in front of   next to   on   opposite_

It's **at the end of** the road.

There's one **behind** here.

The stop is **in front of** a school.

There's a small food shop **on the corner** and the chemist is **next to** that.

**10** Look at the map and the first sentence with the preposition. Then complete the second sentence with the name of the place.

1 There's a pool **in** the sports centre. There's a museum **in** The Park .

2 There's a factory **behind** the station. There's a Car Park **behind** the bank.

3 You can find a taxi **in front of** the station. There's a Bus stop **in front of** the sports centre.

4 The library is **on the corner** near the station. There's a supermarket **on the corner** of Park Avenue and Second Street, next to the bank.

5 There's a chemist in the shopping centre **next to** a shoe shop. The theatre **is next to** a Hotel .

6 There's a path to the car park **between** the cinema **and** the bank. On Saturdays, there's a market in the main square **between** the library **and** the government building.

7 The sports centre is **opposite** the stadium. The theatre is **opposite** Green Park

8 The government building is **at the end of** Park Avenue. The hotel is **at the end of** East Street.

**11** Work in pairs. Look at the map. Ask and answer questions to find places.

*A: Is there a post office near here?*

*B: Yes, there's one opposite the shopping centre.*

**G** See Grammar reference 3A.

## CONVERSATION PRACTICE

**12** You're going to roleplay asking about places in a town. Write five places you want to find and the reason why.

**13** **M** Work in pairs. Choose one of these tasks. Take turns to start.

a Tell your partner where you are looking for and ask how to get there. Your partner needs to give true answers and explain where the place is / how to get there.

b Use the map in this lesson. Imagine you're in the café in the main square. Tell your partner where you want to go and why. Your partner needs to explain where the place is / how to get there.

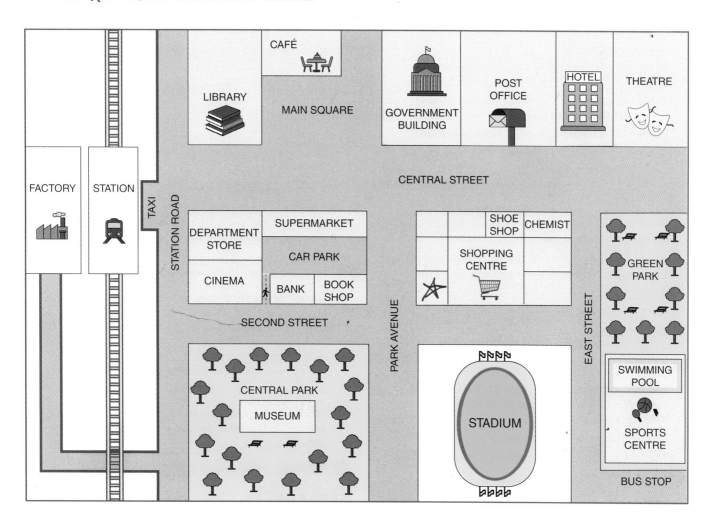

P. 170 فقط

# Family home

## VOCABULARY Homes and family

**V** See Vocabulary reference 3B.

**1** Work in pairs. Why can people be happy / unhappy with their home and home life?

**2** Work in pairs. Read what a student says about their home. Check you understand the words in bold. Use a dictionary if you need to.

1 We don't have our own home. We **rent** it.

2 We live in an **apartment,** but I'd like a house.

3 I have a very small bedroom, so I don't have a lot of **furniture** in it – just a bed and a cupboard to keep my things.

4 I always put my things in the cupboard because I like to **keep my room tidy**.

5 My grandparents live near our home. They often **come round** here for dinner.

6 My grandparents' home is old and has a **broken** window. They want my dad to **repair** it.

7 My dad does a lot of work in our house. He **does most of the cooking and cleaning.**

8 After we have dinner, I usually **wash the dishes**.

9 My sister doesn't do anything to help in the house. She is very **lazy.**

10 My sister never **takes the dog for a walk** or gives it food. My dad or I do it.

**3** Work in pairs. Do you think the person in Exercise 2 is happy with their home? Why? / Why not?

**4** Work with a new partner. Use the words and ideas in Exercise 2 to talk about yourself and your family.

*We don't rent our home.*

*We have an apartment.*

*I have a lot of furniture in my home.*

## READING

**5** Read about two films on page 31. Then work in pairs. Would you like to see these films? Why? / Why not?

*I would (not) like to like to watch My Happy Family.*

*The story sounds funny / sad / boring / interesting / nice.*

**6** Read again. Are these sentences about *My Happy Family* (F) or *What's Eating Gilbert Grape* (G)?

1 There are a lot of visitors to the house.

2 Seven people live in the house.

3 Someone leaves home.

4 Someone in the house can't do cooking or cleaning.

5 Someone in the house is lazy.

6 Someone makes a new friend.

7 They only have one bathroom in the home.

**7** **M** Work in pairs, Say:

1 what you think of Manana and Gilbert.

2 what is the right thing to do for them and their families.

3 what you think happens in the end.

## GRAMMAR

### Possessives

We use **person + 's + noun** and *my / her / their /* etc. + **noun** to show who / what something belongs to.

*Gilbert's mother* became very sad.

*Her husband* plays music.

We can also use a possessive pronoun instead of repeating a possessive form + noun.

*What's your favourite film? This is* **mine**. (= my favourite film)

*The place is old, but she's happy because it's* **hers**. (= her place)

**8** Put the words in brackets in the correct place in the sentences.

1 I share a flat with _____ sister and _____ friend. (my, her)

2 My _____ friend isn't very tidy. She leaves _____ clothes on the bedroom floor. (her, sister's)

3 _____ friend Juan lives alone. I like _____ flat more than _____ . (Juan's, ours, my)

4 I think _____ bedroom is better than _____ . (mine, his)

5 I have a dog, but it stays in my _____ house because there's more space at _____ . (mum and dad's, theirs)

6 _____ house is near to _____ , so I often see _____ dog. (mine, my, their)

**9** Complete the sentences to make them true for you. Use possessives.

1 _____ lives alone.

2 _____ lives with _____ .

3 I like _____ more than mine.

4 _____ is better than _____ .

**10** Work in pairs. One person says a sentence from Exercise 9. The other person asks a question to find out more.

**G** See Grammar reference 3B.

## SPEAKING

**11** Work in groups. Discuss the questions.

1 Do you live in a house or apartment? Where? Do you rent?

2 Who do you live with? What do they do in the house?

3 What's your area like? What places do you have near to you?

4 What's good / bad about your home? Do you like someone else's more?

Tbilisi, Georgia – the home of Manana in the film *My Happy Family*.

# WATCH THIS!

## Share old and new films that you think more people need to see.

**This week, I want to know your favourite film about home life and family. This is mine.**

*My Happy Family* is about Manana, a teacher in Tbilisi, Georgia. She's 52 and lives in her mum and dad's apartment along with her husband, son, daughter and her daughter's husband. There are three bedrooms and one bathroom. Manana and her husband sleep on the sofa in the living room.

Her son spends all day on his computer. Her husband plays music or sits and watches TV. In the evening, their friends often come round and play music and sing until late at night. Manana can't go to bed until everyone leaves. She and her mother also do all the cooking and cleaning. Her children don't help. Her son eats all the food from the fridge and he doesn't put things back in the cupboard.

Manana is tired. She decides to make a change! She rents a small flat in another part of the city. It has a small kitchen, a bathroom, one bedroom, a small living space with a table and two chairs and a small balcony. The place is old and some things are broken, but she's happy because it's hers. She sleeps better and she can keep things tidy. In the evening, she sits and reads, or she just listens to the birds singing in the trees outside. Then her family ask her to come back home – but will she?

**oldfilmfan**  June 7, 21:35

My favourite is an old film called *What's Eating Gilbert Grape*. Gilbert is a young man who lives with his mother, two sisters and brother in a small town in the middle of the US. Gilbert is kind and looks after everyone in his family. His mother became very sad after his father died. Now she just sits on the sofa and watches TV. She's very big and she can't walk very well. Gilbert's little brother is 17 but needs a lot of help too. He can't live on his own. His sisters do the washing and prepare dinner, but they need to study. Gilbert works in a small food shop to earn money. He tries to repair the broken furniture and the roof of their house.

One day he meets a girl, Becky. She's travelling with her grandmother. Their car is broken and it takes time to repair it. Gilbert spends time with Becky. He would like to go with her and travel, but will he?

# Can you help me?

**IN THIS LESSON, YOU:**
- ask someone for help with a problem in a shared house
- describe problems in the home
- practise listening to conversations and say what the problem is
- say what you can't do and ask people to help

## SPEAKING

**1 Work in groups. Discuss the questions.**

1 Are there any broken things in your home at the moment? What?

2 Are you good at repairing things in the home? If you don't repair things, who does?

3 What other jobs do you do in the home?

## VOCABULARY Problems in the home

**2 Match the sentences (1–9) with the follow-up sentences (a–i).**

1 I'm cold.

2 The door was open when I got home.

3 I can't find my glasses.

4 I have some dirty clothes.

5 There's no space on the table.

6 All the baby's toys are **on the floor**.

7 The heating **isn't working**.

8 The fridge is **empty** and there's no milk.

9 There's broken glass on the floor.

a Can you turn **the heating** on?

b We need to **call an engineer**.

c Do you have a **brush**?

d Can I use the **washing machine**?

e Can you **check** it's closed when you go out?

f We need to **pick them up** or someone may fall over them.

g Can you help me **look for** them?

h Can you **move** some things? Put them on the floor or the **shelves** over there.

i We need to go shopping.

**3 Work with a new partner. Say:**

1 how often you have each problem in your home.

2 two other problems you sometimes have.

## LISTENING

**4 Work in pairs. Look at the pictures where people share a home. Answer the questions.**

1 What do you think the problem is in each picture?

2 What do the people want or need to do?

*y eght*

**5** FS ▶ In fast speech, *can't* sometimes sounds like /kɑːn/ and *can* like /kən/. Listen to eight phrases and decide if you hear *can't* or *can*.

**6** ▶ Listen to three conversations about problems in a shared home. Match each conversation (1–3) with a situation from Exercise 4 (a–h).

**7** ▶ Listen again. Complete the sentences with one or two words in each gap.

**Conversation 1**

1 It's a mess. You never keep things _____ .

2 Can you wait? I'm on this _____ .

3 Just move everything to _____ of the room.

**Conversation 2**

4 Yeah, I turned it on ten minutes _____ .

5 We need to call someone to _____ .

6 Your English is better than _____ .

**Conversation 3**

7 Hey, you two. Can you stop _____ ?

8 Can't we watch _____ ?

9 Let's go. We can sit in _____ .

**8** Tell your partner about someone you know who:

1 is untidy or lazy.

2 plays a lot of games on their phone.

3 doesn't like to call people or talk on the phone.

4 talks during a film / TV programme.

## GRAMMAR

### Can / Can't

To ask (someone) to do something, we often use *can* + person + verb.

A: **Can you pick** up your things?

B: Of course, sorry. / Yeah, in a minute.

We use **can + verb** to say something is possible and **can't + verb** to say it's not possible.

I **can tidy** up later.

He **can't hear** the film.

**9** Write the words in the correct order to make sentences.

1 repair / I / can't / it .

2 you / pick up / can / rubbish / the ?

3 brush / find / I / can't / the .

4 you / are / off / check / the / lights / can ?

5 help / can / everyone / me / tidy / the room ?

6 you / can / there / things / leave / your .

7 change / music / you / the / can .

8 where / can / my / hands / wash / I ?

**10** Use these words to write a question to ask for things in class (using *can*) and the reason to ask (using *can't*).

1 I / hear you
you / speak louder
*I can't hear you. Can you speak louder?*

2 you / help me
I / do this exercise

3 I / move to the front
I / see the board

4 I / come to the next class
you / tell me what homework to do

5 I / go to the toilet
I / wait

6 Kenji / find his phone
everyone / help him look for it

7 I / stand on this chair
I / get the book off the shelf

**11** Work in pairs. Have short conversations using your sentences from Exercise 10.

A: I can't hear you. Can you speak louder?

B: Yes, of course. Sorry.

G See Grammar reference 3C. »»

## SPEAKING TASK

**12** M Work in pairs. Do the following:

1 Choose three or four situations from the pictures in Exercise 4.

2 Write a short conversation for each picture. You can start the conversations with these phrases.

Are you OK?

What's the problem?

Can I help you?

Can you help me?

Excuse me. I'm trying to …

3 Practise the conversation. Try to remember your parts and have the conversation without looking at your notes.

**13** Work with another pair. Have your conversations again. Can the other pair guess which pictures you chose?

## ■ MY OUTCOMES ■

**Work in pairs. Discuss the questions.**

1 What conversations did you enjoy most?

2 What new things can you now say about you and your life?

3 Can you understand some spoken English better now?

4 When are you going to practise English this week? How?

# 4
# Time off

## IN THIS UNIT, YOU:

- talk about what you did at the weekend
- talk about holidays / special days you had
- talk about public holidays you enjoyed

## SPEAKING

**1  Work in pairs. Discuss the questions.**

1  Look at the photo. Do you think this is a nice place for a holiday? Why? / Why not?

2  Can you think of three things people do in this kind of place?

3  Do you like doing these things?

**2  Look at these activities. Put ✓✓ next to things you really like doing, ✓ next to things you quite like doing and ✗ next to things you don't really like doing. Then compare your answers with your partner.**

a  spending time outside

b  cooking nice food

c  having interesting things to see and do

d  doing nothing

e  having time to read

f  watching films or TV shows

g  going swimming

h  going out at night

**3  Work with a new partner. Say two more things that you really like doing when you have time off.**

People enjoying time off at the beach in Rio de Janeiro, Brazil.

## 4A

# I had a great weekend

**IN THIS LESSON, YOU:**
- talk about what you did at the weekend
- practise listening to people talk about what they did at the weekend
- share what you like doing at the weekend
- comment on what people tell you

## SPEAKING

1 ▶ **Work in pairs. Listen to the conversation between two friends. Then say it.**

A: Did you have a good weekend?

B: Yeah, it was **great**.

A: What did you do?

B: Well, on Saturday morning I **went to the gym**. Then I **met some friends for lunch** and in the evening, I **went to a party**.

A: That sounds fun.

B: Yeah, it was. Then on Sunday I **just slept** and then **watched TV**. Oh, and I **did my homework** too.

A: Oh, nice!

B: What about you? What did you do?

2 **Change the words in purple. Use a dictionary if you need to. Then practise your new conversation with your partner. Exchange roles and repeat.**

## LISTENING

3 **Look at what four people say about what they did last weekend. Do you think each person had a very good time, an OK time or a bad time?**

a I was ill. I had a bad cold.

b We went to a music festival.

c Some friends came to visit, so I showed them round the city.

d Nothing much, really. I did some shopping on Saturday morning.

4 ▶ **Listen to four conversations. Match the conversations (1–4) with the sentences in Exercise 3 (a–d). Does each person say the weekend was good, OK or bad?**

5 ▶ **Listen again. Match these statements (a–f) with the conversations (1–4).**

a We had a picnic in the park.

b I saw DJ Format on Saturday night. He was good.

c I stayed in bed all weekend.

d I cooked lunch for everyone.

e I played tennis, watched TV … the usual things.

f I needed to relax.

6 **Work in pairs. Do you like these things? Why? / Why not?**

1 busy weekends

2 quiet weekends

3 going to music festivals

4 going to markets

5 cooking for lots of people

6 showing people round your town / area

## GRAMMAR

### Past simple positive

The past simple form is usually verb + -ed. If the verb ends in -e, just add -d.

I **played** tennis and **watched** TV.

I **wanted** to go out yesterday.

She **agreed** with me.

A lot of common verbs are irregular. You just need to learn the past simple forms of irregular verbs.

| | | |
|---|---|---|
| see – saw | take – took | spend – spent |
| get – got | read – read | buy – bought |

7 **Write the past simple form of these verbs.**

1 show    *showed*

2 cook

3 stay

4 go

5 do

6 have

7 come

8 is / are

**8** Complete the sentences about things people did last weekend with the past simple form of these verbs.

be   come   get   go   have   spend   stay   watch

1 I _had_ lunch with my grandparents.
2 I _stayed_ [~~went~~] to the beach with some friends.
3 We _stayed_ at home and relaxed.
4 I _watched_ a football match on Saturday.
5 There _was_ a free concert in town.
6 Some friends _came_ to our house for dinner.
7 I went shopping and I _got_ some new shoes.
8 I _~~been~~ spent_ all weekend studying for an exam.

**9** Write three things you did in the past that were great and three things that were bad / boring. Work in groups. Share your ideas.

> **G** See Grammar reference 4A.

## DEVELOPING CONVERSATIONS

### That sounds ...

We use *that sounds* + adjective to comment on what people say.

A: *Some friends came to visit, so I showed them round the city.*

B: **That sounds nice.**

A: *I played tennis, watched TV, the usual things.*

B: **That sounds OK.**

**10** Write a comment about each sentence using *that sounds* and one of these adjectives.

bad      great      interesting      nice

1 We rented a boat and went on the lake. _That sounds nice_
2 I went for a walk in the countryside. _that sounds great_
3 I had a headache, so I stayed at home. _that sounds bad_
4 I went shopping with my mum. _that sounds nice_
5 I watched a nature show on TV. _that sounds interesting_
6 We had a party at home. _that sounds ~~interesting~~ nice_

**11** Use the ideas from Exercise 10 to have conversations like the ones in Exercise 4.

A: *What did you do at the weekend?*
B: *We rented a boat and went on the lake.*
A: *That sounds great.*

## CONVERSATION PRACTICE

**12** Think about last weekend. Did you have a nice weekend? Choose an answer from the list (a–c). Write down two or three things you did.

a  Yeah, it was great.     b  It was OK.     c  Not really.

**13** Have conversations about last weekend with different people in your class. Use these questions. Comment on people's answers with *that sounds* ... .

*Did you have a nice weekend?*
*What did you do?*

**14** **M** Work in pairs. Which person in the class had the most interesting weekend? Why?

# 4B

# It didn't rain once

IN THIS LESSON, YOU:
• talk about holidays / special days you had
• describe different kinds of holidays
• read messages about a holiday
• discuss holiday activities

## VOCABULARY Holidays

**1 Complete the short texts with the words in bold.**

1 **fantastic, whole, worried**

Before we left, I was _Worried_ about the weather there, but it was _fantastic_. It was lovely and warm the _whole_ time we were there.

2 **fly, trip, wonderful**

It was the best _trip_ ever! It was my 50th birthday and we decided to _fly_ to Sicily. We stayed in a lovely hotel there and had a _wonderful_ time.

3 **castle, sightseeing, tour**

We went _sightseeing_ a lot while we were there. We visited all the museums, and one day we went on a ~~tour~~ _castle_ of the old town and saw the ~~tour~~ _castle_ too.

*tour* <

4 **chat, cycling, relaxing**

I just stayed at home and spent the week _relaxing_. I had time to read, _chat_ with friends, sleep. Oh, and one day I went _cycling_ in the mountains.

**2 Work in groups. Discuss the questions.**

1 Which person in Exercise 1 do you think had the best holiday? Why?

2 How often do you / does your family have a holiday?

3 Do you usually go away somewhere or stay at home?

4 If you go away, do you always go to the same place or to different places?

5 What do you usually do when you are on holiday?

## READING

**3 Read the messages on page 39 between a Danish man, Nicklas, and his Italian friend, Alesia. Number the photos (a–d) in the order they are talked about (1–4).**

**4 Read the messages again. Answer these questions.**

1 Where did Nicklas go? _Cardiff_

2 Did he go on his own? _No_

3 How long was he there for? _three weeks_

4 Was the weather good? _yes_

5 What did he do there? _sightseeing everedary_

6 Do you think it was a good holiday? Why? / Why not? _yes_

**5 Work in pairs. Tell each other the best place in your area / country:**

1 to go sightseeing.

2 to go walking.

3 to go swimming.

4 to spend a week relaxing.

5 to go out at night.

6 for driving around.

## GRAMMAR

### Past simple negative

To make the past simple negative, we use *didn't* + verb.

It **didn't rain** once.

We **didn't stay** long.

For the verb *be*, we use *wasn't / weren't*.

It **wasn't** very expensive.

There **weren't** many people around.

**6 Complete the sentences with the negative form of the past simple verbs in brackets.**

1 I _didn't do_ much on Sunday. (did)

2 I _didn't get up_ until eleven. (got up)

3 I wanted to have breakfast, but there _wasn't_ any coffee or bread in the house. (was)

4 I went to the shop, but I _didn't take_ my keys. (took)

5 The shops _weren't_ open. It was a holiday! (were)

6 I went to a café and I had a coffee, but then I saw that I _didn't have_ any money! (had)

7 I went back to my flat. I broke a window to get in. I _didn't go_ out again after that. (went)

**7 Complete the sentences with the past simple negative form of these verbs.**

| ~~be~~ buy do eat go have see understand |

1 I wanted to buy it, but I _didn't have_ any money.

2 The film was in English. I _didn't understand_ anything!

3 The beach was very quiet. We _didn't see_ anyone there for three days.

4 We went shopping, but I _didn't buy_ anything.

5 I had a very quiet weekend. I _didn't go_ anywhere.

6 We stayed in a small town. There ~~wasn't~~ _weren't_ any shops!

7 I _didn't do_ anything special. I just stayed in.

8 I felt ill, so I _didn't eat_ anything at dinner.

**G** See Grammar reference 4B.

## SPEAKING

**8 Choose one of these things to talk about. Make notes about what you want to say.**

1 the last time you had a holiday

2 your last birthday

3 a special day in your life

**9 Work in groups. Tell each other about your weekend / holiday / day.**

# READING

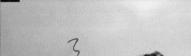

> Hi Alesia. How are you? Hope you and your family are well. Just to let you know Helena and I are back home now after three fantastic weeks in Wales.

Hey Nicklas! Oh wow, that sounds great.

> It was. We had a wonderful time. We flew to Cardiff, the capital, and spent a few days there. It's a really nice city. We went sightseeing every day and visited the museums. Oh, and we went on a tour of the castle. We really enjoyed going out at night too. It's a fun place – and it wasn't very expensive! You'd love it.

I'm sure. I want to visit one day!

> Then after that, we rented a car and spent two weeks driving round the country. It's really beautiful! I was worried about the weather, but it didn't rain once. We stayed in B&Bs and met some really lovely people.

Lucky you! What was the best place you went to?

> I think my favourite place was the south of the country. We went walking in the mountains for a few days. It was lovely and quiet. On the first day we didn't see anyone else – we only saw cows and sheep!

Oh, nice! It's always good to leave the city for a bit, right?

> Yeah, but now we're back in Copenhagen and back at work! Anyway, how was your summer? Did you go on holiday anywhere? Did you have a good time?

I did, yeah. I'm at work now. Are you free later for a chat?

> Sure. Call after seven and tell me everything! And hey, come and visit us soon. Maybe in September? The weather is still OK, then.

# What did you do?

**IN THIS LESSON, YOU:**
- talk about public holidays you enjoyed
- discuss what people do on public holidays
- practise listening to a school podcast about public holidays
- ask and answers questions about past public holidays

## VOCABULARY Public holidays

1 **Work in groups. Discuss the questions.**

   1 How many public holidays do you have in your country?

   2 What's your favourite public holiday? What do you normally do?

   3 Do you know about any other public holidays around the world?

2 **Complete the sentences with these pairs of words.**

| | | |
|---|---|---|
| envelopes / luck | flowers / national | off / picnics |
| paint / dead | sing / laugh | terrible / away |

   1 We _sing_ songs and _laugh_ with our friends.

   2 We have a day _off_ and people often have _picnics_ in the park or in the countryside.

   3 We _paint_ our faces and remember _dead_ people in our family.

   4 We give each other gifts and _flowers_ , and we wear our _national_ clothes.

   5 The traffic's usually _terrible_ because everyone wants to go _away_ for a few days.

   6 Adults give children money in red _envelopes_ and we open all the doors and windows for good _luck_ .

3 **P ▶ Listen to the words from Exercise 2 and practise saying them on their own and in a phrase. Which words / phrases do you find hard to say? Practise saying them again.**

4 **Think of public holidays from last year. Choose four things from Exercise 2 to describe what happened. Tell a partner.**

*Last year, I gave my mum flowers for Mother's Day.*

*Everyone wanted to visit their families for the holiday.*

## LISTENING

5 **FS ▶ In fast speech, questions using *are / were* and *do / did* can often sound similar. Listen to six pairs of questions. In each pair, which question is asking about the past: a or b?**

6 **▶ Listen to part of a school podcast about different public holidays. Answer the questions.**

   1 Which holidays do they talk about?

   2 Where do they happen?

   3 When are they?

7 **▶ Work in pairs. Check you understand these words from the three stories. Then decide which speaker used each group of words. Listen again to check.**

   2 a three – drove – clear – cloud – views – traffic – two

   3 b work – missed – old – remember – prepare – happy – sad

   1 c fire – beach – night – songs – swam – warm – slept

8 **Work in pairs. Say as much as you can about what each speaker did, using the words in Exercise 7.**

*They made a fire on the beach with some friends.*

People celebrate *Día de los Muertos* in South San Francisco Bay, US.

## GRAMMAR

### Past simple questions

We make past simple questions using *did* + subject + verb.

***Did you do*** *anything special?*

*Where **did you go***?

For the verb *be*, make questions with *was / were*.

***Was*** *the weather OK?*

*Where **were** you for this day this year?*

**9** Write past simple questions to ask a friend about what they did for a public holiday. Use these notes.

1 you / go away anywhere?

2 where / go?

3 who / go with?

4 have a good time?

5 how long / there for?

6 where / stay?

7 the weather good?

8 the food good?

**10** Match these answers (a–h) with the questions in Exercise 9 (1–8).

a Yes, I did. I love it there. 4

b Yes, great. I ate lots of fish and chips. 8

c At a friend's place. 6

d Yes, I did. I went to the coast. 1

e Three days. 5

f I went on my own. 3

g A town called Hastings. 2

h It was great, yes. Really hot and sunny. 7

**G** See Grammar reference 4C.

## SPEAKING TASK

**11** Think about what you did on different public holidays in the past. Look at the questions and make notes.

1 Which public holiday was the most special?

2 Where were you?

3 Who were you with?

4 What did you do?

5 Why was it so special?

**12** Talk to at least three different people in your class. Take turns to ask and answer the questions in Exercise 11. With each person, ask three more connected past simple questions to continue the conversation.

**13** **M** Work in pairs. Who was most similar to you? In what way?

### ▪ MY OUTCOMES ▪

**Work in pairs. Discuss the questions.**

1 What conversations were fun to have?

2 What can you now talk about in English?

3 What did you learn about other students and their lives?

4 What part of this unit do you want to look at again and practise?

# Introducing yourself

**IN THIS LESSON, YOU:**
- write a short introduction to yourself for a home stay
- talk about staying in someone's home and renting a room
- read an offer of a home stay and guests' introductions
- improve your writing by joining sentences in simple ways

## SPEAKING

1 **Work in groups. Discuss the sentences and say if they are true for you. Why? / Why not?**

1 On holiday, I like meeting local people.

2 I sometimes do home stays – I stay in other people's homes when I travel.

3 It's good to rent a room in your home to tourists or students.

4 I know someone who rents a room in someone's home.

5 I don't want to rent a room in my family home to anyone.

## WRITING

2 **Read an advertisement on a website for offering a home stay. Answer the questions.**

1 Where is the home? *in santigo de chile*

2 How many people live there? *2, the father, the daughter*

3 What sounds good to you about the place?

4 Can you think of any possible problems with the place?

Hi, I'm Karina. I live an area called Providencia in Santiago de Chile. I'm retired now, but I was a bank manager. I live in an apartment with my daughter Sandra, who is 27, and our small dog.

The apartment is on the third floor. Your room is quite small, but there are two cupboards for your things and there is a bathroom only for you. You can share the kitchen. There's a gym in our building that you can use and there's a park near here too. There's a metro station and lots of shops near our building.

I'm at home most of the day. I like reading, taking the dog for a walk, cooking and playing chess and other games. My daughter works in an office. In the evening she often cooks with me. She loves music and she goes out a lot to see bands. She plays the electric guitar.

From $16/night

3 **Work in pairs. Compare your answers. Would you like to stay in Karina's home? Why? / Why not?**

The district of Providencia in Santiago de Chile.

## WRITING

4 Work in pairs. Read the introductions of two people who are interested in renting Karina's room. Who do you think is the best guest for Karina? Why?

**ANDRZEJ**
Poland
Age 20–25

✓                    2 AUGUST

My name's Andrzej. I'm 22 and I'm from Gdańsk in Poland. I'm coming to Chile to do a music course. I want to stay for about 18 months. I speak Spanish OK. I'm a friendly person, but I'm quiet. I stay at home a lot and I practise the violin and write music. I also like reading and watching movies. I'm clean and tidy.

**Kim Eun-jung**
Korea
Age 55–60

3 AUGUST

I'm Kim Eun-jung. I'm 57. I'm from South Korea. I'm coming to South America to travel. I want to stay in Santiago for a month. I don't speak Spanish. I have two children who are 28 and 32. I worked for a big Korean company, but I retired last year. I like travelling and meeting new people. I also like walking and playing golf.

5 Work in pairs. Complete these sentences from the texts with up to three words or numbers. Don't look back at the texts.

1 My **name's** Andrzej.
2 I'm coming to Chile to do *a music course*
3 I want to stay for *about 18 months*
4 I also like reading *and watching movies*
5 I'm Kim Eun-jung. I'm *57*.
6 I'm coming to South America *to travel*
7 I want to stay in Santiago for *a month*
8 I also like walking *and playing golf*

6 Tell your partner about someone you know who:
- plays music.
- plays a sport.
- plays games at home.
- is quiet.
- is retired.

## USEFUL LANGUAGE

### *And* and *but*

We can join two short sentences with *and* or *but*.

I'm 22. I'm from Gdańsk. → I'm 22 **and** I'm from Gdańsk.

I'm coming to South America to travel. I want to stay in Santiago for a month. → I'm coming to South America to travel **and** I want to stay for a month.

I worked for a big Korean company. I retired last year. → I worked for a big Korean company, **but** I retired last year.

I'm a friendly person. I'm quiet. → I'm a friendly person, **but** I'm quiet.

7 Work in pairs. Answer the questions.

1 How do you say *and* and *but* in your first language?
2 Where do the words come in the sentence – at the start, the middle or the end?

8 Join these sentences using *and* or *but*.

1 I'm at university. I study business. *and*
2 I'm from the UK. I live in Brussels. *but*
3 Our home is near a metro. You can get to the centre in fifteen minutes. *and*
4 My apartment has two bedrooms. There are two bathrooms. *and*
5 Our building has parking. We don't have a space. *but*
6 I have a car. I prefer to cycle in the city. *but*
7 I love going to the cinema. I also like listening to music. *and*
8 I visited the capital last year. I was only there for the day. ~~and~~ *but* I didn't really see anything. ~~but~~ *and*

9 Write four sentences about your home and family. Write two sentences with *and* and two sentences with *but*.

*The kitchen is small, but the bedrooms are big.*
*My brother plays the piano and I play the guitar.*

## PRACTICE

10 Write an introduction to yourself for a home stay as in Exercise 4. Write 50–80 words.

11 Work in pairs. Read your partner's introduction. Discuss the questions.

1 Do you want to know anything else about your partner?
2 How similar are you?

12 Would you change your introduction if you were writing it for one of these reasons? What would you change?

1 for people working together
2 for people travelling together on a group holiday
3 for finding people to share a house / apartment

## VIDEO  Out and about

**1**  Work in groups. What did you do last weekend?

### Understanding accents

Some accents use an /ɪ/ sound instead of an /iː/ sound, so *feel* /fiːl/ may sound more like *fill* /fɪl/.

**2**   Watch six people answer the same question. How many different activities did you hear? Then work in pairs. Did anyone have similar experiences to you?

**3**  Watch again. Match one or two sentences with each speaker.

a  I went for something to eat with friends.

b  I saw a really good film about Ireland.

c  I did something that I don't normally do.

d  I want to do well in my IELTS exam.

e  I recently moved to the city.

f  It rained, but then there was some sun.

g  I was a bit ill.

h  I went out at night with some friends.

i  I went for a long walk.

**4**  Tell your partner about the last time you did four of these things.

1  went for a long walk

2  did something a bit different

3  went out at night

4  did an English exam

5  felt a bit ill

6  went for something to eat

## VIDEO  Developing conversations

**5**  You're going to watch someone asking about places they want to go to. Watch and take notes about where they want to go.

**6**  Work in pairs. Compare what you understood. Watch again if you need to.

**7**  FS  Watch again. Complete the sentences with two or three words in each gap.

1  Excuse me, do you _____ ?

2  There is one. _____ just walk straight ahead and you turn left …

3  But unfortunately, it closes _____ .

4  I'm looking for a quiet place _____ write a birthday card.

5  OK. Perfect. And _____ if they sell pens?

6  But there is a shop just right _____ road.

7  Got it. And the bank is _____ , right?

8  OK. I got it. Thank you so much. _____ kind.

## CONVERSATION PRACTICE

**8**  Work in pairs. You're going to practise a conversation.

1  Choose a Conversation practice from either Lesson 3A or Lesson 4A.

2  Look at the language in that lesson.

3  Check the meaning of anything you don't remember with your partner.

4  Have the conversation. Try to do it better than the last time you did it.

# Grammar and Vocabulary

## GRAMMAR

**1 Choose the correct option to complete the sentences.**

1 There's a café *on / in* the corner of this road.
2 Our house is *in front / next to* a school.
3 *Simon's / Simon* parents live on this road.
4 Can you give *he / him* the keys.
5 I'm sorry, I *can't / can* see the board.
6 Did you *went / go* out last night?
7 They *were / was* both ill at the weekend.
8 My house is *at / in* the end of this road *opposite / between* the church.

**2 Complete the text with the past simple form of the verbs in brackets.**

We ¹_____ (have) a great holiday in Greece. We ²_____ (fly) to Athens and ³_____ (spend) three days there and ⁴_____ (see) all the famous sights. After that, we ⁵_____ (take) a boat to Mykonos and we ⁶_____ (stay) in a small hotel near the beach.

**3 Rewrite the sentences as negatives (–) or questions (?).**

1 I can come to the next class. (–)
2 There was a beach near the hotel. (?)
3 The hotel was very good. (–)
4 He had a nice time. (?)
5 I understood everything. (–)
6 You can look for it later. (?)

**4 Complete the questions in the conversation. Use the words in brackets and a question word if you need to.**

A: ¹_____ a nice weekend? (you / have)
B: Yes, it was great.
A: ²_____ ? (do)
B: I went to stay with my brother.
A: That's nice. ³_____ ? (live)
B: Dublin. We went to the theatre on Saturday night.
A: ⁴_____ ? (see)
B: The Lion King.
A: ⁵_____ ? (it / good)
B: I liked it, but my brother didn't.

**5 ▶ Listen and write the six sentences you hear. Include these words.**

1 think / things
2 can / off
3 bank / road
4 long / there
5 anyone / knew
6 I / what

## VOCABULARY

**6 Match the two parts of the phrases.**

1 sing          a a taxi / an engineer
2 send          b the dishes / my hands
3 go            c our faces / the house
4 call          d my home / a car
5 paint         e a birthday card / someone a gift
6 wash          f songs / Happy Birthday
7 wear          g my glasses / somewhere to live
8 rent          h my room tidy / warm
9 keep          i cycling / for a walk
10 look for     j our national clothes / shorts

**7 Decide if these words are about places for things you need, home or holidays. There are five items in each group.**

| apartment | away | bookshop | castle |
| --- | --- | --- | --- |
| chemist | cleaning | cooking | furniture |
| heating | library | post office | sightseeing |
| sports centre | tour | trip | |

**8 Choose the correct option to complete the sentences.**

1 Do you have a *brush / shelf* so I can clean the floor?
2 Do you want to *pick up / come round* later for dinner?
3 Is there anywhere *quiet / noisy* where I can study?
4 Can I share your book? I *forgot / moved* mine.
5 Can you *repair / check* the window is closed?
6 I put the flowers in the rubbish. They were *broken / dead*.
7 Is there anywhere near here I can *change / find* money?

**9 Complete the text with one word in each gap. The first letters are given.**

I had a week ¹of_____ from work last month and went to Greece for a holiday. I was a bit ²wo_____ because it was my first time travelling alone, but it was fine! I stayed in a hostel in Athens and there were lots of people my age. We sat in the café and ³ch_____ together in the evening and we ⁴la_____ a lot. I also spent two days on an island. One day, the weather was ⁵te_____ , so I stayed inside all day and ⁶re_____ . The next day, I went to the beach and went ⁷sw_____ . I took a picnic and spent the ⁸wh_____ day there. It was ⁹fa_____ .

# 5 Shopping

**IN THIS UNIT, YOU:**

- roleplay choosing and buying food or clothes in a shop
- talk about money and shopping
- ask for and get help in different places in a shopping centre

## SPEAKING

**1 Work in pairs. Answer the questions.**

1 Look at the photo. Is there a market near you?
2 How do you get there?
3 Do you do your shopping there? Why? / Why not?
4 Does the market sell any of these things?

| | | | |
|---|---|---|---|
| bread | cheese | cleaning things | clothes |
| drinks | fish | flowers | furniture |
| meat | plants | shoes | |

**2 Work in groups. Don't use a dictionary. In two minutes, share and write down all the words you know for:**

1 food.
2 clothes.
3 colours.

Selling fruit in the Municipal Market, São Paulo, Brazil.

# How much is that red one?

**IN THIS LESSON, YOU:**
- roleplay choosing and buying food or clothes in a shop
- explain the size and quantity of what you want
- practise listening to people buying food and clothes
- make clear which thing you want

## SPEAKING

**1** ▶ Work in pairs. Listen to the conversation in a market. Then say it.

A: Can I help you?

B: Hi. How much is this **shirt**?

A: **150**.

B: Do you have a **bigger** one?

A: Sorry – only **medium**.

B: What about that **blue** one behind you?

A: That one is **200**. Do you like it?

B: Yeah. Can I try it on?

A: Of course. It looks good.

B: Yeah. I'll take it.

A: Anything else? **A hat**? **A T-shirt**?

B: No, that's all thanks.

A: OK. That's **200** then.

**2** Change the words in purple. Use a dictionary if you need to. Then practise your new conversation with your partner. Exchange roles and repeat.

## VOCABULARY Size and quantity

**3** Work in pairs. Decide which word completes all three phrases.

| bag | bottle | a few | half | litre | kilo |
|-----|--------|-------|------|-------|------|
| pair | piece | size | | | |

1 ~ oranges / ~ bananas / ~ pairs of socks
   *a few oranges / a few bananas / a few pairs of socks*
2 a smaller ~ / a ~ 14 / what ~ are you?
3 a big ~ of water / a ~ of milk / a ~ of tomato sauce
4 a small ~ of sugar / a ~ of pasta / do you need a ~?
5 cut it into ~s / a small ~ of cake / a bigger ~
6 a ~ of potatoes / half a ~ of chicken / a five-~ bag
7 half a ~ / a two-~ bottle / a ~ of oil
8 a ~ of jeans / a new ~ of shoes / get three ~s
9 it's ~ price / ~ a kilo / cut it in ~

**4** P ▶ Listen to the words from Exercise 3 and practise saying them on their own and in a phrase. Which words / phrases do you find hard to say? Practise saying them again.

**5** Work in pairs. Which words from Exercise 3 could you use with these words?

1 lemon
2 cheese
3 T-shirt
4 gloves
5 juice
6 melon

## LISTENING

**6** ▶ Listen to three conversations in markets. Complete the table with one word or a number in each gap. Then listen again and check your answers.

| | Shopper buys ... | Total cost |
|---|---|---|
| 1 | three [1]_____ peaches [2]_____ red [3]_____ | [4]£ _____ |
| 2 | [5]_____ a lemon cake two pieces of [6]_____ | [7]€ _____ |
| 3 | two [8]_____ – one medium and one [9]_____ | [10]$ _____ |

**7** Work in groups. Discuss the price of these things:

| | | | |
|---|---|---|---|
| bananas | cake | coffee | a flat |
| jeans | petrol | shoes | water |

*A cup of coffee in a café is usually three euros.*

## GRAMMAR

### This / These / That / Those

We use *this / these* for things we're wearing or holding. We often use *that / those* to point at things. *This* and *that* are singular. *These* and *those* are plural.

a **This** is really nice.

b Can I have **that** piece?

c I like **those** ones.

d **These** ones are too small.

**8** Look at the examples in the Grammar box. Match the sentences (a–d) with the photos (1–4).

**9** Complete the conversations with one word in each gap.

1 A: How much are _____ jackets behind you?

B: What? These leather _____ ?

A: Yes.

B: Well, it depends. _____ brown one is £100.

2 A: What are _____ called, on my hands?

B: Gloves.

3 A: What do you call _____ thing over there?

B: A plant.

**10** Work in groups. Ask each other the name in English for different things in the classroom.

*What's this called?*

*What's that thing there called?*

*What are these / those things called?*

G See Grammar reference 5A.

## DEVELOPING CONVERSATIONS

### Questions in shops

For common situations like shopping, it's a good idea to learn useful questions and answers.

*Can I help you?*

*Who's next?*

*Anything else?*

**11** Who usually asks these questions: shop assistants (A) or customers (C)?

1 Who's next?

2 Can I have some … ?

3 What are those made of?

4 How much are they?

5 Which one(s)?

6 How much would you like?

7 How many would you like?

8 Anything else?

**12** Match each pair of answers (a–h) with a question in Exercise 11 (1–8).

a Sure. / Of course.

b 50 each. / 1.49 a kilo.

c Me. / This lady, I think.

d A kilo. / Half a litre.

e Those are with chicken. / Leather.

f No thanks, that's it. / Do you have any blue cheese?

g Five or six. / Just one.

h The red ones. / The one behind that.

## CONVERSATION PRACTICE

**13** Work in pairs. You're going to roleplay conversations in a shop. Follow the instructions:

1 Choose a shop from the photos in this lesson or the photo at the beginning of the unit.

2 Roleplay the conversations.

**Student A:** You're the shop assistant. Help your partner buy what they want and decide the price.

**Student B:** You're the customer. Buy two or three different things in the photo.

3 Choose a different photo. Exchange roles and repeat.

# They're having a sale

**IN THIS LESSON, YOU:**
- talk about money and shopping
- read and share information about how two shops are doing
- give reasons why you can't go somewhere with someone

## Vocabulary Money and shopping

**V** See Vocabulary reference 5B.

**1 Complete the sentences with these words.**

| bills | complained | discount | high | in cash |
|---|---|---|---|---|
| low | make | online | sale | save |

1 I don't go to bookshops. I buy books _____ .

2 It's cheap. Some prices are very _____ .

3 Our shop tries to keep prices low, but then we don't _____ a lot of money.

4 I bought a TV online, but they sent the wrong one, so I _____ .

5 I complained to the restaurant manager and he gave me a 50% _____ on my next meal.

6 The shop is having a _____ at the moment and they have some big discounts.

7 I _____ money by buying things in the sales.

8 It's more expensive if you pay by card, so I saved some money by paying _____ .

9 I live with my parents, so I don't pay any _____ .

10 The last bill for electricity was very _____ . I don't know if I can pay it.

**2 Work in pairs. Tell your partner the last time you:**

1 bought something online.

2 complained about something.

3 paid a bill.

4 paid in cash.

5 went to a sale.

6 saved some money.

## READING

**3 Read the introduction to the newspaper article on page 51. Then work in groups. Discuss the questions.**

1 Does the situation sound similar to your country?

2 Which shops are doing badly where you are? Why?

3 Which shops are doing well? Why?

**4 Work in groups of four: two Student As and two Student Bs. Student As read about Ioana. Student Bs read about Esi. Write short answers to these questions about the person in your story.**

1 What does she do?

2 Where does she work?

3 Does she enjoy her job?

4 How's the shop doing?

5 Why does she think it's doing well / OK / badly?

**5 Work in pairs: Student As together and Student Bs together. Compare your answers for Exercise 4.**

**6 M Work with a new partner: one Student A and one Student B. Ask and answer the questions in Exercise 4 to find out about your partner's story.**

**7 With your partner, discuss the questions.**

1 Which shop is doing better?

2 Which job sounds better to you?

3 Are there any similar shops where you live?

4 Can the shops do anything else to get more customers?

## GRAMMAR

### Present continuous

The present continuous shows an action is temporary, and it started but is not finished. We form the present continuous with a present form of *be* + *-ing* form of the verb.

*Today we**'re having** a sale.*

*At the moment, people **aren't going** to the shops so often.*

*How**'s** the shop **doing**?*

Sometimes the action is in the future, but we have the plan now:

*A local singer **is doing** a concert next Thursday. Can we go?*

**8 Look at the examples in the Grammar box. Then find twelve examples of the present continuous in the article.**

**9 Complete the conversation using the words in brackets in the present continuous.**

A: What [1]_____ (you / do) now?

B: We [2]_____ (go) shopping in the city centre. The department store [3]_____ (have) a sale because it [4]_____ (close). They [5]_____ (not make) enough money. Do you want to come?

A: Sorry, I can't. Augusto [6]_____ (come round). I [7]_____ (make) dinner. Also, I [8]_____ (try) to save for a holiday!

B: How [9]_____ (he / do)?

A: He's OK. He [10]_____ (look) for a new job.

**10 Work in groups. Write as many reasons as you can to say *no* to the question *Do you want to go shopping?***

*Sorry, I can't. I'm going to the library.*

*Sorry. Some friends are coming round for dinner.*

**G** See Grammar reference 5B.

## SPEAKING

**11 Work in pairs. Tell your partner about the following.**

1 when you're going shopping next and where

2 somewhere which is having a sale

3 a place which is closing / opening near you soon

4 something you're saving for or looking for at the moment

5 something which is doing well / badly at the moment

Winter sales in Harvey Nichols, Edinburgh, UK.

# HOW'S THE SHOP DOING?

**Life is difficult for local shops at the moment. Customers aren't going to them as often because people are worried about their bills at home and high prices in the shops. They're looking online for things at lower prices. We talk to two shop workers and ask, 'How's the shop doing?'**

**Ioana Radu** works at the biggest clothes shop on High Street. She started as a shop assistant five years ago, but now she's a manager. She says they're busy and the company is doing very well. 'I think people always like great fashion and they love it more when it's cheap. We sell clothes from famous names, but they have big discounts – often half-price or more. We also sell other things at low prices, like soaps and perfume and things for the house. Also, we change what we sell all the time, so customers come once or twice a week to see what there is. They don't always buy anything, but if they find something they like, they know they have to buy it quickly, because it might not be there next week.' So, does Ioana like her job? 'Most of the time, but I don't like working on Saturdays. It's always crazy! There are so many customers. They're really untidy. They look at things and don't put them back on the shelf. They complain because they wait a long time to pay. It's not my favourite day.'

**Esi Jones** is an assistant in the only bookshop in town after two other bookshops closed last year. How does her shop stay open? 'We do a lot of different things so that people come into the shop. Today, we're having a sale – 10% off everything. We also give customers a card and if they buy a book, they get a stamp on the card. When they have eight stamps, they get a free book. There's also a café and we have new books there which people can read while they drink their coffee. Sometimes they then buy the book. We also stay open late on Wednesdays and Thursdays. On Wednesdays, we have different writers in to talk about their books. Keith Lowe is coming next week. I'm reading his new book at the moment and it's really interesting. On Thursdays, we have music. A local singer is doing a concert next week. Your readers can still get tickets!' So is it working? The shop seems quite busy. 'The shop's doing OK, but it's not making a lot of money and I don't earn much. I love it here, but I can't save any money, so I'm looking for a new job. It's a shame.'

# Do you sell . . . ?

**IN THIS LESSON, YOU:**
- ask for and get help in different places in a shopping centre
- talk about shopping centres where you live and what's there
- practise listening to four conversations in a shopping centre
- use *a*, *an* and *the* in short conversations to ask for help

## SPEAKING

**1** **Look at the photo and read the short text. Would you like to go to Central World? What would you do there?**

Central World (centralwOrld) is Thailand's biggest shopping centre. It's eight floors high. It has a very large department store and over 500 local, national and international shops. There are all kinds of fashion at low and high prices. There are lots of places that sell TVs, phones and other technology. And there's everything else from furniture to gifts for tourists. There's also a hotel (five stars), a supermarket, a very big cinema, places for kids and families to play and lots of places to eat and drink. You can even learn to make Thai food at a cooking school there.

**2** **Work in groups. Discuss the questions.**

1 Is there a shopping centre near you? Where?
2 Is it bigger or smaller than Central World? What can you buy / do there?

## VOCABULARY In a shopping centre

**3** **Work in pairs. Check you understand the words in bold. Use a dictionary if you need to.**

1 A: Is this the main **entrance**? I'm meeting a friend here.
   B: **I'm afraid not**. It's on the other side of the building – through these doors and **straight on**.

2 A: Can I try on this shirt somewhere?
   B: Of course. There are **changing rooms** at **the back** of the shop.

3 A: Do you have chargers for these kinds of **batteries**? I can't see any on the shelves.
   B: I'm afraid not. We only sell normal batteries like the ones on this shelf.

4 A: I'm looking for birthday cards.
   B: Oh right. They're over here. **Follow** me and I can show you what we have.

5 A: I think I left my phone here when I paid. It's pink.
   B: I can't see anything. Wait here and I'll ask my **manager**.

6 A: **Let's** have a coffee. There's a nice place on the top floor.
   B: The **lift** isn't working and I don't want to walk up the **stairs**. Let's go home.

7 A: Can I pay for this here?
   B: Sorry, this is for information. You pay **downstairs**. Take those stairs and go right at the **bottom**.

8 A: Is there somewhere I can **change the baby**?
   B: Sure. There's a place downstairs next to the toilets.

**4** **Work in pairs. Practise the conversations.**

**5** **Work with a new partner. Write four similar conversations using the words in bold in Exercise 3.**

*A: Can you help me? I'm looking for the entrance.*

*B: It's downstairs. At the bottom of the stairs, go right*

Central World shopping centre, Bangkok, Thailand.

## LISTENING

**6** ▶ Listen to four short conversations in a shopping centre. Match each conversation (1–4) with one of these situations (a–f). There are two extra situations.

a They're sitting in a café.

b They're in a lift.

c They're waiting to pay.

d They're in a clothes shop.

e They're in a technology shop.

f They're at an information place.

**7** FS ▶ We often say phrases with prepositions fast. Listen to nine phrases from the conversations. Which of these prepositions do you hear in each one?

| for | in | of | on | to |
|-----|----|----|----|----|

**8** ▶ Are the statements true (T) or false (F)? Listen again and check your answers.

**Conversation 1**

1 The customer gets what they want.

2 The assistant wants to sell the customer something else.

**Conversation 2**

3 The man is going to the top floor.

4 The doors aren't opening.

**Conversation 3**

5 Only one person is buying something.

6 One of the women asks for a dress in a different colour.

**Conversation 4**

7 The man wants a computer.

8 The technology shop is on the top floor.

**9** Work in groups. Discuss the questions.

1 Do you like shopping with other people or do you go alone?

2 Do you ever ask for help from shop assistants? What for?

3 Have you had a problem in a lift? When? How long were you in the lift? How many people were in it?

## GRAMMAR

### A, an and the

We use a / an + (adjective) + noun. It shows we're talking about one thing, but it's not important exactly which one.

*Is there **a** chemist in here?*

*Do you want **an** apple?*

We use the (+ adjective) + noun / one(s). It makes clear exactly which thing we're talking about.

*Where are **the** changing rooms?*

*Can I try **the** red ones?*

**10** Put the articles in the correct place in the sentences.

1 A: I'm looking for place to change some money. (a)

B: There's a bank on second floor. When you get to the top of stairs – turn left. (the / the)

2 A: I'm looking for phone with good camera. (a / a)

B: I think this is best one, but I'm sorry, it's not in sale. (the / the)

3 A: Can you help me? Where's exit to car park? (the / the)

B: Take that lift. It's on bottom floor. When you come out of lift, it's in front of you. (the / the)

4 A: I want to get bus to city centre. (a / the)

B: The stop is next to bank, near main entrance. Go straight down there. (a / the)

5 A: That's nice dress. Ask assistant if you can try it on. (a / the)

B: Is there place I can try this? (a)

C: Of course – changing rooms are at back of the shop. (the / the)

G See Grammar reference 5C.

## SPEAKING TASK

**11** Work in pairs. Look at the map of the shopping centre in File 8 on page 201. Discuss what shops you usually go to and decide which ones you'd like in a shopping centre. Complete A–G on the map with the shops you'd like.

**12** M You're going to roleplay some situations in the shopping centre. Follow the instructions:

1 Choose how to do the roleplay.

a In pairs, between a customer and shop assistant: both speak English.

b In groups of three. The customer or assistant doesn't speak English, so the third person needs to translate for them!

2 Read the role cards and think about what you're going to say.

**Customer (and translator):** Look at File 1 on page 199.

**Assistant:** Look at File 8 on page 201.

3 Roleplay the situations. Exchange roles and repeat.

## ■ MY OUTCOMES ■

**Work in pairs. Discuss the questions.**

1 What conversations were most useful?

2 What grammar did you study in this unit?

3 What can you remember about the reading texts?

4 How are you going to practise new language from this unit?

# 6
# Education

**IN THIS UNIT, YOU:**

- roleplay conversations about what you're studying
- compare education now and in the past
- describe and discuss four different courses

## SPEAKING

**1 Work in pairs. Discuss the questions.**

1 Look at the photo. What do you think they're studying?

2 What do you think is good about this kind of class?

3 What was the same / different in your school when you were this age?

**2 Work in groups. Discuss the questions.**

1 What are / were the three best things for you about school?

2 What is / was your favourite subject at school?

3 What do you think is the best thing about being a teacher?

4 What do you think is hard for teachers?

A class of students in Bahrain.

# What are you studying?

**IN THIS LESSON, YOU:**
- roleplay conversations about what you're studying
- discuss issues connected to education
- practise listening to three conversations about studying
- talk about courses people are doing

## SPEAKING

1 ▶ **Work in pairs. Listen to the conversation between two people talking about studying. Then say it.**

A: So what do you do?

B: I'm a student at university.

A: Oh, OK. What are you studying?

B: **French and Spanish.**

A: Oh right. So what year are you in?

B: **My first. I only started this year.**

A: And how's the course going?

B: **Really well, thanks. I'm really enjoying it.**

2 **Change the words in purple. Use a dictionary if you need to. Then practise your new conversation with your partner. Exchange roles and repeat.**

## VOCABULARY Studying

3 **Replace the words in bold with these words.**

chemistry  classmate  college  course  pass  popular  term

1 I'm sure I'm going to **fail** this exam. *Pass*
2 My mum is a **maths** teacher. *chemistry*
3 I'm studying at a local **language school**. *college*
4 It's a very **modern** school. *popular*
5 I'm doing a **degree** in French. *course*
6 I share an apartment with a **colleague** of mine. *classmate*
7 This is the second **year** of three. *term*

4 **P ▶ Listen to the words from Exercise 3 and practise saying them on their own and in a phrase. Which words / phrases do you find hard to say? Practise saying them again.**

Students learning English at EC Boston, US.

**5** Work in pairs. Say which you think is better. Explain why.

1 thinking you're going to fail an exam or thinking you're going to pass
2 studying maths or studying chemistry
3 a modern school or a popular school
4 doing a degree in English or doing an English course
5 sharing an apartment with a classmate or a colleague
6 studying a language for a year or for a term

## LISTENING

**6** ▶ Listen to three conversations. What is the second person in each conversation studying?

**7** ▶ One thing is wrong in each sentence. Listen again and write the correct information.

**Conversation 1**
1 Orla is in her second year. ~~B~~
2 The course is boring.
3 The teachers are very nice and friendly. ~~B~~

**Conversation 2**
4 Tom is at college.
5 His course is going very well.
6 He's in his third year.

**Conversation 3**
7 José is doing a French course.
8 It's quite easy.
9 He has an exam in July.

**8** Work in pairs. Discuss the questions.

1 Do you know anyone at university / college at the moment?
2 What are they studying?
3 What year are they in?
4 Are they enjoying it?

## DEVELOPING CONVERSATIONS

### How's the course going?

We can ask *How's the course going?* to find out if someone is enjoying their course or not.

A: **How's the course going?**

B: *Really well. It's great. I'm really enjoying it.*

**9** Look at these answers (1–9) to the question *How's the course going?* Complete each answer with *Really well, OK* or *Not very well.*

1  OK , but it's not very easy.
2 *not very well*  , I find it boring.
3 *Very well* . It's very interesting.
4 OK ~~very well~~ , but it's a lot of work.
5 *not very well* . I don't really like the school. It's not very modern.

6 *very well* . The other students are very nice and friendly.
7 *very well* . I did very well in my exams. I found them easy.
8 *not very well* . I think I chose the wrong subject!
9  OK , I suppose, but I'm not sure it's what I really want to do.

**10** Work in groups. Discuss the questions.

1 How's your English course going?
2 What are you enjoying most?

## CONVERSATION PRACTICE

**11** M Work in pairs. Use the guide to have four conversations about studying. You can invent answers or use the ideas in the table. Explain how the course is going. Take turns to start.

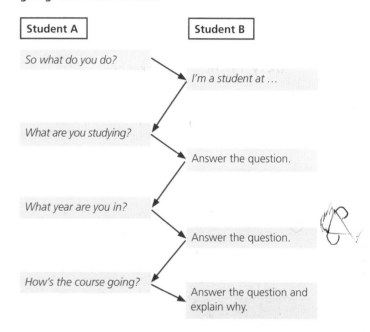

**Student A**

*So what do you do?*

*What are you studying?*

*What year are you in?*

*How's the course going?*

**Student B**

*I'm a student at …*

Answer the question.

Answer the question.

Answer the question and explain why.

| Place | Course | Year | How's it going? |
|---|---|---|---|
| University of Rome, Italy | Biology | 1 | Very well |
| Middlesex University, UK | Business | 2 | Not very well |
| University of the Andes, Colombia | Spanish | 3 | OK |
| University of Copenhagen, Denmark | Geography | 3 | |
| Concordia University, Canada | Chinese | | |

## 6B

# Two is better than one

**IN THIS LESSON, YOU:**
- compare education now and in the past
- talk about different languages
- read an article about languages and education
- compare different things

## SPEAKING

**1 Work in pairs. Discuss the questions.**

1 Can you think of a country or area in the world where each of these is an official language?

| | | | | |
|---|---|---|---|---|
| Arabic | Bengali | English | French | German |
| Hindi | Mandarin Chinese | Portuguese | Spanish | Urdu |

2 Which languages do you think are most important? Why?

3 How many of these languages can you say something in?

4 Do you know anyone who speaks more than one language very well?

## READING

**2 Read the article about languages and education on page 59. Which of these sentences best describes the main idea?**

a If students at a school speak different languages, it's difficult to teach them.

b Lots of students in the UK don't speak English at home.

c There are lots of good things about speaking more than one language.

d More than half the people in the world speak two or more languages.

**3 Read the article again and find:**

1 two ways Kensington Primary School works with students' home languages.

2 the number of schoolchildren in the UK that don't speak English at home.

3 two reasons it's important for children to use their first language at school.

4 four good things about growing up with two languages.

**4 Complete the sentences with the words and phrases in bold in the article.**

1 I don't _belive_ using your first language can help you learn English.

2 I didn't go to any after-school _clubs_ .

3 I always got good _marks_ at school.

4 When I was _growing up_, I didn't meet anyone who spoke English as a first language.

5 I'm good at _solving_ problems. People often ask me for help.

6 Most of the _pupils_ at my school only spoke one language.

7 After English, I want to learn _at least_ one more language.

8 I like reading about new _research_ and how it can help learning.

**5 Work in pairs. Say which sentences in Exercise 4 are true for you.**

**6 Work in groups. Discuss the questions.**

1 What do you think of the way Kensington Primary School works with its students?

2 Do you agree with everything the article says?

3 Are there any bilingual schools in your city / region? Do you think they are good? Why? / Why not?

## GRAMMAR

### Comparatives

To compare two things, we can use a comparative adjective (+ *than*).

We add -er to short one-syllable adjectives.
*They usually finish school with **higher** marks in their exams.*

For adjectives ending in -y, we change -y to -ier.
*Languages are **easier** for me **than** science subjects.*

For longer adjectives of two or more syllables, we use *more*.
*My last course was **more difficult than** this one.*

The comparative adjective forms of *good* and *bad* are irregular.
*Growing up like this is **better than** only knowing one language.*
*Things are **worse than** they were ten years ago.*

**7 Choose the correct option to complete the sentences.**

1 My English is better than his. I get *higher* / *lower* marks.

2 They're better students than me. I'm *more popular* / *lazier*.

3 Her new book is worse than her first one. It's *funnier* / *more boring*.

4 I think maths is better than English. It's *more interesting* / *more difficult*.

5 This car is worse than mine. My one's *slower* / *faster*.

**8 Write sentences using comparatives and these ideas.**

1 I'm / good at / swimming / you.

2 My house is / near to / the school / your place.

3 My sister / old / me.

4 You're / interested / in history / me.

5 My school was / small / yours.

**9 Work in pairs. Find three ways you're different.**

*A: How far can you swim?*

*B: Not far. Maybe 100 metres.*

*A: So I'm better at swimming than you. I can do 800 metres.*

G See Grammar reference 6B.

## SPEAKING

**10 M Are these things better or worse now than they were in the past? Think of reasons why. Then work in groups and share your ideas.**

| | | |
|---|---|---|
| class sizes | degree subjects | exams |
| the hours you study | schools | school subjects |
| universities | ways of teaching | |

more ≠ Less

# The World in One School

*Today, we look at the benefits of knowing more than one language.*

The students at Kensington Primary School in east London speak over 40 different languages. Teachers find that the best way to help students with their English is to work with the languages they bring with them. For example, **pupils** can write in their first language and then explain their ideas to their classmates in English. The school tries hard to include parents too. Many come to after-school **clubs** and teach different languages to the children.

In the UK, around one in five children speaks a different language to English at home. Some people think this is a problem. They **believe** teaching is more difficult with kids who don't speak English at home and that these children aren't going to do well in *any* subject.

Of course, it's true that starting school can be difficult for some children like this. It's not easy to learn new information and a new language at the same time.

**Research** tells us it's better for these kids to learn how to do things in their first language before learning to do them in English. Also, language is a big part of who we are and kids sometimes feel sad if they can't use their first language at school. Schools can do a lot to help. It's clear that students feel happier about school and their new lives if they can sometimes do things in their first language – like they do at Kensington Primary. Oh, and they learn English faster too.

Most children who speak two different languages don't actually have any problems at school. In fact, **growing up** like this is usually *better* than only knowing one language. Research shows that bilingual children – children who can use two languages well – are better at **solving** problems and they usually finish school with higher **marks** in their exams. That's because they can see things in different ways and they're often better at explaining ideas. That's good news for everyone, because **at least** 50% of the world's population speak two or more languages!

# Learning and training

## VOCABULARY Courses

**1** Complete the short texts with the words in bold.

1 **borrow, lasts, pilot**

My brother's studying to become a ___pilot___.
The course ___lasts___ three years and it's very
difficult. It costs about £100,000 altogether and my
family needed to ___borrow___ money to pay for it.

2 **hope, improve, useful**

I'm doing a course at the moment. It's for my work,
so the company is paying for it. It's about ways to
___useful___ sales. I'm learning a lot. It's very
___improve___ and I ___hope___ it helps me
get better at my job.

3 **advice, beginner, photography**

I'm doing a ___advice___ course at the moment. I'm
really enjoying it and I'm learning a lot. The teacher helps
us and always gives us good ___photography___ When I
started, I was a ___beginner___, but I'm much better
now.

4 **fun, level, repeat**

I started learning French last year. I went to a class on
Wednesday evenings. It was ___fun___, but
I was quite lazy and failed the exam at the end of the
course. Now, I can't do the next ___level___. I
don't want to ___repeat___ the course, so I'm going
to stop.

**2** Work in pairs. Take turns to use the words in bold
from Exercise 1 to say things about your English class.
How many of the words can you use?

**3** Work with a new partner. Which of the four courses in
Exercise 1 sounds best / worst to you? Why?

## LISTENING

**4** Match these words and phrases with the photos (a–d).
Think of one more word for each photo.

a   d   b   c
fashion   a horse   an online course   a training course

**5** **FS** ▶ In fast speech, people often say *a*, *to* and *for*
with a schwa – /ə/ – so you often just hear /ə/, /tə/ and
/fə/. Listen to ten phrases and decide which word you
hear: *a*, *to* or *for*.

**6** ▶ Listen to four people talking about the courses in
the photos. Match the speakers (1–4) with the photos
(a–d).

**7** Work in pairs. Were all of the learning experiences in
Exercise 6 good? Why? / Why not?

**8** ▶ Listen again. Are the statements true (T) or
false (F)?

**Speaker 1**

1 The course is 6:30 to 10 twice a week. F

2 He wants to get a job in fashion. T

**Speaker 2**

3 The woman's boss told her to go to the training session. T

4 She learned how to write better emails. F

**Speaker 3**

5 The woman always rides twice a week. F

6 She rode horses when she was younger, but then
stopped. F

**Speaker 4**

7 The man's wife didn't like the course because there were
too many people. T

8 The man is hoping to work for a newspaper. F

**9** Work in groups. Discuss the questions.

1 Do you know anyone who changed jobs? If yes, why did they change?

2 Do you do any training courses at work? Does anyone you know? What kind?

3 Are there things you wanted to do when you were young, but didn't?

4 What do you think is good / bad about doing open online courses?

## GRAMMAR

### Modifiers

*Very*, *really* and *quite* are modifiers. We use them before adjectives.
*Very* and *really* mean 'a lot'.

*It's **very useful**.*
*It's **really good**.*

We often make adjectives negative by adding *not very*.
*It was**n't very long** – only about an hour.*

*Quite* means 'a bit'.
*It's **quite expensive**.*
*I'm getting **quite good** now.*

**10** Choose the correct option to complete the sentences.

1 Some of my classmates aren't *very / quite* friendly.

2 The course is *quite / really* difficult! I don't understand anything!

3 It's a great university. It's *very / not very* popular.

4 She's nice, but she's *quite / not very* lazy.

5 Most of the students are really friendly, but one or two aren't *really / very* nice.

6 It's a good course. It's *quite / not very* interesting.

7 He's a good teacher, but he's *not very / quite* patient.

8 It's a great university, but it's *quite / really* expensive! I can't study there.

**11** Work in groups. Tell each other about things – or people – that you think are:

1 really expensive.

2 very popular at the moment.

3 quite boring.

4 not very modern.

5 quite interesting.

**G** See Grammar reference 6C.

## SPEAKING TASK

**12** Work in pairs. You're going to read about four different courses.

**Student A:** Read File 2 on page 199.

**Student B:** Read File 7 on page 200.

Find out the answers to these questions.

1 What kind of course is it?

2 How long does it last?

3 How much does it cost?

4 When are the classes?

**13** **M** Tell each other about the courses you read about. Then decide which of the four courses sounds best to you. Explain why.

## ■ MY OUTCOMES ■

Work in pairs. Discuss the questions.

1 What did you find interesting in this unit?

2 How many new words can you remember?

3 What other conversations about education do you want to have?

4 What part of this unit do you want to practise?

# Writing adverts

## SPEAKING

**1 Work in groups. Discuss the questions.**

1 Look at the photo. Do you have places for adverts like this where you live?

2 What kinds of things do you think people usually offer / look for?

3 Do you ever buy / sell things like this – or online? If yes, what kind of thing?

## WRITING

**2 Work in pairs. Look at the titles for online adverts (a–d). Discuss the questions.**

a Sofa Bed for Sale

b Spanish Teacher Available

c Small TV

d Language Partner Wanted

1 Which adverts:
- look interesting to you?
- don't look interesting to you?
- are maybe interesting to you?

2 What else do you want to know about each advert?

**3 Read the adverts (1–4). Match the adverts with the titles in Exercise 2 (a–d).**

**1**

**Do you need help with your school exams?**

**Do you want to practise some simple conversations before a holiday?**

I can help. I give one-to-one or group lessons – online or at your home. Try a **FREE** 30-minute class on a topic of your choice before booking.

Send a message for more **details** – including prices.

¡Gracias!

**2**

Hi there. I'm Ewa and I'm from Poland. Polish is my first language, but I'm learning English.

I think my level is B1. Ten years ago, it was maybe B2, but I don't practise enough.

I want to meet someone I can talk to about daily life, interests and so on. Maybe 45 minutes a week in English, and the same in Polish?

Message me or **text**: 07791-336-199

**3**

It's black, less than one year old and looks new.

It's big enough for two people to sleep on.

We're selling it because we need more space.

You need to come and **collect** it.

€100. Cash only please.

Message me or contact 777-4246

**4**

It's 75cm by 45cm and **nearly** new.

It's in very good **condition** and **works** fine.

I'm selling because I just don't have time to watch it.

It's $40 if you can collect it, but I can deliver at an extra **cost**.

Message me for details or call 248-821-848.

**4 Work in pairs. Think about your discussions in Exercise 2. Then answer these questions.**

1 Did you find all the information you wanted?

2 Do you still feel the same way about each one?

**5 Match two sentences with each advert (1–4).**

a You can't pay by card.

b You can try before you buy.

c I don't use it because I'm very busy.

d I'm not doing this to make money.

e I work with children and adults.

f I can bring it to your place.

g I was better in the past.

h You need to come to my place.

**6 Complete the sentences using the words in bold in the adverts.**

1 It's only six months old and it _____ well.

2 I bought it two years ago, but it's in very good _____ .

3 I don't need it anymore, so it's _____ to anyone who wants it.

4 I don't have a car so you need to come and _____ it from here.

5 If you're interested, please _____ me on 0782760582.

6 If you want more _____ , call me on 0772679999.

7 I bought it three months ago, so it's _____ new.

8 If you live near me, I can deliver at no extra _____ .

Woman taking a contact number from an advertisement.

**7 Look at the adverts in Exercise 3 again. Number these things in the order they usually appear.**

a   how to contact us

b   more details about what we're offering / looking for

c   the price

d   a simple title to tell readers what the advert is about

e   what we're offering / looking for

**8 Number the lines of this advert in the best order.**

a   Free if you can collect.

b   This is a good book for low-level learners of Italian.

c   Message me or text on 07832-222-969

d   English–Italian Dictionary

e   It has 168 pages. It's small and easy to carry. I used it for my university exams, so there's some writing in it.

## USEFUL LANGUAGE

### If

We often use *if* in adverts. *If* often introduces a situation that might be real. We also often talk about the results of this situation.

*It's $40 **if** you collect it.* ( = but it's more expensive if you can't)

**9 Match the beginning of the sentences (1–5) with the endings (a–e).**

1   If you want to speak great French,

2   I want €20 for it, or €30

3   It's free

4   If you need me to,

5   If you pay cash,

a   I can deliver at an extra cost.

b   I can sell it for €50.

c   if you take two.

d   if you collect it.

e   I can help.

**10 Work in pairs. Think of two ways to complete each sentence.**

1   Please text me if _____ .

2   I can sell it for less money if _____ .

3   If you're looking for a great teacher, _____ .

4   If you collect, _____ .

## PRACTICE

**11 Think of one thing to sell and one thing you are looking for. Write an advert for each. Write 30–60 words. Use Exercises 7 and 8 to help you.**

**12 Work in pairs. Read your partner's adverts. Do they do the following? Tell your partner.**

1   Are the titles simple and clear?

2   Do the adverts explain what the writer is selling / looking for?

3   Do they give more details?

4   Do they give the price and contact details at the end?

## VIDEO Out and about

**1 Work in groups. Discuss the questions.**

1 How often do you go shopping?

2 How often do you buy things online?

3 Which do you prefer?

### Understanding accents

Some accents use a /d/ sound instead of a /ð/ sound, so *they* /ðeɪ/ may sound more like *day* /deɪ/.

**2** 🎥 **Watch six people answer the same questions. Then work in pairs. How much can you remember about what they said? Did anyone have similar answers to you?**

**3** 🎥 **Watch again. Match one or two sentences with each speaker.**

a I go to a shopping centre maybe once or twice a month.

b I prefer shopping online because it's easier and faster.

c I don't buy clothes online because the size might be wrong.

d I choose what I want and click and then it comes a day or two later.

e I don't enjoy shopping for clothes – I only like buying food.

f I try not to go shopping too often.

g I only go shopping when my father tells me I have to.

h I'm not really interested in fashion.

**4 Work in groups. Discuss the questions.**

1 Is there a shopping centre near where you live? Do you like it?

2 Which online shopping sites do you use? Why?

3 Do you prefer buying clothes or buying food?

4 What problems can happen when you shop online?

## VIDEO Developing conversations

**5** 🎥 **You're going to watch two people talking about a university course. Watch and take notes on what they say.**

**6** 🎥 **Work in pairs. Compare what you understood. Watch again if you need to.**

**7** FS 🎥 **Watch again. Complete the sentences with two words in each gap.**

1 Are you home for _____?

2 It's really good to _____.

3 How's the _____ at the university?

4 It's great … um … but it's also _____.

5 Oh, I'm sorry to _____.

6 Are you learning a lot about _____?

7 Yeah, very interesting, but I'm learning more about _____.

8 You can visit Mount Fuji and the _____ cities.

## CONVERSATION PRACTICE

**8 Work in pairs. You're going to practise a conversation.**

1 Choose a Conversation practice from either Lesson 5A or Lesson 6A.

2 Look at the language in that lesson.

3 Check the meaning of anything you don't remember with your partner.

4 Have the conversation. Try to do it better than the last time you did it.

# Grammar and Vocabulary

## GRAMMAR

**1 Choose the correct option to complete the conversations.**

1 A: Can you pass me *that / those* cups over there?
  B: Sure. Here.

2 A: *You are / Are you* waiting to pay?
  B: No. Go ahead.

3 A: How was the exam?
  B: Bad! It was *more difficult / difficult* than last year.

4 A: Hello. Can I speak to Isabel Lopez, please?
  B: Sorry, *she works / she's working* from home today.

5 A: Did you enjoy the film?
  B: It was *quite / very* good, but not great.

6 A: I'm looking for *a / the* new camera.
  B: OK. Well, there's this one here – or this one if you want something *more cheap / cheaper*.

7 A: Do you want to try some of *this / that* soup?
  B: Oh, it's really nice. It's *more good / better* than mine.

**2 Complete the questions in the conversation. Use the words in brackets and a question word if you need to.**

A: So ¹_____ ? (studying)
B: Business management.
A: ²_____ ? (it / going)
B: Great. I'm really enjoying it. I really like marketing.
A: ³_____ ? (doing / that)
B: In Rotterdam. There's a really good school there.
A: So ⁴_____ business management? (doing)
B: My parents want me to manage their factory.
A: And ⁵_____ (living)? Do you have your own place?
B: No. I share with three friends.

**3 Complete the sentences with one word in each gap. Contractions (*he's, don't,* etc.) count as one word.**

1 She lost her job last month. She's _____ working at the moment.

2 I can't help you now. _____ doing my homework.

3 What _____ all those people looking at?

4 Do you have a coat? _____ raining outside.

5 I love _____ shoes. They're _____ nice.

6 I can't do _____ exercise. Can you help me?

7 A: Are you _____ this book?
  B: Yes, I am, but it's not _____ good. Her last book was much _____ interesting.

**4 ▶ Listen and write the six sentences you hear. Include these words.**

1 son's / law / university
2 to / a horse / moment
3 for / changing
4 my classmates / friendly
5 English / mine
6 warmer / summer

## VOCABULARY

**5 Match the two parts of the phrases.**

| | | | |
|---|---|---|---|
| 1 | borrow | a | in cash / the bills |
| 2 | do | b | sales / my English |
| 3 | hope | c | good advice / your opinion |
| 4 | last | d | your pen / some money |
| 5 | buy | e | a course / a degree |
| 6 | give | f | a few oranges / things online |
| 7 | improve | g | a long time / two years |
| 8 | pay | h | it helps / you get the job |

**6 Decide if these words are about shopping centres, studying, or sizes and quantities. There are five items in each group.**

| | | | |
|---|---|---|---|
| beginner | changing rooms | college | downstairs |
| entrance | fail | half | kilo |
| lift | litre | manager | maths |
| pair | piece | term | |

**7 Choose the correct option to complete the sentences.**

1 Lots of people do it. It's very *popular / high*.

2 I *failed / passed* my exam, so I have to take it again next month.

3 I need a new *bag / battery* for my watch.

4 She's got a very good job. She *pays / makes* a lot of money.

5 Prices are really *high / big* at the moment. If we wait, they might go down.

6 My phone bill was really *low / modern* last month, which was nice.

**8 Complete the text with one word in each gap. The first letters are given.**

I work in a ¹la_____ school in the centre of town and yesterday after work, I went for a coffee with a ²co_____ of mine. We talked about work and our families and everything. It was ³f_____ . On my way home, I went into a shop to buy a ⁴b_____ of water. I also needed the toilet, which was on the third floor in the café. The lift wasn't working, so I had to go up the ⁵st_____ and then walk to the ⁶b_____ of the shop. Then the man in front of me needed to ⁷ch_____ his baby and he took a long time!

After that, I was walking out of the shop and I saw some really nice shoes. They were quite cheap and they had my ⁸s_____ . There was one problem – one shoe had a bit of paint on it. I ⁹co_____ to the shop assistant and they gave me a 50 per cent ¹⁰d_____ . It was great because I ¹¹sa_____ a lot of money. I might go back there next week because they're having a ¹²s_____ – and you can never have too many shoes!

# 7
# People
# I know

## IN THIS UNIT, YOU:

- find out about each other's families
- give opinions about home life, parents and kids
- describe friends to other people

## SPEAKING

**1 Work in pairs. Look at the photo and discuss the questions.**

1 Do you ever hold hands with any of these people? When? Did you in the past?
- a friend – man or woman
- your wife / husband
- your mum or dad
- your son or daughter
- your brother or sister

2 Do you ever hold someone's hand in these situations? Can you give an example?
- in a dangerous situation
- when someone is sad
- when someone is worried
- when someone is sick
- before someone takes an exam
- when watching a film / series

**2 Work with a new partner. Discuss the questions.**

1 Who is your best friend?
2 What things do you do together?

Mother and daughter at a carnival in Hong Kong, China.

# 7A

# Cousins, aunts and uncles

IN THIS LESSON, YOU:
- find out about each other's families
- practise listening to conversations about people's families
- ask questions about people and give short answers
- add information to a short answer

## SPEAKING

**1** ▶ **Work in pairs. Listen to the conversation between two friends. Then say it.**

A: What did you do yesterday?

B: I went to see **my big sister**. *my brother*

A: Oh nice. Where **does she** live? *he*  (neighbour)

B: In a flat near the university.

A: Right. Do you often go and see **her**? *him*

B: Yes, I do. We meet most weeks.

A: **That's nice**. So what did you do together? *cool*

B: We went to the cinema.

**2** **Change the words in purple. Use a dictionary if you need to. Then practise your new conversation with your partner. Exchange roles and repeat.**

## VOCABULARY Relationships

**3** **Complete the table with these words.**

| aunt | boyfriend | cousin | grandma |
|------|-----------|--------|---------|
| grandson | neighbour | partner | step-mum |

| Male | Female |
|------|--------|
| granddad | ¹ *grandma* |
| ² *grandson* | granddaughter |
| step-dad | ³ *step-mum* |
| ⁴ *boyfriend* | girlfriend |
| uncle | ⁵ *aunt* |
| parent, ⁶ *cousin*, ⁷ *neighbour* ⁸ *partner* | |

**4** **Complete the sentences with words from Exercise 3.**

1 Stefan is my *uncle* . He's my mum's big brother.

2 Maria is my *cousin* . She's my aunt Stella's daughter.

3 I have six *aunts* and uncles and fifteen cousins.

4 Enrique and César are my *partner* . They live on the same floor in our block of flats. They're good friends.

5 Taylor is my youngest *granddaughter* . She's three. She's my daughter's little girl.

6 My friend Ashok lives with his *partner* , Mariko. I don't know if they're married or not.

7 My mum's *parent* are both dead now, and so is my dad's dad, but my *grandma* is still alive. She's 98!

8 Ha-yoon was my first *girlfriend* I met her when I was at high school and it lasted about six months.

9 Henrik is my *step-dad* . My mum got married to him last year. I like him. He's a nice guy.

**5** **Work in pairs. Look at the photo. Say who you think the people are.**

*Maybe she's the grandmother of these two – and the mother of her there.*

*Maybe these five are brothers and sisters – or cousins.*

**6** **With your partner, choose five people from Exercise 3. Think of one or two questions you might ask about each person.**

*Where does your grandma live? How old is she?*

A family in the village of Lengeri, Svanetia, Georgia.

## LISTENING

**7** ▶ Listen to three conversations about families. Which relationships do they mention?

**8** ▶ Listen again. Answer the questions about the different family members.

**Conversation 1**

1 Who is 19?

2 Who is a teacher?

**Conversation 2**

3 How long have Ted and his wife been married?

4 Who is studying to be a nurse?

**Conversation 3**

5 In what two countries do members of Alain's family live?

6 Who were colleagues in a company?

## GRAMMAR

### Short answers

We don't usually repeat the whole verb phrase when we answer a *yes / no* question. We either:

- Only say *yes* or *no*.
- Say *yes* or *no* + subject + auxiliary verb (e.g. *be, do, can*).

A: *Do you have any children?*

B: **Yes** ~~I have children.~~ / **Yes, I do**.

A: *Did you go out yesterday?*

B: **Yeah, I did** ~~go out~~.

A: *Are they visiting from France?*

B: **No, they're not** ~~visiting from France~~.

**9** Complete the conversations with the correct auxiliary verbs.

1 A: Do you have any brothers or sisters?
   B: Yeah, I _do_ .

2 A: Does she have a partner?
   B: Yes, she _is_ .

3 A: Are you and your sister similar?
   B: Yes, we _are_ .

4 A: Do your children still live with you at home?
   B: Yeah, my son _does_ , but my daughter _doesn't_ .

5 A: Are your grandparents still alive?
   B: Yeah, my mum's parents _are_ , but my dad's _aren't_ .

6 A: I'm going for a coffee with my cousin. Can you come?
   B: No, sorry, I _can't_ .

7 A: Did you do anything nice at the weekend?
   B: Yes, I _did_ .

8 A: Did it rain?
   B: No, it _didn't_ .

**10** Work in pairs. Take turns to read the questions in Exercise 9, but this time give opposite answers.

A: *Do you have any brothers or sisters?*

B: *No, I don't.*

**G** See Grammar reference 7A.

## DEVELOPING CONVERSATIONS

### Adding information

In conversations, we don't usually just give short answers to questions. We add information to help the conversation continue.

A: *Do you have any other cousins here?*

B: *No, I don't,* **but I have twelve back in Italy**.

A: *Really? So how many aunts and uncles do you have?*

**11** Match the extra information (a–h) with the questions and short answers in Exercise 9 (1–8).

a It wasn't very hot, but it stayed dry. _8_

b My grandfather had his 80th birthday party. _7_

c A younger brother. _1_

d They died a few years ago. _5_

e She's studying in the US. _4_

f We both like a lot of the same things. _3_

g I'm meeting a friend of mine. We're going shopping. _6_

h He's a really nice guy. I like him. _2_

**12** Work in pairs. Practise reading the conversations in Exercise 9, adding the information above. Your partner should then ask one more question.

A: *Do you have any brothers or sisters?*

B: *Yeah, I do. A younger brother.*

A: *How old is he?*

B: *Six.*

## CONVERSATION PRACTICE

**13** Work in pairs. Use this guide to have conversations about family. Use your questions from Exercise 6.

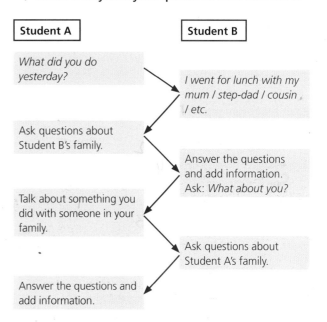

| Student A | Student B |
|---|---|
| What did you do yesterday? | I went for lunch with my mum / step-dad / cousin / etc. |
| Ask questions about Student B's family. | Answer the questions and add information. Ask: *What about you?* |
| Talk about something you did with someone in your family. | Ask questions about Student A's family. |
| Answer the questions and add information. | |

# I have to look after the kids

**IN THIS LESSON, YOU:**
- give opinions about home life, parents and kids
- describe what parents and kids are like
- read about parents' experiences
- say things you have to do in different situations

## VOCABULARY Parents and kids

**1** **Work in pairs. Check you understand the words in bold. Use a dictionary if you need to.**

1  I can't sleep because the baby**'s crying**.

2  She's getting too big to carry, but she complains when I **push** her in the pushchair.

3  She comes in and **jumps** on top of me in the morning.

4  Before bed, he gives everyone a **kiss** goodnight.

5  I have a headache because the kids are **shouting** and making so much noise.

6  He cried because another boy pushed him when they were in the **playground**.

7  I usually take her to school in the morning and my wife **collects** her in the afternoon.

8  She has a mobile and a laptop, so she spends a lot of time looking at a **screen**.

9  Kids just want love. It **doesn't matter** if they don't have a lot of things.

10  I'm **glad** I can spend a lot of time with my grandchildren. They keep me young.

11  **Unfortunately**, I don't see my kids much because I travel a lot for work. I really **miss** them when I'm away.

**2** **P ▶** Listen to the words from Exercise 1 and practise saying them on their own and in a phrase. Which words / phrases do you find hard to say? Practise saying them again.

**3** **Work in pairs. Take turns to act or draw a word in bold in Exercise 1. Your partner says the word.**

## READING

**4** **Work in pairs. Read Robin99's main forum post on page 71. Discuss what you think about these questions.**

1  Will Robin's situation get better? Why? / Why not?

2  Is Robin's experience usual? Why? / Why not?

3  Is it better for one parent to stay at home? Why? / Why not?

**5** **Read the forum replies. Match the replies (1–5) with these sentences (a–e).**

a  I don't want to stop working. 2

b  I look after my grandchild. 4

c  Some parents don't look after their kids well. 5

d  I'm happier staying at home with my child. 1

e  My child is happy at nursery. 3

**6** **Work in pairs. Discuss the questions.**

1  Do you think Robin is going to stay at work or not? Why? / Why not?

2  Do you think each comment is helpful or not?

3  Which comment do you like best?

## GRAMMAR

*Have to*

*Have / Has to* + verb is similar to *need(s) to* + verb. They show something is (not) necessary.

We **have to** pay for the nursery.

She **has to** work two jobs to earn enough money to live.

It's good that you **don't have to** stay at home.

**Does** your partner **have to** work too?

**7** **Complete the sentences with the correct form of have to.**

1  I'm glad I ___have to___ work with kids. They make too much noise.

2  My kids have a lot of exams at school that they ___have to___ pass.

3  She's glad she ___doesn't   have to___ share a room with her brother. He's very untidy.

4  A: ___Do you have to___ pay for the nursery?
   B: I do, unfortunately. And it's really expensive.

5  I ___have to___ travel a long way to work, so unfortunately my son ___has to___ be at nursery from 7:30 till 6.

6  My friend Ada ___has to___ to help her parents cook and clean, but a lot of my friends ___don't have to___ do anything!

7  Do we have time for a coffee? What time ___do you have to___ be back?

8  Unfortunately, we can't come. We both ___have to___ work tomorrow.

**8** **Work in groups. Say two things you have to / don't have to do:**

- at home.   • at work / school.   • this week.

**G** See Grammar reference 7B.

## SPEAKING

**9** **M** **Work in groups. Decide if each of these situations is good, bad or it doesn't matter. Do you all agree?**

1  Both parents have to work.

   *A: I think it doesn't matter if both parents have to work.*
   *B: I agree.*
   *C: I don't agree. Kids miss their parents.*

2  Little kids shout and push when they play.

3  Parents pick up and carry their baby a lot.

4  Kids have to go to bed before eight in the evening.

5  Kids don't have to do jobs in the home.

6  Kids spend a lot of time looking at a screen.

7  Families don't eat together.

A mother hugs her little girl as she leaves her at the nursery.

# WORKING PARENTS

**Robin99** So I went back to work last week and I left my little daughter at the nursery. She didn't want me to go and she cried a lot. The whole day I felt bad and I worried about her. When I picked her up in the evening, the teacher said she was happy and played with the other kids, but she was angry with me. She didn't want to give me a kiss and she cried and shouted when I put her in her pushchair to go home. She was better when she saw my partner. He gave her a bath and read her a story. But I feel terrible. Does it get any better? What do you think about being a working parent? Is it better to stay at home?

## MESSAGE BOARD

**1 bobbijo** Do you have to work? When I went back to my job after my kid was born, I felt the same as you. I decided to leave my job – and I'm glad I did!

>> **Robin99** It's a good question. My partner doesn't earn a lot, so we do need the extra money. But then we have to pay for the nursery and it costs most of what I earn!

**2 legalkate** Looking after kids is important work – maybe the most important – but you have to think about yourself too. I worked very hard to become a lawyer and I'm good at it. It's part of who I am.

>> **Robin99** I'm a shop manager. It's OK. I like my colleagues, but it's not so important to me.

**3 chazwashere** The same thing happened with my son. He cried and shouted every day for three months, but now he loves nursery. When we arrive, he doesn't kiss me goodbye, but it's because he jumps out of his chair and **runs** to see his friends.

>> **Robin99** Thanks, that's good to know.

**4 grannycool62** It's good that you don't have to stay at home. When I became a mum, I left my job and I really missed it. I'm glad I can help my daughter with her child now, so she can work. Do you have a parent that can help?

>> **Robin99** Unfortunately, my parents don't live near, so we have to take our daughter to the nursery.

**5 tigerdad** It's better for the kids to be at nursery with other kids. I see so many parents pushing their kids' chair while looking at a mobile phone. And the kids are sitting and looking at a screen too!

>> **Robin99** I don't think I'm one of those parents, but maybe you're right about kids playing together.

## 7C

# A good friend

**IN THIS LESSON, YOU:**
- describe friends to other people
- explain how you know people
- talk about relationships with friends and family
- practise listening to five people talk about family and friends

## SPEAKING

**1** **Make a list of six friends that you met in different ways. Write sentences like these:**

1 I've known **Ali** all my life. We were neighbours. We lived in the same building.

2 I've known **Hassan** all my life. My parents were friends with his parents.

3 I've known **Salma** for ten years. We met at school. We were in the same class.

4 I've known **Aisha** for two years. We met at university. We're doing the same degree.

5 I've known **Khalid** for five years. We met at work. We work in the same department.

6 I've known **Helen** for a few months. We met online.

**2** **Tell your partner about your friends from Exercise 1. If you have a photo, show it to your partner. Ask each other one of these questions for more information.**

1 How often do you see each other?

2 When was the last time you saw each other?

## VOCABULARY Talking about friends

**3** **Work in pairs. Check you understand the words in bold. Which sentences do you think show something good? Which show something bad? Say why.**

1 She has some **health problems**.

2 She didn't **offer to help** me.

3 She **'s like** my mum.

4 She doesn't **think about herself**.

5 She **believes she can** do anything.

6 They often **invite me** to dinner.

7 We **grew up together**.

8 He's **easy to talk to**.

**4** **Choose six words or phrases from Exercise 3 to talk about people you know.**

*My cousin invited me to her birthday party.*

*My friend Aisha is like my big sister.*

*My uncle has health problems.*

**5** **Complete the descriptions about seeing friends with these words.**

| clever | fit | funny | kind | quiet | stupid |
|---|---|---|---|---|---|

1 I visited Poland and stayed with a friend of a friend, called Hanna. She was like my mum. She was so _____ . She drove 100km to collect me from the airport. She cooked for me and did my washing. I offered to pay for things, but she always said no. On the last night I invited her to have dinner to say thanks.

2 I saw my friend Xavi yesterday. He usually talks a lot. He's _____ and we laugh a lot. But yesterday he was very _____ . He didn't say very much at all. I hope he's OK.

3 I have a colleague called Olena. I like her a lot. She's very friendly and easy to talk to. But sometimes she only thinks about herself and she often forgets things. Last week, I was a bit _____ and I asked her to get me a ticket for a concert we wanted to go to together. But she forgot and only got a ticket for herself! Now there are no tickets left.

4 I saw my friend Bian yesterday. She was a neighbour and we grew up together. I invited her for dinner because she passed all her exams. I know she's very _____ , but she doesn't always believe she can do things, so I'm really pleased for her.

5 I saw my friend Tia last week. Unfortunately, she has some health problems. She was in hospital last year and the doctor says she needs to do more exercise. She's not very _____ . We went for a walk, and she had to stop and sit down. I worry about her.

**6** **Work in pairs. Don't look at the descriptions in Exercise 5. How many of these questions can you answer?**

1 In what ways was Hanna kind?

2 How was Xavi different yesterday to what he's normally like?

3 What's good about Olena? What's bad?

4 Why did Bian go for dinner? What doesn't she believe?

5 In what ways is Tia not fit?

**7** **Explain which adjectives in Exercise 5 describe:**

1 you.

2 members of your family.

3 your friends from Exercise 1.

## LISTENING

**8** ▶ **Listen to five speakers talking about friends and family. Match the speakers (1–5) with who / what they're talking about (a–e).**

a a possible boyfriend

b a brother or sister

c an old friend

d a partner

e a dog

**9** **FS** ▶ **In fast speech, *not* is often said *n't* and sometimes you don't hear the *t*. Listen to eight phrases. Which ones include *not / n't*?**

**10** ▶ **Listen again. Choose the correct option (a–c) to answer the questions.**

1 What does the man say he did?
  a bought something expensive
  b borrowed a jacket
  c gave someone a present

2 Why did the woman go to bed late?
  a Someone called her at night.
  b She was studying.
  c She visited New York.

3 Why was the woman unhappy about her evening out?
  a She ate bad food.
  b She had to pay for dinner.
  c She didn't like the guy she met.

4 What was Django like?
  a friendly
  b stupid
  c beautiful

5 What does the man say about Andrea?
  a He's like her.
  b He doesn't believe she can dance.
  c She isn't very friendly.

**11** **Work in pairs. Choose three sets of questions to discuss.**

1 Do / Did you borrow things from a family member? What?

2 Do you know anyone who lives in a different country? How often do you speak?

3 Do you know anyone who says stupid things? What kinds of things do they say?

4 Are dogs good friends? Have you ever had one?

5 Do you know anyone who has a partner who is very similar? Or who is very different?

## SPEAKING TASK

**12** **Work in pairs. Each think of a friend – not a family member. Interview each other about your friend using these questions. You can ask more questions if you want.**

*What's the name of your friend?*

*How long have you known each other?*

*How did you meet?*

*What's he / she like?*

*What does he / she do?*

*Where does he / she live?*

*Do you go out together a lot?*

*When did you last see each other?*

**13** **M** **Work with a new partner. Tell them what you found out about your partner's friend in Exercise 12. Then discuss these questions.**

1 How many things are the same for both your friends and the friends of your partners?

2 Which two friends would you introduce to each other?

### ■ MY OUTCOMES ■

**Work in pairs. Discuss the questions.**

1 What new language did you learn?

2 How many different questions can you now ask about people?

3 Which listening activity did you most enjoy?

4 Can you think of two people you can talk / write to in English this week?

# 8
# Plans

**IN THIS UNIT, YOU:**

- discuss plans
- say how you feel about government plans
- decide how to improve places you know

## SPEAKING

**1 Work in pairs. Discuss the questions.**

1 Look at the photo. Do you ever do things like this?

2 Where do you most like to spend your free time? Who do you usually spend it with?

3 Are you happy with how much free time you have? If not, why not?

4 What different ways of enjoying yourself are there where you live?

5 How often do you go out in the evening? Where to?

**2 Work with a new partner. Which of these things do you enjoy doing? Which are you planning to do this week?**

1 doing some shopping  2
2 going to the library  4
3 tidying your flat / house  7
4 paying a bill  6
5 going to the cinema  5
6 going swimming / cycling / running  3
7 doing some drawing / painting  8
8 going for a walk  1

Old friends play video games together.

# What are your plans?

## SPEAKING

1 ▶ **Work in pairs. Listen to the conversation between two friends. Then say it.**

A: What are your plans for today?

B: I'm going to **do some shopping** this afternoon and then **just go home**. What about you?

A: I'm going to **go to the gym**. Then I'm going to **meet some friends**.

B: What about tomorrow? Do you want to go out somewhere?

A: Yes. Great. Where?

B: How about the **Old Town**?

A: OK. Fine. What time?

B: How about **twelve**?

A: Perfect.

2 **Change the words in purple. Use a dictionary if you need to. Then practise your new conversation with your partner. Exchange roles and repeat.**

## VOCABULARY Plans for the week

3 **Complete the sentences with these words.**

5 ~~4~~  4  A8  2  7  9  3
appointment  book  camping  gas  lift  mind  pack
show  trip  wedding
B 8        6        1

1 I need to buy some clothes for a friend's _wedding_ I want to look my best.

2 I need to pay my _gas_ bill today – before I forget.

3 I'm going away for a few days so I need to _pack_ my things tonight.

4 I want to visit my parents this weekend, so I have to _book_ a train ticket.

5 I can't come to class tomorrow because I have a doctor's _appointment_

6 My wife is away on a business _trip_ this week.

7 I have my car with me, so I can give you a _lift_ to the shops if you want.

8 A: We're planning to go _camping_ next weekend. Do you want to come with us?

B: I can't. I have tickets to a _show_ at the theatre that Saturday.

9 A: So what time do you want to meet?

B: I don't _mind_. What time's best for you?

4 P ▶ **Listen to the words from Exercise 3 and practise saying them on their own and in a phrase. Which words / phrases do you find hard to say? Practise saying them again.**

5 **Work in pairs. Look at Exercise 3 and say:**

1 which things you often do.

2 which things you never do – or don't often do.

3 which things you're planning to do this week.

4 which things you most / least enjoy doing.

## LISTENING

**6** ▶ Listen to three conversations about plans. Match the conversations (1–3) with the places where they happen (a–c).

a at work **3**
b at university **1**
c on holiday **2**

**7** ▶ Listen again. Write the correct conversation (1, 2 or 3).

a Someone is going to go to a restaurant. **3**
b Someone arranges where to meet. **2**
c Someone invites another person out for dinner. **1**
d Someone has to go and get another person. **3**
e Someone doesn't want to meet. **1**
f Someone is going to fly somewhere soon. **2**

## GRAMMAR

### Going to

We use the present form of the verb *be* + *going to* + verb to talk about the future – and especially the plans we have.

I**'m going to go** running by the river later.

She**'s not going to have** time today.

What about tonight? **Are** you **going to be** busy then?

**8** Complete the sentences with the correct form of *going to* and the verbs in brackets.

1 A: My parents are going to take me for dinner tonight. (take)
 B: That's nice. Where you going ? (go)
2 A: I'm going to leave tomorrow. My flight is at six in the morning! (leave)
 B: Really? That's early. What time are you going to get up ? (get up)
3 A: Some friends are going to visit next week. (visit)
 B: That's nice. How long are they going to stay ? (stay)
4 A: I spoke to Tymofiy. He is not going to come . He's got another bad headache. (not come)
 B: Really? I hope it isn't anything serious are you going to go to the doctor's? (go)

**9** Work in pairs. Say which of these things you are going to do today / tomorrow / this week / this month. Say when. Ask each other questions to find out more.

When are you going to...?

1 meet a friend
2 cook dinner / lunch
3 go on holiday
4 write some emails
5 watch TV
6 do some studying / homework
7 go shopping
8 get up early / late

A: I'm going to meet some friends tonight.
B: Really? Nice. Where are you going to meet?
A: In the centre of town. We're going to have dinner.

**G** See Grammar reference 8A.

## DEVELOPING CONVERSATIONS

### Making suggestions

We often make suggestions using *How about …?*
A: Do you want to meet somewhere?
B: Yes, OK. Where?
A: **How about** in the main square at eight?

**10** Number the sentences in the correct order (1–9) to make a conversation.

a How about in the main square, under the big clock?
b Is six OK?
c Oh, sorry. Well, how about seven thirty?
d What are your plans for later?
e Perfect! See you later. Bye.
f Yes. Great. Where?
g I don't have any. Why? Do you want to meet somewhere?
h It's quite early.
i Yes, fine. What time?

**11** ▶ Listen and check your ideas.

**12** Respond to each question by writing a suggestion with *How about …?*

1 What do you want to see at the cinema?
2 What are we going to get her for her birthday?
3 What do you want to eat tonight?
4 Do you know a good place to have a party?

## CONVERSATION PRACTICE

**13** Work in pairs. Have conversations about plans. Use this guide to help you. Take turns to start.

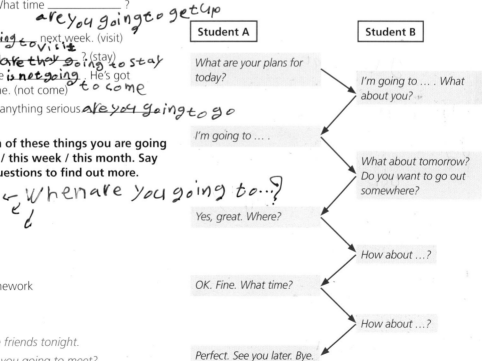

| Student A | Student B |
|---|---|
| What are your plans for today? | I'm going to … . What about you? |
| I'm going to … . | |
| | What about tomorrow? Do you want to go out somewhere? |
| Yes, great. Where? | |
| | How about …? |
| OK. Fine. What time? | |
| | How about …? |
| Perfect. See you later. Bye. | |

# For and against

**IN THIS LESSON, YOU:**
- say how you feel about government plans
- talk about changes your town / city needs
- look at ways of agreeing / disagreeing with plans
- read a local website discussion

## SPEAKING

**1** Work in groups. Discuss the questions.

1  How important are the changes below for your town or city?

2  Say if they are very important, quite important or not very important. Explain why.

- a new airport
- a new shopping centre
- a bigger library
- a new museum
- better roads
- better wi-fi
- a new stadium
- a new hospital
- a new metro line
- more street lights
- better water
- more schools

## VOCABULARY  Discussing plans

**2** Complete the conversations with these pairs of words.

2 🌼
build / crowded          3 economy / government
4 education / digital     environment / complete
6 nothing / save          use / employ 🌼 5

1  A: If more people travel by train, it's better for the **environment**

   B: Yes, maybe, but it's a big plan. It's going to take a long time to **complete**

2  A: I don't want them to **build** new houses in the countryside.

   B: But people need to live somewhere – and most cities are already very **crowded**

3  A: I think it's good for the **economy** if people work longer.

   B: Yes, and the **government** doesn't want to look after a lot of people who aren't working.

4  A: Libraries are important. They're good for **education**

   B: Yes, but we don't need them. Everything is **digital** now – you can find everything online.

5  A: I'm glad they're going to build a new shopping centre. It's a good **use** of money.

   B: Yes, I agree. I hope they're going to **employ** a lot of local people.

6  A: **nothing** is going to change if they build these new stations.

   B: Really? I think they're going to improve transport and **save** time for everyone.

**3** Work in pairs. How many words from Exercise 2 can you use to talk about the changes in Exercise 1?

*A new airport is going to be bad for the environment.*

*A new stadium is (not) a good use of money.*

**4** Work in groups. Discuss the questions.

1  Are they building anything in your city or area at the moment? What? Where? Is it a good idea?

2  Can you think of something that was a good use of public money?

3  Can you think of something that took a very long time to complete?

4  Can you think of something that was good for the environment?

5  What's the most crowded part of your town / city?

6  Can you think of three things that save people time?

## READING

**5** Look at the article on page 79. Read the opinions about the local government's plans. What do you think the plans are? Complete the headings (1–3) with your ideas.

**6** Work in pairs. Compare your ideas for Exercise 5. Who has the best heading for each plan?

**7** Read again. Answer the questions.

1  Who would like more tourists? Gloria Jamila

2  Who would like to improve education? Selina Elijah

3  Who wants to save time? Jamila

4  Who wants to save money? Gavin

5  Who likes sport? Gloria

6  Who is worried about the environment? Cass

**8** Work in pairs. Which opinions do you agree with? Which do you disagree with? Why?

## SPEAKING

**9** Decide which of these plans and ideas you think are good and which you think are bad. Write one reason why for each.

1  The government is planning to build new high-speed train lines.

2  The government wants to stop people building in the countryside or next to the sea.

3  The government is going to change the age when people can stop working from 65 to 68.

4  The local government is going to close all the libraries and put digital books online for free.

5  The local government wants to build a shopping centre in your area with 100 shops and a car park.

**10** **M** Work in groups. Discuss your opinions about the plans.

*A: I think building new high-speed train lines is good. There are going to be more jobs.*

*B: I agree – and it's going to save everyone time.*

*C: I think it's a bad idea. It's going to be bad for the environment.*

Building Titanic Belfast – a museum about the famous ship, Belfast, Northern Ireland, UK.

# WHAT DO YOU THINK?

There's a lot happening in our local area and we always love hearing how you feel about changes that are being planned. We spoke to some local people to hear their opinions about three big new plans.

**1** The local government wants to _~~by~~ build a new airport_ .

**FOR** I think it's a good idea. It's going to help business and more people are going to come here. At the moment, people have to fly to the capital and then get the train. It takes hours.
– *Jamila*

**AGAINST** I don't think it's a good idea. It's not going to be near my house, but I still don't want all those planes to come here. There's going to be a lot of noise and it's not going to be good for the air. They want to build it in some nice countryside outside the city too.
– *Cass*

**2** The government is planning to _~~is going to spend~~ Less money_

**FOR** It's going to improve things. The government is spending too much money at the moment. They need to do something about it and I don't want to give the government more of my money. I worked hard to earn it.
– *Gavin*

**AGAINST** If this happens, there are going to be a lot of problems because lots of doctors, police officers and teachers are going to leave their jobs. Maybe some people can pay to see a doctor, or pay for extra classes for their children, but for most people, it's going to be bad for their health and their children's education.
– *Selina*

**3** Our government wants to _build a new ~~st~~ stadium._

**FOR** It's going to be good for our country and our economy. Lots of people are going to come here and spend money in the hotels and restaurants. And they're going to meet local people and learn about our country too. I think it's great. And for me, it's going to be good because I really want to go and see some matches – I hope the tickets aren't going to be very expensive.
– *Gloria*

**AGAINST** I don't think it's a good use of money. We could spend the money on better things. There are more important things in life than sport. How about giving every student a laptop or giving them free English lessons? Those are better ways of spending all that money.
– *Elijah*

# Hopes and dreams

## LISTENING

1 You're going to hear four people talking about things they want to do. The photos show what each person is thinking. Work in pairs. What do you think each person wants to do?

2 ▶ Listen and match the speakers (1–4) with the photos (a–d). Then work in pairs. Compare your ideas.

3 FS ▶ In fast speech, the word *to* often just sounds like /tə/. Listen to eight phrases. Which include *to*?

4 ▶ Listen again. Are the statements true (T) or false (F)?

**Conversation 1**

1 The man is from Manchester. F

2 He already does Brazilian jiu-jitsu. F

**Conversation 2**

3 The woman is planning to leave her job this year. F

4 She wants to have children before starting a business. F

**Conversation 3**

5 The woman thinks not working is going to be good. F

6 She wants to grow flowers. F

**Conversation 4**

7 The man wants to be rich. T

8 He wants to drive a big expensive car. F

5 Work in groups. Would you like to do any of the things the people talk about? Why? / Why not?

*A: I wouldn't like to do that. It looks difficult.*

*B: I'd like to be famous and have lots of money.*

## VOCABULARY In my life

**6** **Work in pairs. Check you understand the words in bold. Use a dictionary if you need to.**

1 I **joined** a golf club last year.
2 I travelled across Indonesia on a **motorbike**.
3 I started going to the **opera**.
4 I was the **star** of the school play.
5 I was **single** until I was 32.
6 I got my **driving licence** when I was 16.
7 I want to go in a **helicopter**.
8 I just want to have a **normal** life.
9 I want to be famous **everywhere** in the world.
10 I'm going to change the colour of my hair. I want it **blonde**.
11 I'm going to make my own **album**.
12 I'm going to start my own YouTube **channel**.

**7** **Work with a new partner. Say which things from Exercise 6 you think are good and which aren't. Explain why.**

**8** **With your partner, use words from Exercise 6 to talk about your life up to now and your plans for the future.**

*I went to the opera once – and I don't want to go again. It's not for me!*

## GRAMMAR

### *Would like to*

We use *would like to* + verb to talk about things we want to do – or hope to do. We often write (and say) *would* as *'d*.

*I'd like to go to Japan one day. I'm sure it's really interesting.*

*He'd really like to learn Spanish.*

We make negatives using *wouldn't like to* + verb.

*I wouldn't like to do his job! It's hard!*

We make questions using *Would* + person + *like to* + verb.

*Would you like to go in a helicopter?*

**9** **Use the notes to make sentences with the correct form of *would / wouldn't like (to)*.**

1 I / really / spend a year in India.
2 I / really / meet him sometime. I loved his last album!
3 My brother / learn how to cook.
4 She / change jobs sometime soon.
5 I / not / be famous!
6 It's a nice apartment, but I / not / live in that area.
7 you / join a band?
8 you / come shopping with me tomorrow?

**10** **Work in pairs. Discuss which of these things you'd like to do sometime in the future. Explain your decisions.**

1 buy my own house / flat
   *I'd really like to buy my own house one day.*
   *I'm OK just renting. I think it's easier.*
2 make a lot of money
3 get fitter
4 move to a different country
5 speak really good English
6 buy a motorbike
7 stop working at 50
8 write a book
9 eat less meat
10 learn another language

**11** **Work in groups. Tell each other about:**

1 a place you'd really like to visit.
2 a person you'd really like to meet.
3 something you'd really like to do.
4 something you'd like to learn.
5 something you'd like to stop doing.

**G** See Grammar reference 8C. ≫

## SPEAKING TASK

**12** **Work in pairs. You are going to think of different ways to improve one of the places below. Choose the place you want to talk about. Discuss what you'd like to change – and why.**

a your classroom
b your school
c your area
d your country

*I'd like to have more windows in this classroom. It's very dark.*

*I'd like to start school a bit later. We start very early.*

*We need more jobs in this area – more jobs that pay well.*

*We need to spend more money on schools and hospitals in this country.*

**13** **M** **Tell the rest of the class about your ideas. As a class, decide what the best plan for each place is.**

## ▨ MY OUTCOMES ▨

**Work in pairs. Discuss the questions.**

1 Which of the texts are you going to read / listen to again?
2 What plans and opinions can you now share in English?
3 How many words from the vocabulary exercises can you remember?
4 What can you do to remember more vocabulary?

# WRITING 4
# Writing invitations

## SPEAKING

1 Work in pairs. Use these ideas to tell your partner about things you did with friends recently and things you are planning to do. Ask questions to find out more.

1 My friend **Ben** invited me to …

2 I invited my friend **Aisha** to …

3 I'm going to invite my friend **Pablo** to …

*My friend Sayuri invited me to go to the cinema last week and we went to see* Past Lives.

*I invited my friend Aisha to dinner and we went to a place called Pasha.*

## WRITING

2 Work in pairs. Read the messages inviting people to do things. Match two sentences (a–f) with each message (1–3).

**1**

Hi James. What are you doing on Tuesday? I'm going to be in your area in the afternoon because I have a meeting for work. Would you like to meet me for a drink or something to eat – maybe at the place near your house? My meeting finishes at 4, so I could meet you any time after that. Let me know what you think.

8:29 ✔

**2**

Hi Luisella. How are things? Are you free next Wednesday? I'm going to a meeting against the plans to build a new airport. I know you are unhappy about the idea, so would you like to come with me? The meeting is in the library and it starts at 7. I could meet you there. Anyway, let me know what you think!

17:33 ✔

**3**

Hi. How's the family? Are you free next Saturday? Yago is going to be four next week and we're going to Clissold Park for a picnic. Would you and Jess like to bring Phoebe? We're going to be next to the playground from about 12 p.m. till about 2. Let us know if you can come.

10:45 ✔

*3* a They want to meet at the weekend.

*2* b They want to meet in the evening.

*1* c They're going to do something else on the same day.

*2* d They want to stop something.

*3* e They're inviting someone to a birthday party.

*1* f They're going to do what the other person wants to do.

3 Work in pairs. Complete the phrases from the messages with three words in each gap. Don't look back at the messages.

1 What *are you going* on Tuesday?

2 I *could meet you* any time after that.

3 *Would you like* to come with me?

4 The meeting is in the library and *it is starting*

5 *Are you free* next Saturday?

6 *Let me know* if you can come.

4 Work in pairs. Discuss the questions.

1 Which activities in the messages would you say *yes* to?

2 How do you normally plan things with friends?
- do it with messages
- call them and talk
- do it when you see them
- another way

## USEFUL LANGUAGE

### Inviting people

When we send a message to invite people, we often follow the same pattern with the same phrases.

| | |
|---|---|
| 1 Ask if they're free | *Hi. What are you doing / Are you free …?* |
| 2 Say the main plan (why) | *I'm going to … (with + person) / we decided to …* |
| 3 Invite them | *Would you like to …?* |
| 4 Say place / time of plan | *I'm going to / It starts / It finishes …* |
| 5 Give an idea of how to meet | *I could meet you …* |
| 6 Tell them to answer | *Let me know …* |

**5** Number the parts of the message in the correct order.

a I saw Lana last night and we decided to go for a walk in the mountains on Sunday. *2*

b We're going to leave around 10 a.m. ~~~~ *3*

c Hi. What are you doing next weekend? *1*

d Lana is going to drive, so we could collect you from your place. *4*

e Let me know if you can come. *6*

f Would you like to come too? *5*

**6** Complete the phrases with your own ideas.

1 Are you free *today* ?

2 I saw *Ali* yesterday and we decided to *go to London*

3 Would you like *to come to*

4 We're going to *London tower*

5 We could meet you *in London*

6 Let me know *if you can come* ✓

**7** Match the beginning of the sentences (1–6) with the endings (a–f).

1 I'm afraid we

2 Unfortunately, I'm

3 Yes! That sounds

4 Sure. Thanks for inviting

5 That's a good

6 What a

*5* a idea. I'd love to go.

*2* b busy then. Let me know next time you go.

*3* c lovely. But why don't you come round to mine?

*1* d can't. We're going to see my parents next weekend.

*4* e me. Let's meet there at 6:30 and we can chat before the meeting.

*6* f shame. I'm away. Have a good time.

## Answering invitations

To say *no* to an invitation, we usually explain why with phrases like *I'm afraid / What a shame / Unfortunately* ... .

**I'm afraid** I can't. I have a meeting that day.

To say *yes*, we often use phrases like *I'd love to / That sounds great*. We sometimes ask a question to get details of the plan or offer to help.

*Yes,* **I'd love to**. *Do you want me to bring anything?*

**8** Write one *yes* and one *no* answer to the invitation in Exercise 5.

*I'd love to go with you to go to*

## PRACTICE

*Your ~~y~~ conzry*

**9** Work in pairs. Make a plan to do something together. Think about:

• what you're going to do.

• the place and time of the plan.

• where / when other people could meet you.

**10** Write a message inviting someone else to join you in your activity. Write 40–80 words.

**11** Work in pairs. Read your partner's message. Do they do the following? Tell your partner.

• ask if the person is free *Hi, are you free tomrrw*

• say the main plan *I'm going to London in the*

• invite the person *would you like to come with us weekend*

• say the place / time

• give an idea of how to meet

• tell the person to answer

**12** Work in groups. Share your messages. Write a reply to each one.

## VIDEO  Out and about

**1  Work in groups. Discuss the questions.**

1  Do you come from a big family?

2  Who's more important to you – friends or family?

### Understanding accents

Some accents use an /p/ sound instead of an /f/ sound, so *fat* /ʃæt/ may sound more like *pat* /pæt/.

**2  🎥 Watch five people answer the same questions. How much can you remember about what they said? Then work in pairs. Did anyone have the same answers as you?**

**3  🎥 Watch again. Match one or two sentences with each speaker.**

a  I'm very close to my mum.

b  My husband has a brother and sister who are both married.

c  I have 16 aunts and uncles on my mother's side of the family.

d  My family and friends are both important.

e  I have one grandparent.

f  My family affected how I am.

g  I have pets.

h  I have a big brother.

**4  Tell your partner about four people you know. Give examples.**

1  They are very close to a parent.

2  They aren't very close to their family.

3  They have a lot of aunts and uncles.

4  They have a grandparent living with them.

5  They have a pet.

## VIDEO  Developing conversations

**5  🎥 You're going to watch two people planning to do something. Watch and take notes.**

**6  🎥 Work in pairs. Compare what you understood. Watch again if you need to.**

**7  FS 🎥 Watch again. Complete the sentences with two or three words in each gap.**

1  I need to talk with my friends. Can you come around to _____ ?

2  I can do that. What day is _____ ?

3  I'm _____ . I have drama class on Tuesday.

4  Oh I'm afraid I _____ Wednesday.

5  I think Friday's fine. _____ with us anyway?

6  Oh yes. _____ flatmates, Stephen and Michael.

7  And also Ian as well. Yeah, I think you met him _____ , right?

8  OK, great, so we have a plan. I'll talk with my flatmates _____ .

## CONVERSATION PRACTICE

**8  Work in pairs. You're going to practise a conversation.**

1  Choose a Conversation practice from either Lesson 7A or Lesson 8A.

2  Look at the language in that lesson.

3  Check the meaning of anything you don't remember with your partner.

4  Have the conversation. Try to do it better than the last time you did it.

# Grammar and Vocabulary

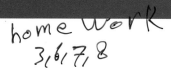
home work
3, 6, 7, 8

## GRAMMAR

**1** Complete the sentences with one word in each gap.

1 A: Are you _going_ to be here for lunch today?

  B: Yes, I'_m_____ . I'm going to leave at about four o'clock.

2 A: Do you have to work at the weekends?

  B: No, I _don't_____ .

3 A: Who's going _to_____ make the dinner?

  B: We _are_____ .

4 A: Your grandfather's 98! Wow! Can he still walk OK?

  B: Yes, he _can_____ . But he's very slow.

5 A: Do you enjoy studying?

  B: No, I _don't_____ .

6 A: Does anyone speak Spanish in your family?

  B: Yes, my wife _does_____ .

7 I can't talk now. I have _to_____ speak to my boss.

8 I _'d_____ like to visit Costa Rica next year, but tickets are very expensive.

**2** Rewrite the sentences as negatives (–) or questions (?).

1 I'm going to see him today. (–)

2 She has to come to the meeting. (–)

3 You'd like to be famous some day. (?)

4 I'd like to work for that company. (–)

5 He's going to stay here. (?)

6 I have to wait. (?)

7 We have to go to right now. (–)

8 She'd like to go to university. (?)

**3** Put the words in brackets in the correct place in the sentence.

1 She have to drive me to the station. I can take a taxi. (doesn't)

2 A: Do you all speak Chinese well?

  B: No, my older brother, but I don't. (does)

3 It's OK. You don't to do it. You decide. (have)

4 Would you like have your own restaurant? (to)

5 My husband is going to, but I'm not. (go)

**4** ▶ Listen and write the six sentences you hear. Include these words.

1 she / idea

2 I / tomorrow

3 time / arrive

4 stop / travel

5 like / something

6 daughter / stay / dad

## VOCABULARY

**5** Match the two parts of the phrases.

| 1 push | 4 | a | a table for two / my train ticket |
| 2 jump | 7 | b | a reading group / a golf club |
| 3 offer | 6 | c | a lot of time / electricity |
| 4 book | 8 | d | local people / new workers |
| 5 build | 1 | e | the door open / them in a pushchair |
| 6 save | 3 | f | to help / me their seat |
| 7 join | 2 | g | on top of me / up and down |
| 8 employ | 5 | h | new houses / a new airport |

**6** Decide if these words and phrases are about relationships, kids or city plans. There are four items in each group.

| aunt | complete | cousin | cry |
|---|---|---|---|
| economy | environment | government | grow up |
| neighbour | partner | playground | shout |

**7** Choose the correct option to complete the sentences.

1 It doesn't *matter* / *mind* if kids spend a lot of time inside.

2 I think kids spend too much time looking at *digital* / *screens*.

3 My son loves singing. He wants to become an opera *show* / *star*.

4 I didn't get the flight because I forgot my passport. I felt so *stupid* / *funny*!

5 I don't like him. He only *thinks* / *believes* about himself.

6 He's a lovely guy. Do you know if he's *single* / *alone*?

7 My friend has invited me to her *appointment* / *wedding* next year.

8 The government should spend more on *education* / *school*.

**8** Complete the text with one word in each gap. The first letters are given.

I met my friend Athia on a business ¹tr_____ . We were on the same train and we chatted for most of the journey, because she is very ²ea_____ to ³ta_____ to. She actually lives quite near me and so we became friends. We both like sport and for a long time we played badminton together. She is very ⁴fi_____ , so she usually won! ⁵Un_____ , I had to stop playing because I had some ⁶he_____ problems, so now we just go walking together or sometimes we meet for dinner. We're going to go ⁷ca_____ in a few weeks. We're going in her car, because I don't have a ⁸dr_____ licence. In fact, she often gives me a ⁹li_____ to places. She's a very kind person. I'm really ¹⁰gl_____ she's my friend.

# 9 Experiences

## IN THIS UNIT, YOU:

- roleplay a conversation with a tourist about their visit
- compare experiences you've had or would like to have
- share experiences of when you got help

## SPEAKING

**1 Work in pairs. Discuss the questions.**

1 Look at the photo. Are there any running races where you live? Are they popular?

2 Do you think running a long race would be a good or bad experience? Explain why, using some of these ideas.

> *It's very hard.*
> *You meet lots of people.*
> *It's nice to share the experience with other people.*
> *It hurts to do it.*
> *It depends if you complete it.*
> *You feel bad if you fail.*
> *People watch you.*
> *You travel and see a beautiful place.*
> *You have to do a lot of practice before it.*

**2 Work with a new partner. What might be good or bad about these experiences?**

1 travelling round a country by bus
2 being in a show in a big theatre
3 going to university away from home
4 working on a farm for a year
5 having a baby

Runners at the end of a 10 km run. London, UK.

## 9A

# Have you ever been there?

**IN THIS LESSON, YOU:**
- roleplay a conversation with a tourist about their visit
- give reasons to (not) visit a place
- practise listening to a local person talk with tourists in Istanbul
- find out where people have been to and things they've tried

## SPEAKING

1 ▶ **Work in pairs. Listen to the conversation between a local person and a tourist. Then say it.**

A: Have you been here before?

B: Yeah. Once, a few years ago.

A: Well, welcome back! So what places have you been to?

B: **The centre of the city, the market square, the old bridge**.

A: Have you been to **the main museum**?

B: No, I haven't.

A: Oh, you should! **It's free to go in**.

B: OK. Maybe I'll go there tomorrow.

2 **Change the words in purple. Use a dictionary if you need to. Then practise your new conversation with your partner. Exchange roles and repeat.**

## VOCABULARY  Visiting places

3 **Complete the sentences with these words.**

| | | | |
|---|---|---|---|
| adventures ⁶ | carefully ³ | crowds ⁴ | go in ⁷ |
| guidebook ² | history ¹ | lie ⁵ | view ⁸ |

1 I'm interested in places with a lot of _____ and culture.

2 I'm not interested in sightseeing. I never take a _____ or go on a tour.

3 I like to plan my trip _____ so I can see as much as possible.

4 I don't like places with _____ . I prefer somewhere quieter.

5 I don't like to do much. I prefer to _____ by the pool or on the beach.

6 I like _____ , so I usually go to places where other tourists don't go.

7 I don't _____ museums or castles if you have to pay.

8 If there's a tall building, I usually go up it to see the

_____ .

4 🎴 **Decide if each statement in Exercise 3 is true for you or not and why. Then talk to other students to find the person who shares the most ideas with you.**

## LISTENING

5 ▶ **Listen to a conversation between two tourists in Istanbul and someone who lives there. Number the questions (a–h) in the order you hear them.**

a How long did you spend there?

b Have you been to Topkapı Palace?

c What are you doing later?

d Did you go up the Galata Tower?

e Have you been to Istanbul before?

f Have you tried the fish here?

g Where have you been?

h When did you arrive?

6 ▶ **Work in pairs. Do you remember how the speakers answered the questions in Exercise 5? Listen again and note down the answers.**

7 **Work in groups. Discuss the questions.**

1 Would you like to visit Istanbul? Why? / Why not?

2 What kind of places do you like to go to when you visit a new city?

## GRAMMAR

### Present perfect questions (*been, tried*)

We use the present perfect – *Have / Has* + subject + past participle (e.g. *been / tried*) – to ask about experiences in someone's life. We often give simple short answers.

A: **Have** you **been** to Istanbul?

B: **No** (*I* **haven't**). / **Yes** (*I* **have**).

A: **Have** you **tried** the fish here?

B: **No** (*we* **haven't**). / **Yes** (*we* **have**).

We can also add *ever* to the question.

*Has your partner* **ever** *been there?*

8 **Complete the conversation with these words.**

| | | | |
|---|---|---|---|
| been | has | have | haven't |
| never | once | times | tried |

A: ¹ have you been to Bangkok before?

B: No, ² never , so I'm really excited about going.

A: What about the friend you're going with – ³ has she ever been?

B: Yes, ⁴ once before, so she knows a couple of places to visit.

A: Have you ever ⁵ tried Thai food?

B: Yeah, lots of ⁶ times . That's one reason I want to go there.

A: I know, I love it. Have you ⁷ been to the Thai restaurant in Market Street?

B: No, I ⁸ haven't.

A: Oh, you should go! It's really nice.

9 Write a list of eight places in your country or city. Then work in pairs. Find out if your partner has been to the places or knows anyone who has. What do they think of the places?

*Have you been to …?*
*Yes, I have. / Yes, once. / Yes, a few times.*
*No, I haven't. / No, never. / No. Have you?*

**G** See Grammar reference 9A.

## DEVELOPING CONVERSATIONS

### Recommending

When someone hasn't been somewhere or tried something, we often say *You should!* because we think it's good or *Don't!* because we think it's bad. We usually explain why.

*A: Have you tried the fish here?*
*B: No, we haven't.*
*A: Oh, **you should! It's very good – very fresh.***

*A: Have you visited the palace?*
*B: No, I haven't.*
*A: **Don't! It's really boring.***

10 Think of four places you think are good to visit – and four places that you think are bad. Think about why.

11 Work in pairs. Have conversations about your places.

*A: Have you been to the Thai restaurant in town?*
*B: No, I haven't.*
*A: Oh, you should! It's really nice. I love their red curry.*

*B: Have you been to Jeffer's department store?*
*A: No, but I'd like to go.*
*B: Don't! It's very expensive!*

## CONVERSATION PRACTICE

12 Work in pairs. You're going to roleplay a conversation between a local person and a tourist.

**Student A:** You're a local person. Ask these questions.

*Have you been here before?*
*When did you arrive?*
*Where have you been?*
*Did you like it?*
*Have you been to / tried …?*
*What are your plans for this evening?*

**Student B:** You're a tourist. Answer Student A's questions.

**Exchange roles and repeat.**

Galata Tower in İstanbul, Turkey.

# New experiences

**IN THIS LESSON, YOU:**
- compare experiences you've had or would like to have
- talk about experiences people you know have had
- read a blog post about bucket lists
- notice words that go together in a text

## SPEAKING

**1** Complete these sentences with the name of someone you know to make true statements.

1 _____ has visited our capital city many times.

2 _____ has never seen a *Star Wars* film.

3 _____ has travelled abroad once or twice.

4 _____ often gives money to people on the street.

5 _____ has never swum in the sea.

6 _____ always says thank you to the bus driver.

7 _____ has met a famous person.

**2** Work in pairs. Share your ideas from Exercise 1 and add more information.

**3** Tell your partner which things in Exercise 1 you:

1 sometimes / often do.

2 have never done in your life.

3 have done once or twice.

4 have done several / many times.

## GRAMMAR

### Present perfect positive and negative

The present perfect is subject + *have / has* (*not / never*) + past participle. We use it to to talk about experiences in our life. We don't usually say when – it's just before now.

**I've travelled** abroad once.

My mum **has visited** the capital many times.

He's **never seen** a Star Wars *film.*

We **haven't met** anyone famous.

Most past participles are the same as the past simple form, e.g. *met, tried, travelled.*

There are a few forms which are different to the past form, e.g. *been, seen, swum.*

**4** Look at these past participles. Make two lists – *same* as the past simple form or *different.*

| | | | |
|---|---|---|---|
| broken | changed | come | done |
| eaten | failed | flown | forgotten |
| given | had | lived | lost |
| made | met | moved | read |
| seen | stayed | swum | taken |

**5** Complete these sentences (1–8) with the present perfect form of the verbs in brackets.

1 She ~~has~~ *failed* her driving test ten times. (fail)

2 You ~~have~~ *broken* my glasses. (break)

3 My uncle ~~has~~ *been married* three times. (be married).

4 My grandma ~~has~~ *never moved* house. She lives in the same house she was born in. (never move)

5 ~~have~~ *I met* him lots of times and we always chat, but I don't remember his name. (meet)

6 My friends ~~haven't~~ ~~don't read~~ *read* any of the *Harry Potter* books, but ~~have~~ ~~they~~ *seen* the films. (not read / see). *haven't*

7 *We visited* over sixty countries, but we ~~don't travel~~ *travele(d)* much in our country. (visit / not travel) *haven't*

8 He *has made* millions of dollars, but he ~~hasn't~~ any of it to his children. (make / not give) *given*

**6** Complete the sentences with a phrase using the present perfect.

1 _____ , but I'd love to one day.

2 _____ and I don't ever want to.

3 _____ because it's just too expensive.

4 _____ once, but I wouldn't do it again.

5 _____ – it's great.

**G** See Grammar reference 9B.

## READING

**7** Read the introduction to the blog post on page 91. Are these statements true (T) or false (F)?

F 1 A bucket list is a list of things someone has done in their life.

T 2 *The Bucket List* was the name of a film.

T 3 There are a lot of websites about bucket lists.

F 4 The writer doesn't really like bucket lists.

**8** Read the rest of the blog post. Decide if the writer likes (L) or doesn't really like (DL) bucket lists which include these things.

DL 1 dangerous activities

DL 2 places which are far from your country

L 3 activities that anyone can do

L 4 doing nice things for other people

L 5 experiences that are sad or difficult

**9** Work in pairs. Look at the blog post again. Find the verb or adjective that goes with these nouns.

1 *funny* phrase    4 animals    7 success

2 *giving* advice    5 nothing    8 heart

3 activities    6 someone

**10** Work in groups. Which of the author's views about bucket lists do you agree with?

## SPEAKING

**11** Create your own bucket list of eight activities. Include:

- four important experiences you've had in your life.
- four experiences you'd like to have.

**12** Work in groups. Has anyone in your group done something on your list or done something similar?

*home work*

# Bucket lists

*home work*

**Have you heard of a *bucket list*? The phrase was made popular by a 2007 American film about two men who meet in hospital, called *The Bucket List*. The men are dying and they start to talk about what they've never done in their lives but would like to do before they *kick the bucket* (a funny phrase which means *die*). Most people have never seen the film, but the idea has become very popular. There are now millions of websites with people sharing their bucket lists, showing the things they hope to do, or giving advice on how to complete a list. I like some of these lists more than others.**

Many lists include a lot of dangerous activities – jumping out of a plane, climbing high mountains, swimming with sharks – those kinds of things. I don't like this, because when you do these activities, you can easily die. And if you die, you can't do all the other things on your list, which seems stupid!

Most lists also include visiting lots of places – the pyramids in Egypt, Machu Picchu, anywhere which looks good on social media. I like seeing new places, and I have actually walked to Machu Picchu, but I understand now that travelling to places far from home is bad for the environment. And we can't all go to the Galápagos Islands to see the amazing animals, so maybe no-one should! We all need to travel less, so I prefer a bucket list of places near home, that you can get to by bike, bus or train.

The other problem with bucket lists is they're often very expensive. In the film, the characters can do all their activities because one of them is very, very rich and pays for everything. So I think the best lists of experiences are cheap or cost nothing. Here's a list of things from one website which anyone can do:

- make a cake for someone special
- do something kind for a stranger
- stay up all night talking

- tell a family member you love them
- spend time with an old person

This is a good list, but I'd like to add something else. Most bucket lists only have good experiences, but many people who've had great success say they learned more when they failed. So if a bucket list is about living a full life, then I would add some bad experiences: lose money, feel sad, get a broken heart, wait ten hours for a flight – that kind of thing.

What do you think? Leave your comments below.

Tourists swim with Great White Sharks in Port Lincoln, South Australia.

# Thank you so much

**IN THIS LESSON, YOU:**
- share experiences of when you got help
- talk about when and why you say *thank you*
- learn words that have more than one meaning
- practise listening to people sharing experiences of getting help

## SPEAKING

**1 Work in groups. Discuss the questions.**

1 Who was the last person you said *thank you* to? Why?

2 How often do you think you say *thank you* in a day?

3 Who do you normally say *thank you* to? What for?

4 Have you ever given a gift to say *thank you*? What was the gift?

## VOCABULARY
## Words with different meanings

**2 Complete each pair of sentences (1–8) with one of these words. Then translate the word's meaning in each sentence into your first language.**

| afraid | fell | join | left | lost | pull | saved | way |
|--------|------|------|------|------|------|-------|-----|

1 a We stayed in their house for free, so we *saved* a lot of money.

   b I was very ill, but the doctors *saved* my life.

2 a She bought me some flowers on the _way_ home.

   b The teacher taught us a _way_ to relax before the exam, which helped a lot.

3 a I got __lost__ on the way there, but someone helped me to find the place.

   b He was upset because his team __lost__ , so I bought him some ice cream.

4 a I was alone, so they asked me to __join__ them for dinner.

   b I wanted to __join__ a gym to get fit and my dad offered to pay.

5 a She _felt_ __fell__ and hurt herself, so we called an ambulance.

   b I borrowed a jacket because the temperature really _fell_ __afraid__ at night and I didn't have any warm clothes.

6 a You need to __pull__ to open it, not push!

   b I have a bad tooth. I think I need the dentist to __pull__ it out.

7 a Thanks for the invitation, but I'm __felt__ _afraid_ I can't come.

   b She stayed with me because I was __felt__ _afraid_ of being alone.

8 a I __lost__ _left_ my bag on the train, but someone sent it to my home.

   b There were no tickets __lost__ _left_ for the concert, so he gave me his.

**3** Work in pairs. Compare your answers. When you translate the words in each sentence, does your first language use the same word or different words?

**4** 🅿 ▶ Listen to the words from Exercise 2 and practise saying them on their own and in a phrase. Which words / phrases do you find hard to say? Practise saying them again.

**5** Work in groups. Discuss the questions.

1 In what jobs can you save lives?

2 What things do people often pull?

3 What things are people often afraid of? What about you?

4 When was the last time you fell? Were you OK?

5 Have you ever joined a club or gym?

6 Have ever you got lost? Where were you going?

7 Have you ever left a bag on a train – or something similar? Did you get it back?

## LISTENING

**6** ▶ Listen to a part of a radio show. What is the show about?

**7** ▶ Work in pairs. Choose the correct option (a–c) to answer the questions about the story of Bao Lam. Then listen again and check your answers.

1 Why did Bao Lam go to the river?

a to swim

b to walk

c to take a boat

2 Who / What saved Bao Lam's life?

a an old man

b a dog

c a woman

3 What did Bao Lam do next?

a go to hospital

b call an ambulance

c give someone money

**8** Work in pairs. Discuss the questions.

1 Do you know any radio shows or podcasts where people share stories or experiences?

2 Would you call a show like this? Why? / Why not?

**9** 🄵🅂 ▶ Sometimes, the subject or object of a verb is a group of words. These groups of words are often said faster. Listen to six phrases and write down what you hear.

**10** ▶ Listen to the rest of the radio show. Choose the correct option (a–c) to answer the questions (1–3).

1 What was the problem for Mo?

a He missed his flight.

b He was very worried about the bad weather.

c The woman next to him talked a lot.

2 How did the woman change Jess's life?

a She helped Jess change her behaviour.

b She saved Jess when she was in a fight.

c She helped Jess pass her exams for university.

3 Why did the man offer to pay for Noah's shopping?

a Because Noah left his cards and money at home.

b Because Noah didn't earn any money and needed to eat.

c Because the machine was broken, so Noah couldn't pay by card.

**11** Work in pairs. Complete these sentences with the people in the radio show to say who gave most help.

1 _____3_____ was helpful.

2 _____1_____ was more helpful.

3 _____2_____ was the most helpful.

## SPEAKING TASK

**12** You're going to tell a story about getting help. Use these questions to organize your story. Use a dictionary if you need to.

1 When was it?

*when I was younger / a few days ago*

2 Where were you?

*I was on holiday. / I was on my way to work.*

3 Who were you with?

*I was alone. / I was with my family.*

4 What was the problem?

*I lost my wallet. / I wanted to sit down, but there were no seats left.*

5 Who helped you?

*There was a guy near / a woman next to me.*

6 What did they do?

*They gave me a lift. / They offered me their ticket.*

7 What happened next?

*I went with them. / I went and had a great time.*

8 Did you thank them? How?

*I said thanks. / I sent them some flowers.*

**13** 🄼 Work in groups. Do the following:

1 Tell your stories to each other.

2 Choose the story with the person who gave most help.

3 Retell the story you've chosen to the class.

4 As a class, choose the story with the person who gave most help.

## ■ MY OUTCOMES ■

**Work in pairs. Discuss the questions.**

1 What was fun to do in the unit?

2 What useful language have you learned?

3 What did you think of the reading text?

4 What are you going to do outside the classroom to practise?

# 10
# Food

**IN THIS UNIT, YOU:**

- roleplay ordering in a restaurant
- explain food and drink culture in your country
- explain a menu from your country

## SPEAKING

**1 Work in pairs. Discuss the questions.**

1 Look at the photo. Does the food look good to you? Why? / Why not?
2 What kind of street food is famous where you live?
3 Do you like eating outside?
4 Do you like sharing a table with people you don't know?
5 Do you ever eat standing up or while you're walking?
6 Do you ever take photos of food?

**2 What's important for you when deciding where to eat? Number these things in order from 1–8: 1 = very important, 8 = not important at all.**

a It's in a nice place.
b It's cheap.
c It has lots of different kinds of food.
d You get a lot of food.
e People say good things about it.
f You don't have to wait long.
g It's nice and quiet.
h You know the place and have eaten there before.

**3 Work in groups. Compare your ideas. Explain your choices.**

Enjoying great food together on Yaowarat Road, Bangkok, Thailand.

# 10A

# Are you ready to order?

**IN THIS LESSON, YOU:**
- roleplay ordering in a restaurant
- look at common things people say in restaurants
- practise listening to two tourists in a restaurant in France
- use different phrases to order food and drink

## SPEAKING

**1** ▶ **Work in pairs. Listen to the conversation. Then say it.**

A: Hello. Do you have a table for **one**?

B: Have you booked?

A: No, I'm afraid not.

B: That's OK. Come with me. This is your table – and here's the menu.

A: Thank you.

B: Are you ready to order?

A: Yes. I'd like **the chicken salad**, please.

B: Of course. And to drink?

A: **Just some water**.

**2** Change the words in purple. Use a dictionary if you need to. Then practise your new conversation with your partner. Exchange roles and repeat.

## VOCABULARY In a restaurant

**3** Complete the sentences with these words.

| | | | |
|---|---|---|---|
| bill | course | decide | dessert |
| include | order | per cent | ready |
| soup | steak | table | vegetarian |

1 Hello there. Do you have a _____ for two?

2 Are you _____ to order?

3 What do you have without meat in it? I'm _____ , you see.

4 For starters, I'll have the _____ , please.

5 Can I take your _____ next please, sir?

6 Sorry, but we need more time. We're still trying to _____ what we want.

7 How do you want your _____ cooked?

8 For my main _____ , can I get the fish, please?

9 Would you like any _____ or coffee?

10 Can we just get the _____ , please?

11 Oh! It's quite expensive. Does this _____ service?

12 We add ten _____ , but you don't have to pay it if you don't want to.

**4** **P** ▶ **Listen to the words from Exercise 3 and practise saying them on their own and in a phrase. Which words / phrases do you find hard to say? Practise saying them again.**

**5** Work in pairs. Who do you think says each sentence in Exercise 3 – a waiter / waitress (W) or a customer (C)?

## LISTENING

**6** ▶ **Listen to two British tourists in a restaurant in France. What does each person order?**

**7** ▶ **Listen again. Answer the questions.**

1 What three problems do the tourists have in the restaurant?

2 Do they enjoy the meal?

3 Do you think they're going to leave any extra money for the waiter? Why? / Why not?

**8** Work in groups. Which of these sentences do you agree with? Why?

1 French food is the best in the world.

*A: I haven't tried French food, so I don't know. Maybe it's true.*

*B: I've tried it, but I prefer Japanese food.*

2 It's always better to book a table before you go out for dinner.

3 Waiters and waitresses usually just recommend expensive things.

4 It's better to have a starter and a main course than a main course and a dessert.

5 It's better if restaurants include service in the bill.

## DEVELOPING CONVERSATIONS

### Ordering food and drink

We can use different phrases to order food and drink. They all mean the same thing.

For starters, *I'll have* the soup, *please*.

*I'd like* the chicken, *please*.

*Can I get* a steak, *please*?

*Can I have* the ice cream?

**9 Number the parts of the conversations in the correct order.**

**Conversation 1**

a  Yes. Thanks. I'll have the salad for starters, please.

b  Can I get the chicken, please?

c  Are you ready to order?

d  Really? Oh. OK. Well, can I have the fish then, please?

e  Certainly. And for your main course?

f  I'm afraid the chicken's finished.

**Conversation 2**

a  Yes, please. Can I get the ice cream?

b  Without, please, so just black.

c  Would you like any dessert?

d  I can't eat anything else. I'll just have a coffee, please.

e  Of course. And for you, madam?

f  With milk – or without?

**10** ▶ **Listen and check your answers. Then work in pairs. Practise reading the conversations.**

## CONVERSATION PRACTICE

**11 Work in pairs. You're going to roleplay a conversation like the one you heard in the listening.**

**Student A:** You're a customer. Look at File 3 on page 199. Decide what you'd like to have.

**Student B:** You're a waiter / waitress. Choose questions from this lesson to ask. Remember them.

**12 Roleplay the conversation. Use this guide to help you. Exchange roles and repeat.**

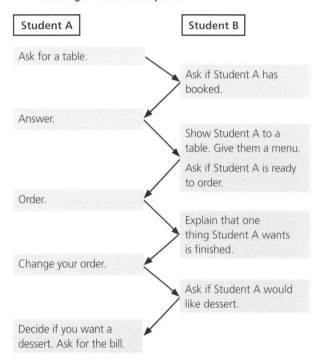

| Student A | Student B |
|---|---|
| Ask for a table. | |
| | Ask if Student A has booked. |
| Answer. | |
| | Show Student A to a table. Give them a menu. |
| | Ask if Student A is ready to order. |
| Order. | |
| | Explain that one thing Student A wants is finished. |
| Change your order. | |
| | Ask if Student A would like dessert. |
| Decide if you want a dessert. Ask for the bill. | |

A restaurant in an 18th-century palace the 'Casa de los Azulejos', Mexico City, Mexico.

## 10B

# A change for the better

**IN THIS LESSON, YOU:**
- explain food and drink culture in your country
- read an article about public health in Finland
- explain quantity using *how much / how many*
- discuss what you eat

## SPEAKING

1  **Work in groups. Look at the five countries with the best levels of health. Then discuss the questions.**

| 1 | Spain |
| 2 | Italy |
| 3 | Iceland |
| 4 | Japan |
| 5 | Switzerland |

1  What kind of things are important for the health of a country?

2  How healthy do you think people in your country are? Why?

3  What do you know about the food and drink from the countries above?

4  What food / drink from your country do you think is very healthy?

## READING

2  **Work in pairs. Read the first paragraph of the article on page 99. Then discuss these questions.**

1  What was the problem in Karelia?

2  Why do you think this problem happened?

3  What do you think Pekka Puska did to change things?

3  **Read the rest of the article. Check your ideas for Exercise 2.**

4  **Are the statements true (T) or false (F)?**

1  Women in North Karelia had worse heart problems than men.

2  Generally, people there didn't eat a lot of fruit or vegetables.

3  Puska told local people to stop cooking the things they usually cooked.

4  One local company saved money by making healthier food.

5  It became harder for cigarette companies to sell their products.

6  After all the small changes, the situation improved a little bit.

5  **Work in pairs. Discuss the questions.**

1  What do you think was the most important change in Karelia? Why?

2  Can you think of any other ways of improving the health of a country?

3  Did / Do you talk about food and health at school or with your family?

## GRAMMAR

### Explaining quantity

There are some words we often use to show quantity when we talk about how much / how many.

They ate **a lot of** meat.

They ate **quite a lot of** animal products.

I try to eat **some** fruit / vegetables every day.

I don't eat **much** meat.

We don't have **many** eggs in the fridge.

Do we have **any** coffee in the house?

6  **Work in pairs. Look at the examples in the Grammar box. Answer these questions.**

1  Which words in bold go with both countable and uncountable nouns?

2  Which word only goes with countable nouns?

3  Which word only goes with uncountable nouns?

4  Which words do we often use in negative sentences and questions?

7  **Complete the sentences with one word in each gap.**

1  I'm vegetarian. I don't eat _____ meat or fish.

2  I don't eat _____ chocolate bars – maybe just one or two a month.

3  I had _____ biscuits half an hour ago, so I'm not very hungry.

4  Most days, I don't have _____ time to cook, so I just do something quick and easy.

5  Did you add _____ salt to this? I can't taste it.

6  A: Do you eat _____ rice?
   B: Yeah, quite a _____ , but I sometimes have pasta or potatoes instead.

8  **Choose six things of these things. Tell a partner how much or how many you have every day / week.**

| chicken | eggs | fish | fruit |
| mushrooms | pizza | sausages | soup |
| tea | tomatoes | vegetables | water |

*I eat a lot of fruit – maybe three or four pieces a day.*

G  See Grammar reference 10B. »»»

## SPEAKING

9  M  **Work in pairs. How can you explain what people in your country usually eat and drink to someone who's never been there?**

10  **Work with another pair. Compare your ideas. Do you think the things people eat and drink have changed in your country? If yes, how?**

A farm in Finland.

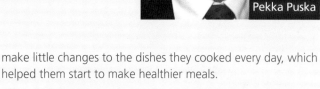

Pekka Puska

# CHANGING MEALS
# CHANGING
# LIVES

## How changes in one small area helped a whole country get healthier

Today, North Karelia is a popular tourist area in the east of Finland, famous for its beautiful countryside. But 50 years ago, the area was famous for a very different reason: bad health. It was one of the unhealthiest places in the world. A lot of people there – especially men – died early from heart problems. Local people were upset and angry about the situation, so in 1972, the government asked a young doctor called Pekka Puska to find out why it was happening and how they could improve things.

Puska and his team found that a big part of the problem was the food people ate – and men in Karelia had strong ideas about food. Because they worked on farms, they ate a lot of animal products – meat, milk and butter – which had a lot of fat in them. They also used quite a lot of salt in their cooking. Some men didn't eat any vegetables, because they said vegetables were for animals, not real men. People didn't eat much fruit, either, and farmers didn't grow any.

Changing these ideas – and changing what people ate – wasn't easy. First, Puska and his team talked to schools and parents about food and cooking. They showed them how to make little changes to the dishes they cooked every day, which helped them start to make healthier meals.

They also worked with local companies. After talking to the team, one local sausage factory started using local mushrooms instead of animal fat. The result? Sausages that were healthier *and* cheaper to make. The government also gave less money to farmers for milk and butter, and helped them grow healthier food. For example, they gave advice about the kinds of fruit that grew well in the area.

Food wasn't the only reason for heart problems. Most of the men in the area smoked. Again, the team used education to change people's behaviour and the government stopped cigarette advertisements.

The results of these small changes were so good that the government asked Puska and his team to help the whole country. Today, the number of men in Finland who die from heart problems is 80% lower and people in North Karelia live ten years longer. Other governments have used the same ideas to improve the health of millions more people around the world.

# What's this on the menu?

**IN THIS LESSON, YOU:**
- explain a menu from your country
- describe different kinds of foods
- practise listening to three conversations connected to food
- agree and disagree with statements

## VOCABULARY Food

V   See Vocabulary reference 10C.

1   **Work in groups. Say how often you eat / drink things in the photos – or how often you use the different things when you cook.**

*I eat vegetables every day. I always have salad for lunch.*

*I sometimes eat meat if I go to a restaurant, but I don't cook it very often. It's expensive.*

*I never buy drinks like this. They have a lot of sugar in them. I prefer water.*

2   **Work in pairs. Decide which word does not go in each group (1–6). Use the correct sentence from a–f to explain why.**

1   salt / water / **pepper** / sugar

   *They're all things that we add for flavour except water.*

2   **yogurt** / cheese / **mango** / cream

3   apples / oranges / eggs / **melons**

4   juice / carrots / hot chocolate / tea

5   **lemons** / potatoes / **onions** / garlic

6   chicken / **beef** / **pasta** / steak

a   They're all kinds of meat except …

b   They're all kinds of vegetables except …

c   They're all things that we add for flavour except …

d   They're all kinds of drinks except …

e   They're all milk products except …

f   They're all kinds of fruit except …

3   **Which of the foods from Exercise 2 can you see in the photos?**

4   **Work in pairs. Practise asking about and explaining the names of different foods.**

**Student A:** look at File 4 on page 199.

**Student B:** look at File 10 on page 202.

Vegetables

Nuts

Milk products

Drinks

Beans

Seafood

Fruit

Meat

PETITE STEAK
$6.99

## LISTENING

**5** ▶ Listen to three conversations connected to food. Match each conversation (1–3) with one sentence (a–e). There are two extra sentences.

a They're choosing a place to go on holiday.

b They're discussing things on a menu.

c They're talking about which food programmes on TV they like the most.

d They're discussing where to go and eat.

e They're talking about what food someone is going to cook.

**6** FS ▶ In fast speech, when one word ends in a consonant sound like /t/ or /k/ and the next starts with a vowel sound like /iː/ or /e/, the two sounds usually join together. Listen to nine pairs of words and write what you hear.

**7** ▶ Listen again. For each conversation, say which sentence (a–c) is true.

**Conversation 1**

a One of the speakers is vegetarian.

b One of the speakers is Italian.

c One of the speakers doesn't eat meat.

**Conversation 2**

a Two people ask to try the food.

b One person explains why they can't eat a kind of food.

c They all laugh about the barbecue.

**Conversation 3**

a They all say they love seafood.

b They all order different dishes.

c They all watch food programmes on TV.

**8** Work in groups. Discuss the questions.

1 Do you know anyone who's vegetarian? Do you know why they are?

2 What different restaurants are there near your home? What are they like?

3 Have you ever tried Mexican food? If yes, did you like it?

4 What other food from different countries do you like?

5 What food programmes do you know? Do you watch them? How often?

## GRAMMAR

### *Me too, me neither* and auxiliaries

We can use *me too* or *me neither* to agree with other people.

*A: I can't decide.   B: **Me neither**.   (= I also can't decide)*

*A: OK. That's fine with me.   B: **Me too**.   (= That's also fine with me)*

We can use an auxiliary verb like *do, have, would*, etc., to disagree with other people.

To disagree with a negative sentence, we use a positive auxiliary.

*A: Oh, I **don't like** seafood.   B: Really? I **do**!*

To disagree with a positive sentence, we use a negative auxiliary.

*A: I**'d** really **like** to try that.   B: Oh, I **wouldn't**.*

**9** Complete the conversation with one word in each gap. Contractions like *can't* count as one word.

1 A: I love mangoes.

   B: Oh, me _____ . They're one of my favourite fruits.

2 A: I've never tried German food.

   B: Me _____ . What kind of things do they eat there? Do you know?

3 A: I can't cook very well.

   B: No? I _____ . I love cooking.

4 A: I've never eaten in there.

   B: Oh, I _____ . I don't go there often, but sometimes I just want a burger.

5 A: I'd really like to go to Iceland.

   B: Oh, I _____ . I prefer hot countries.

6 A: I loved that restaurant we went to last week.

   B: Hmm. I _____ . My main course wasn't very good – and it was quite expensive.

**10** Complete the sentences to make them true for you.

1 I love _____ .

2 I've never had _____ food.

3 I can't _____ very well.

4 I've seen _____ several times.

5 I'd really like to _____ .

6 I _____ last weekend.

**11** Work in pairs. Read your sentences out to each other. Your partner should agree or disagree. Try to find out more by asking a question.

*A: I've never tried Greek food.*

*B: Oh, I have.*

*A: Really? Was it nice?*

*B: Yes. Delicious.*

**G** See Grammar reference 10C.  ⟩⟩⟩

## SPEAKING TASK

**12** In your first language, write a menu for a restaurant in your country. Include six to eight dishes.

**13** M Work in pairs. Ask your partner to explain what the things on their menu are in English. Then decide:

1 what you would eat.

2 who has the best menu.

## ▇ MY OUTCOMES ▇

**Work in pairs. Discuss the questions.**

1 What classroom activities did you enjoy doing?

2 What can you do better now?

3 How many things to say in restaurants can you remember?

4 What part of this unit do you want to practise?

# Writing a restaurant review

**IN THIS LESSON, YOU:**
- write reviews of restaurants you have eaten in
- discuss positive and negative restaurant experiences
- think of good titles for reviews
- decide what to put in reviews

## SPEAKING

**1 Work in groups. Discuss the questions.**

1 How often do you eat in restaurants?

2 Do you have a favourite restaurant? If yes, why is it so special?

3 What do you usually eat when you go out for a meal?

4 Do you ever read online reviews before choosing where to eat?

**2 Work in pairs. Discuss the questions.**

1 Which sentences (a–j) do you think come from positive reviews (P)? Which do you think come from negative reviews (N)?

a I can't believe they call this place a Mexican restaurant. It really isn't. *N*

b The waiter explained the menu to us. *P*

c The food is simple but excellent. *P*

d There was enough space for a big group of us. *P*

e Our food came very quickly. *P*

f There weren't many things to choose from. *N*

*N* g They used a lot of salt in the cooking – and I mean A LOT!

h I don't know why it was so busy. Maybe there's nowhere *N* else to eat in town.

*P* i We can't wait to go back.

*N* j They asked us to leave before we finished our desserts.

2 Have you ever had any similar feelings / experiences? If yes, when? Where? What happened?

## WRITING

**3 Read the two reviews (A and B). Choose the best title (1–5) for each one.**

1 If you like good food, don't eat here!

2 Not for vegetarians!

3 You really should visit

4 The best starters in town

5 Not bad, but not great

## A

**Dan W.** ~~3~~
Sydney         ☆☆☆☆☆    April 12

We came here for lunch one day while we were on holiday and we loved it. The staff were very **friendly**, the food was **delicious** and we had a great view of the river from our table. For our main course, two of us had chicken and two had fish – and then we all had dessert and coffee. It wasn't **expensive** and the bill included service too. I really recommend this place.

## B

**Sofia M.** ~~5~~
Rio de Janeiro      ★★☆☆☆    July 29

We stopped and had dinner here **while** driving home from the coast. It was **busy** and we had to wait fifteen minutes for a table. Our **waiter** was tired and not very friendly. After we ordered, we waited half an hour for our food. I'm vegetarian and I quite liked my salad. Actually, all of the food was OK, but not really amazing. It wasn't cheap either. I've been to worse places, but I'm not sure I want to come here again.

**4** Work in pairs. Answer these questions about each review.

1 When / Why did they go to the restaurants?
2 What did they think of the staff?
3 What did they think of the food?
4 What did they think of the price?
5 What else do you learn about the restaurants?
6 Do they recommend the places?

**5** Work in pairs. Check you understand the words in bold in the two reviews. Use a dictionary if you need to.

**6** Now complete this review using the words in bold from the two reviews.

We came here [1] _While_ visiting family in the area. The restaurant is on a hill and we wanted a nice view, but our table wasn't near the window. It was in a dark corner. It was lunchtime and we knew something *busy* was wrong because it wasn't very [2] ~~delicious~~. There were only three other people there, but we still waited almost half an hour for the [3] _waiter_ to bring us a menu – and when he did, he wasn't very [4] _friendly_. We both had soup for our starter and it was [5] _delicious_, but the main courses were awful. My partner's pizza was almost cold and my steak wasn't cooked enough. Terrible. Oh, and it was [6] _expensive_ too. Not a place I recommend.

**7** Work in pairs. Think of a good title for the review in Exercise 6.

**8** Work in groups. Look at the good and bad things that the three reviews describe. What do you think was the best / worst thing about each restaurant? Why?

## USEFUL LANGUAGE

### *While*

We can use *while* to introduce an action or situation that continues when another action happens.

We can use *while* + *-ing* form of a verb.

*We came here **while visiting** family in the area.*

We can also *use while* with a clause that contains *was / were*.

*We came here one day **while we were on holiday**.*

**9** Complete the sentences with these words / phrases.

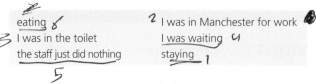

| eating | I was in Manchester for work |
| I was in the toilet | I was waiting |
| the staff just did nothing | staying |

1 We came here while _staying_ in a hotel on the same street.
2 I had dinner here while _I was in Manchester for work_
3 The waiter took my drink away while _I was in the toilet_
4 While _I was waiting_ for my partner to arrive, the waitress brought me some delicious snacks.
5 We waited a long time for the menu while _the staff just did_
6 While _staying_ our delicious main courses, we enjoyed ~~eating~~ *Nothing* the live band playing there.

**10** Work in pairs. Think of three different ways to complete each sentence.

1 While we were on holiday, we …
2 We waited to order for a long time while …
3 While we were waiting for our food, …
4 While we were eating dessert, …

## PRACTICE

**11** Think of two restaurants you've eaten in – one good and one bad. Make notes about:

- why / when you went there – and who you went with.
- what you ate.
- why you thought the restaurant was good / bad – think about the staff, the food and the price.

**12** Use your notes to write a review for each restaurant. Write 50–80 words. Your reviews should have a title and finish with a short sentence explaining your feelings about the place.

**13** Work in pairs. Read your partner's reviews. Discuss the questions.

1 Do your partner's reviews include all the things in Exercise 11?
2 Can you think of one thing to improve your partner's reviews?
3 Would you like to eat in the restaurants your partner reviewed? Why? / Why not?

## VIDEO Out and about

**1** Work in groups. What's your favourite restaurant? Why?

### Understanding accents

Some accents use a /ʃ/ sound instead of a /tʃ/ sound, so *choose* /tʃuːz/ may sound more like *shoes* /ʃuːz/.

**2** Watch five people answer the same question. Then work in pairs. How much can you remember about what they said? Which restaurant sounds best to you?

**3** Watch again. Match two sentences with each speaker.

a The food looks great and tastes great too.

b I really recommend the lunch box there.

c I like the lamb there.

d I like trying lots of different kinds of things.

e I know the woman who owns it.

f There are lots of different restaurants in my street.

g My favourite restaurant is just on this street.

h I went there six times in one week.

i They do traditional Arabic food.

j It's in the south of the country.

**4** Work in groups. Discuss the questions.

1 What's more important for you – how food looks or how it tastes?

2 What do you usually have for lunch?

3 Do you know anyone who owns – or works in – a restaurant?

4 What's the best traditional food from your country?

## VIDEO Developing conversations

**5** You're going to watch two people talking about places in their area. Watch and take notes on what they say.

**6** Work in pairs. Compare what you understood. Watch again if you need to.

**7** FS Watch again. Complete the sentences with two words in each gap.

1 Wow! Your sandwich _____ .

2 I have been there a few times, but I don't _____ often because it's dangerous.

3 I _____ with my friends last night.

4 Do you know that _____ on West Street?

5 I've _____ it, but I've not been.

6 Have you _____ that new Italian place on Mina Street?

7 Oh, the place _____ the pizza and pasta?

8 There are some places that have opened that we _____ think about trying.

9 It's one of my _____ .

10 They have so many _____ there.

## CONVERSATION PRACTICE

**8** Work in pairs. You're going to practise a conversation.

1 Choose a Conversation practice from either Lesson 9A or Lesson 10A.

2 Look at the language in that lesson.

3 Check the meaning of anything you don't remember with your partner.

4 Have the conversation. Try to do it better than the last time you did it.

# Grammar and Vocabulary

## GRAMMAR

**1** Complete the conversation with one word in each gap. Contractions (*hasn't, can't,* etc.) count as one word.

A: Have you [1]_____ tried Moroccan food?

B: Yeah, I [2]_____ – lots of [3]_____ . I love it.

A: Oh, me [4]_____ . I've eaten [5]_____ a lot of different foods, but Moroccan is maybe my favourite.

C: Really? I've [6]_____ tried it. I think Indian is probably my favourite. I eat it a lot at home.

B: Oh, I [7]_____! A lot of it is too hot for me. I can't eat [8]_____ very hot food.

A: Can't you? I don't eat [9]_____ , but I love Mexican and Thai.

B: Really? I don't.

C: Me [10]_____ .

**2** Complete the conversations with the correct form of the words in brackets. Use the present perfect in the questions and the past simple in the answers.

1 A: _____ to Brazil? (you / ever / be)

B: Yes. _____ there last year on holiday. (I / go)

2 A: _____ the new Disney film? (your son / see)

B: Yes. _____ it at the weekend, actually. (he / see)

3 A: _____ the US before? (they / visit)

B: Yeah, _____ to see us here two years ago. (they / come)

4 A: _____ your parents yet? (she / meet)

B: Yes. _____ lunch with them on Sunday. (we / have)

5 A: _____ Indian food? (you / try)

B: Once, in London, but _____ it. (I / not / like)

**3** Correct the underlined mistake in each sentence.

1 Have you ever <u>saw</u> *Dune*?

2 He <u>have</u> done this hundreds of times before.

3 He makes <u>a lot money</u>.

4 I've never <u>readed</u> anything by Günter Grass.

5 I've had <u>quite lot of food</u> already.

6 We didn't have <u>many</u> money when I was young, but we were happy.

7 I've never <u>eat</u> this kind of food before.

8 <u>I've played</u> a really good video game yesterday.

9 He doesn't have <u>much</u> friends – just one or two.

10 They're vegetarian, so they don't eat <u>much</u> meat or fish.

**4** ▶ Listen and write the six sentences you hear. Include these words.

1 tried / but / like

2 been / but / go

3 drink / coffee / tea

4 been / few

5 eat / lot / chicken

6 met / parents / now

## VOCABULARY

**5** Match the two parts of the phrases.

| | | | |
|---|---|---|---|
| 1 | save | a | my bag at school / home |
| 2 | lie | b | and hurt yourself / into a river |
| 3 | leave | c | a tooth out / someone out of the river |
| 4 | include | d | on the beach / by the pool |
| 5 | fall | e | lost / something to eat |
| 6 | pull | f | a museum / a castle |
| 7 | get | g | money / my life |
| 8 | go in | h | service / three new words in your story |

**6** Decide if these words and phrases are about food, holidays or restaurants. There are five items in each group.

| | | |
|---|---|---|
| add ten per cent | adventure | beef |
| bill | crowd | garlic |
| great view | guidebook | a lot of history |
| main course | mango | onion |
| order | table for four | yogurt |

**7** Choose the correct option to complete the sentences.

1 I need to get some milk on my *road* / *way* home.

2 It wasn't a good game for me because my team *lost* / *failed*.

3 We're still trying to *know* / *decide* what to order.

4 It's hot during the day, but the temperature *falls* / *loses* at night.

5 I'm *sorry* / *afraid* of spiders and snakes.

6 Do you want to *come* / *join* us for lunch?

**8** Complete the text with one word in each gap. The first letters are given.

I'm [1]ve_____ , so I don't eat any meat or fish. I like to plan where I eat very [2]ca_____ . Reading about places online is usually a good [3]w_____ to learn about other people's experiences, but sometimes things go wrong. Last night, we went to a terrible place. We got the menu, looked at it and were [4]r_____ to order, but no one came to our table. We waited for half an hour! Then, for my starter, I tried to order the tomato [5]so_____ , but then the waiter said, 'I'm [6]a_____ we sold the last one five minutes ago!' How annoying! For my main course, I ordered a salad, but they brought me a beef [7]st_____ ! My husband ordered a [8]pa_____ dish, which was OK, but they put a lot of [9]cr_____ in the sauce – and they added a lot of [10]le_____ juice too. There was salt on our table, but no [11]pe_____ and when we asked for some, they said they didn't have any more. Then we tried to order fruit for dessert, but all they had were [12]me_____ .

# 11

# Travel

## IN THIS UNIT, YOU:

- roleplay a conversation buying travel tickets
- discuss solutions to traffic problems
- choose places for a guided tour and explain your choices

## SPEAKING

1 **Work in pairs. Don't use a dictionary. How many words about the photo can you write in one minute?**

2 **Work with a new partner. Discuss the questions.**

1 Does the situation in the photo ever happen where you live? Why? / Why not?

2 What reasons for being late have you experienced? Use these ideas to help you.

   a **My flight** was late because of the weather.

   b The journey took a long time because of **all the traffic**.

   c We were late because someone on **the train** was ill.

   d **There was a fight**, so the driver had to stop the bus and **call the police**.

   e There were **people** in the road stopping the traffic.

3 Have you been late on a journey recently? What happened?

A lorry is delayed by sheep on a road in New Zealand.

# When's the next train?

**IN THIS LESSON, YOU:**
- roleplay a conversation buying travel tickets
- learn common questions and answers for buying tickets
- practise listening to someone buying a train ticket
- say the time of trains, buses, etc., and what time you do things

## SPEAKING

1 ▶ **Work in pairs. Listen to the conversation. Then say it.**

A: Hi. I'd like a ticket to **Bilbao**, please.

B: **Bilbao**. Certainly. Single or return?

A: **Single**.

B: And do you want the fast train or the regular service?

A: What's the difference in price?

B: The fast train is **58.30** and the regular service is just **18.50**, but it takes **an hour and a half** longer.

A: OK. I'll take the **regular service**.

B: That's **18.50** then. The next train is at **11:25** and it leaves from **platform 4**.

2 **Change the words in purple. Use a dictionary if you need to. Then practise your new conversation with your partner. Exchange roles and repeat.**

## VOCABULARY Travel and tickets

V **See Vocabulary reference 11A.**

3 **Work in pairs. Check you understand the words in bold. Then decide who usually asks each question – someone travelling (T) or someone who works for the train company (C).**

1 Would you like a **single** or **return**?

2 Do I get a discount with a **student card**?

3 Which **platform** is it?

4 Is it a **direct** train?

5 Why is there a **delay**?

6 Which stop do we **get off at** to visit the science museum?

7 Can you **touch** the top of the machine with your card?

8 How much is a **first-class** ticket?

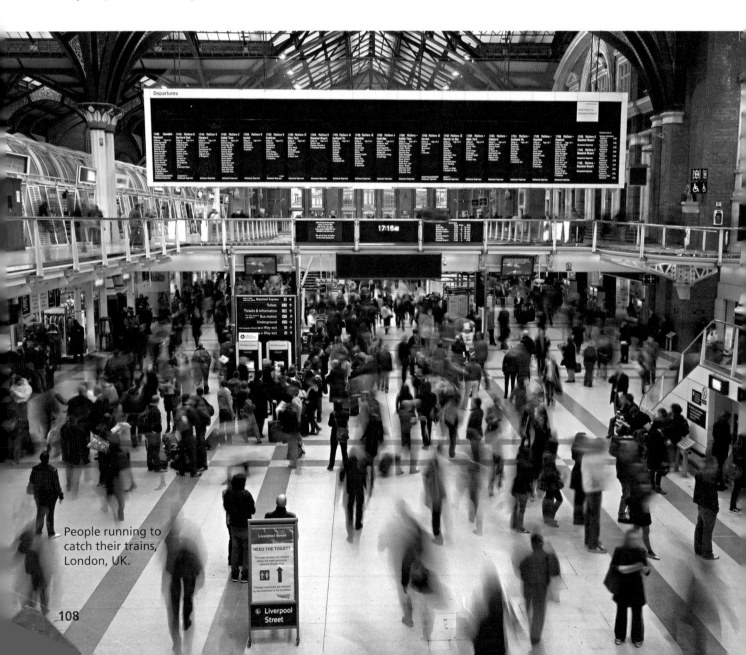

People running to catch their trains, London, UK.

**4 Match the questions in Exercise 3 (1–8) with these answers (a–h).**

a  I don't think it's working. Shall I put it in and use my number?

b  No, you have to **change** in Cuzco.

c  64 – and second-class is 45.

d  A return, please, **coming back** tomorrow.

e  Uruguaiana. Not the next one, but the one after that.

f  Number three. Take the stairs over there and cross the bridge.

g  There's a problem at the next **stop**. We have to wait for the train to leave the platform.

h  Yes, you get 15 per cent off.

**5 Work in pairs. Which of the words in bold in Exercises 3 and 4 can we use to talk about travel and tickets by bus or plane?**

**6 P ▶ Listen to the words from Exercises 3 and 4 and practise saying them on their own and in a phrase. Which words / phrases do you find hard to say? Practise saying them again.**

## LISTENING

**7 ▶ Listen to a conversation in a train station in The Hague, Netherlands. Answer the questions.**

1  What time is their train?

2  What kind of tickets do they buy – single or return, first or second class?

3  How do they pay?

4  Which platform do they need?

**8 ▶ Listen again. Complete the sentences with one word in each gap.**

1  _____ can I help?

2  It's probably _____ to buy a single.

3  It hasn't _____ . Can you put it in the machine and use your number?

4  Five. It's the train to Enschede and you _____ at Amersfoort.

5  I see. How long does it _____ then?

6  You'll _____ in Groningen around quarter to five.

7  Thanks for your _____ .

**9 Work in groups. Discuss the questions.**

1  Is the train service good or bad in your country? Why? What about the bus service?

2  What's the longest train / bus journey you've taken?

3  Do you have a favourite train / bus journey?

4  Are there any train / bus journeys you'd like to make?

## DEVELOPING CONVERSATIONS

### Telling the time

We can say times in different ways.

| | | |
|---|---|---|
| 1:15 = *one fifteen* | or | *quarter past one* |
| 1:30 = *one thirty* | or | *half past one* |
| 1:40 = *one forty* | or | *twenty to two* |

These ways are all very common.

**10 Match the times (1–8) with the pictures (a–h).**

1  half past three  ~~f~~ f

2  quarter to four  a

3  four fifteen  d

4  five to nine  b

5  five past nine  c

6  six twenty-five  g

7  nine o'clock  e

8  two thirty  h

 a
 b
 c
 d
 e
 f
 g
 h

**11 Work in pairs. Without looking at 1–8 in Exercise 10, say the times in the pictures (a–h).**

**12 Work in groups. Discuss the questions.**

1  What time is it now?  11:30

2  What time do you usually get up?  8:00

3  What time did you go to bed last night?  12:00

4  What time do you usually leave home in the morning?  8:30

5  What time do you usually get home in the afternoon / evening?  3:00

6  What time do you usually have dinner?  5:00

## CONVERSATION PRACTICE

**13 Work in pairs. Roleplay conversations between someone travelling and someone who works for the train company. Take turns to ask about and buy tickets.**

**Student A:** Look at the information in File 5 on page 200.

**Student B:** Look at the information in File 9 on page 202.

# 11B

# Getting around

**IN THIS LESSON, YOU:**
- discuss solutions to traffic problems
- talk about your experiences of using different types of transport
- read and share information about cities' solutions for traffic
- explain what's bad about transport and cities

## SPEAKING

**1** **Work in groups. Discuss the questions.**

1 Do you use buses much? If yes, which buses and why? If no, why not?

2 Is it safe to cycle where you live? Do people often steal bikes there? Have you ever fallen off a bike?

3 Is driving easy where you live? Do you have a car? Have you ever rented a car?

4 Are taxis good where you live? Why? / Why not? Have you had any good / bad experiences in a taxi?

## READING

**2** **Read the introduction to an article about solutions to traffic problems on page 111. What do you learn about:**

1 traffic in London?

2 dirty air?

**3** **Work in groups. What solutions to the problems of traffic and dirty air do you know of? Make a list. Use a dictionary if you need to.**

**4** **Work in groups of four: two Student As and two Student Bs.**

**Student As:** Read about the places on page 111.

**Student Bs:** Read about the places in File 6 on page 200.

**Answer these questions.**

1 Which places tried a solution from your list for Exercise 3? What was the solution?

2 What different solutions did you read about?

3 Which do you think is the best solution? Why? Are there any solutions you think aren't a good idea? Why?

**5** **Work in pairs: Student As together and Student Bs together. Compare your answers for Exercise 4.**

**6** **M Work in your groups of four. Share your answers from Exercise 4 and discuss these questions.**

1 Which do you think is the best solution from all the places?

2 Would the solution work where you live? Why? / Why not?

**7** **In your group, complete each set of phrases with words in bold from the different parts of the article you read.**

1 have a safe ~ / use the car for short ~s / a long ~ *journey*

2 have clean ~ / dirty ~ / go out and get some fresh ~ *air*

3 need to find a ~ / a simple ~ / a good ~ to the problem *solution*

4 it ~ how busy it is / it ~ on the weather / the price ~ on your age ~~system~~ *depends*

5 ~ you to park / ~ extra money / ~ people to enter *depends charge*

6 a cycle ~ / a bus ~ / the road has three ~s *lanes*

7 a taxi ~ / use their ~ / a regular bus ~ *services*

8 the transport ~ / a ~ to reduce traffic / improve the ~ *system*

9 ~ a special area / ~ new jobs / ~ a better system *creating*

**8** **Work in pairs. Use one phrase from each set in Exercise 7 to say something about where you live.**

## GRAMMAR

### *Too much, too many* and *not enough*

**Too much / many** shows a situation is bad because it's more than we want.

**Too much** traffic is bad for the economy.

There are **too many** delays.

It costs **too much** to take a helicopter.

**Not enough** shows a situation is bad because it's less / fewer than we want.

There are**n't enough** safe places to cross.

People do**n't** have **enough** money for that.

People do**n't** walk **enough**.

**9** **Look at the examples in the Grammar box. Complete these rules with *too much*, *too many* or *not enough*.**

1 We use *too many* with plural nouns.

2 We use *too much* with uncountable nouns and verbs.

3 We use *not enough* with uncountable nouns, plural nouns and verbs.

**10** **Choose the correct option to complete the sentences.**

1 There *aren't enough* / are too many trains. They should come more often.

2 There are *too much* / *too many* accidents. We should stop drivers going so fast.

3 There *is* / are too much crime on public transport.

4 There *isn't* / *aren't* enough buses at night. You have to get a taxi after 11 p.m.

5 Too *much* / *many* people are flying these days. Flights are too cheap.

6 I'm selling my car. I don't use it *enough* / too much and it costs *enough* / *too much*.

**G** See Grammar reference 11B.

## SPEAKING

**11** **Work in groups. Talk about traffic, transport and air quality where you live. Think about these things.**

| | | | |
|---|---|---|---|
| accidents | airport | buses | cyclists |
| drivers | flights | places to park | pollution |
| roads / motorways | taxis | traffic | trains |

*The trains in my city are OK, but there aren't enough trains at night. They stop at midnight.*

**12** **In your groups, think of possible solutions to the different problems.**

# SOLUTIONS to CITY TRAFFIC
## from around the world

**T**raffic has become a big problem in cities all over the world. A study by TomTom found that travelling by car in many cities is very slow. The situation was worst in London, where a short car **journey** of 10 km takes over 35 minutes on average. Travel by car is difficult in London because some streets are small and there are many vans that deliver online shopping. Too much traffic is bad for the economy because people have to spend a lot of time in their car doing nothing; too many cars are also bad for the environment and people's health. Another study found that in 2019, 1.8 million people around the world probably died from dirty air in cities. So what's the solution? Here's what some places are doing.

## SINGAPORE

In 1975, Singapore became the first city in the world to **charge** drivers to enter the main city area. The cost to drive into the centre **depends** on how busy the roads are. Drivers can now pay easily using technology. The result of charging drivers was that traffic fell by almost 54% and it became quicker to travel by road.

## COPENHAGEN, DENMARK

Denmark's capital has reduced traffic and pollution by choosing the bicycle as the main way to get around. When the city decided to do this, there weren't enough cycle **lanes** or places to park bikes, so they chose to spend more money on cycling. They built new bridges for cyclists, new cycle lanes (over five metres wide) and did other things to make cycling quick, safe and comfortable for everyone. Now over 60% of Copenhageners go to work and school by bike.

## MEXICO CITY, MEXICO

The local government of Mexico City doesn't charge drivers, but it has a **system** to stop people driving some days. For example, if your car number ends in a 5 or 6, you can't drive in the city on a Monday. It has helped improve the **air** in the city. More people now use other types of transport, but a few people buy an extra car with a different number so they can drive every day.

## MALTA

In 2022, the government of Malta made it free to travel on most buses on the island, except the fastest and most direct **services**. Some say it's not a good **solution** to traffic problems. In the first year, more people used the bus, but the free buses cost around €6 million a month and car use only fell 1% – from 75.6% to 74.5%. People say they still use their cars because there aren't enough buses and there are too many delays.

Most people in Copenhagen, Denmark, use bikes instead of cars to get to work.

## 11C

# Where's the best place to go?

**IN THIS LESSON, YOU:**
- choose places for a guided tour and explain your choices
- talk about guided tours and places you visit
- practise listening to parts of a guided tour
- compare descriptions of a place

## SPEAKING

**1 Work in groups. Discuss the questions.**
1 How might you travel on a guided tour? Which is the best way?
2 What kind of places do you see on a guided tour?
3 What makes a good tour guide?
4 Have you ever been on a guided tour of a museum / a castle / a city / a country? Where? Was it good? Why? / Why not?

## VOCABULARY Guided tours

**2 Complete the sentences with these pairs of words.**

entering / gate    fire / collection    indoor / roof
paintings / artists    unusual / designed    walls / century
writer / play

1 The old city ~~entering~~ **walls**, which you see on the left, are 15 metres high and were built in the 15th ~~gate~~ **century**.
2 We are now ~~writer~~ **entering** the old town. This is the north ~~play~~ **gate**, which was built in the 16th century – it's the only one left – all the others were destroyed.
3 The Orsay Museum, which we're passing now, has a big collection of **paintings** from many 19th-century **artits**, including Van Gogh and Monet.
4 The National Museum of Brazil was very important for science and history, but unfortunately there was a **fire** here a few years ago which destroyed most of the **collection**.
5 The building on our right was the home of the **writer** Federico García Lorca. You might know his **play** The House of Bernada Alba.
6 What you see there is Caesars Superdome – the biggest **indoor** stadium in the world. The **roof** is 83 metres high.
7 The **unusual** building you see on your left is Markthal – an indoor market. The artists Arno Coenen and Iris Roskam **designed** the inside of the roof.

**3 Work in pairs. Discuss the questions.**
1 Do you know any places with high walls? How many gates are there?
2 Are there any buildings near you from the 19th century? From what century is the oldest building?
3 Which artists do you like? Are they still alive?
4 Who's your favourite writer? What did they write?
5 Can you think of an unusual building? Where is it? Why is it unusual?
6 Are there any museums near you? What's in the collection? Is it good?

## LISTENING

**4 ▶ Listen to the introduction to a guided tour. Answer these questions.**
1 How are the people travelling? **Bus**
2 What city are they in? **Madrid**
3 How long is the tour? **90 minute.**

**5 FS ▶ In fast speech, people often don't say a letter at the end of the word – especially the letter t. Listen to eight phrases. Write them down.**

**6 ▶ Listen to three parts of the tour. Choose the correct option (a–c) to answer the questions (1–6).**

**Part 1**
1 When did the Prado museum open?
   a 1890
   b 1819 ✓
   c 1785 ✗
2 When can you enter for free?
   a on Mondays
   b after 6 p.m. ✓
   c at 8 p.m.

**Part 2**
3 What does the Barrio de Salamanca area of Madrid have?
   a 21 roads
   b three stadiums
   c two basketball teams ✓
4 What happened in the indoor stadium?
   a Spain won a world cup.
   b There was a fire. ✓
   c There was a big fight.

**Part 3**
5 When was the Casa de la Panadería built?
   a 18th century
   b 17th century
   c 16th century ✓
6 What was the building first used for?
   a selling bread ✓
   b offices
   c a hotel

**7 ▶ Listen again. Can you find one more piece of information about each place? Then compare your ideas in groups.**

**8** Work in pairs. Discuss the questions.

1 Are museums free in your country? Do you think it's better to pay to enter or for museums to be free? Why?

2 Has your country ever won a world cup in a sport? Which sport?

3 Have you ever been to an indoor stadium? What did you see?

4 Do you know any famous places that had a fire? What happened?

5 Do you know any buildings that have changed their use? What was their use before and now?

## GRAMMAR

### Superlatives

To compare more than two things, we can use *the* + superlative adjective.

To form the superlative, we add *-est* to short, one-syllable adjectives.

*It has paintings by our **greatest** artists.*

*This is one of the **richest** areas.*

For adjectives ending in *-y*, we change *-y* to *-iest*.

*It is maybe **the loveliest** square in Madrid.*

For longer adjectives of two or more syllables, use *the most* + adjective.

*We will see some of **the most famous** places.*

The superlative form of *good* is **the best**, and the superlative form of *bad* is **the worst**.

**9** Complete the questions (1–8) by using the superlative form of the adjectives in brackets.

1 Where's _the best_ place to live in your town / city? (good)

2 Where's _the worst_ place to live in your town / city? (bad)

3 Where's _the oldest_ part of your town / city? (old)

4 What's _the easiest_ way to get around your town / city? (easy)

5 Where's _____ place to eat in your town / city? (cheap) _the cheapest_

6 What's _the most beautiful_ part of your country? (beautiful)

7 Who's _the most famous_ person from your country? (famous)

8 What's _the most delicious_ food from your country? (delicious)

**10** Work in groups. Discuss the questions from Exercise 9. Do you agree with the other people in your group?

**G** See Grammar reference 11C.

## SPEAKING TASK

**11** On your own, think of at least five places for a guided tour of your country or area. Write the names of places and one or two pieces of information about them. Include somewhere which:

• is old

• has lots of art

• is beautiful

• was / is the home of someone famous

• has nature

• is for sport

**12** **M** Work in pairs and do one of the following:

a If your partner is from the same place: explain your choices to each other. Together, decide on one set of places for your tour.

b If your partner is from a different place: explain to each other what you're going to see on the tour. Your partner can ask you questions to find out more. They should say what they think is the most interesting thing on the tour.

## ■ MY OUTCOMES ■

Work in pairs. Discuss the questions.

1 What reading or listening texts did you find most interesting?

2 What different things did you talk about and do in this unit?

3 How are you feeling about your listening in English now?

4 How will you practise new language from this unit?

People on a guided tour of Belém, Lisbon, Portugal.

# 12
# Feelings

**IN THIS UNIT, YOU:**

- talk about health problems and give advice
- explain what happened in a news story
- discuss how happy you think people in your country are

## SPEAKING

**1 Work in pairs. Discuss the questions.**

1 Look at the photo. How do you think the people are feeling?

2 Why do you think they're feeling like this? What happened?

3 Can you remember the last time you felt like this?

**2 Work with a new partner. Think of three different times people might feel:**

1 really happy.

2 a bit sad.

3 really angry.

4 quite worried.

5 wonderful.

6 really bad.

**3 Work in groups. Choose one of the adjectives from Exercise 2. Talk about a time you felt like this. Explain why.**

K-pop fans at the London Korean Festival see their favourite band, UK.

## 12A

# Are you OK?

## SPEAKING

**1** ▶ **Work in pairs. Listen to the conversation. Then say it.**

A: Are you OK?

B: No, not really. I don't feel well. **I have a headache**.

A: Oh no. Maybe you should **go home and have a sleep**.

B: No, it's OK. I just need **something to drink**.

A: Are you sure?

B: Yes, thanks. I'll be fine.

A: Well, I hope you feel better soon.

**2** **Change the words in purple. Use a dictionary if you need to. Then practise your new conversation with your partner. Exchange roles and repeat.**

## VOCABULARY  Health problems

**V** See Vocabulary reference 12A. ≫

**3** **Complete the sentences with these words.**

| accident | alright | badly | cold | cut |
|---|---|---|---|---|
| hurts | ice | knee | lie down | matter |
| medicine | sick | stomach ache | | |

*(handwritten numbers: accident B5, alright 8, badly 8+, cold 1, cut 5, hurts 7, ice B7, knee 7, lie down 8B, matter 6, medicine 9B, sick 3, stomach ache 4)*

1  I'm going to take the day off. I have a _cold_ and I don't want anyone else to get it.

2  You shouldn't carry that if your back _hurts_ . Let me help you.

3  I feel really _____ . I'm going to call my boss to say I can't come in today.

4  I think I ate some seafood that was bad. I have a really bad _stom_ .

5  A: What happened to your hand – did you have an _____ or something?

   B: Yeah, I _____ it on a piece of glass.

6  A: What's the _____ with your leg?

   B: I fell in the park.

7  A: I hurt my _____ playing volleyball.

   B: Oh no. You should put some _____ on it. That usually helps.

8  A: I'm tired. I slept really _____ last night.

   B: Maybe you should go and _____ . Have a little sleep.

9  A: Are you _____ ?

   B: Yeah, I'm OK, thanks. I just need to take this _____ . It always helps.

**4** **P** ▶ **Listen to the words from Exercise 3 and practise saying them on their own and in a phrase. Which words / phrases do you find hard to say? Practise saying them again.**

**5** **Work in groups. Discuss the questions.**

1  Have you had any accidents recently? If yes, what happened?

2  Have you ever fallen over? If yes, what happened?

3  When was the last time you felt sick or had a stomach ache or cold? Did you go to the doctor? If yes, what did they say / do?

4  What do you usually do when you have a cold?

5  Can you think of three reasons why people sleep badly?

## LISTENING

**6** ▶ **Listen to five conversations about health problems. What is the health problem in each conversation?**

**7** **Work in pairs. Match these pairs of words (a–e) with the conversations (1–5).**

a  sick / fresh air  _3_

b  doctor / medicine  _4_

c  lie down / hungry  _1_

d  tennis / start  _5_

e  boss / day off  _2_

**8** ▶ **Listen again and check your ideas. With your partner, explain what the people said. Use the words in Exercise 7.**

## GRAMMAR

### *Should / Shouldn't*

We use *should(n't)* + verb to give advice. We often say *maybe* before so the advice doesn't sound too strong.

*Should* shows we think it's a good idea to do the action. *Maybe you **should lie** down.*

*Shouldn't* shows we think it's a bad idea. *Maybe he **shouldn't play** tennis today.*

**9** **Complete the sentences with *should* or *shouldn't*.**

1  A: That looks bad. Maybe you _should_ see a doctor.

   B: No. I'm fine.

2  A: You _shouldn't_ carry that if you have a bad back. Let me take it.

   B: Oh, thanks.

3  A: You _shouldn't_ sit in the sun for so long. It's not good for you.

   B: It's fine. I've put on some sun cream.

4  A: I feel terrible.

   B: Yeah, you don't look very well. Maybe you _should_ go and see a doctor.

5  A: He looks really tired.

   B: I know. Maybe he _shouldn't_ work so hard.

   A: Yeah. He _should_ take some time off or let someone else do some of his work.

**10** Work in pairs. Give two or three pieces of advice to someone in each situation. Use *should / shouldn't*.

1 My back hurts.    *You shou*
2 I feel sick.
3 I hurt my knee running.
4 I have a terrible cold.
5 I'm so tired. I slept really badly last night.
6 My dad fell over in the street and hurt his arm.

**G** See Grammar reference 12A.

## DEVELOPING CONVERSATIONS

### Saying *no*

When we say *no* to offers and advice, we often use words and phrases like *it's OK / really* and then give a reason. It's polite.

A: *Maybe you should lie down.*

B: **No, it's OK.** *I think I'm just hungry.*

A: *Are you sure?*

B: *Yeah.* **Really**. *I'll be fine after I have something to eat.*

**11** Write four similar conversations starting with these sentences (1–4). Say *no* to the advice / offers and give reasons. Use the phrases below to help you.

1 Maybe you should go to hospital.
2 Would you like any more to eat?
3 Maybe you should take the day off.
4 You shouldn't stay here alone.

*No, it's OK. / No, thanks. / I'm alright. / Really.*

**12** Work in pairs. Practise reading your conversations from Exercise 11.

## CONVERSATION PRACTICE

**13** **M** Have conversations about health problems with different students. Use this guide to help you. For each new conversation, work with a new partner and choose a different problem.

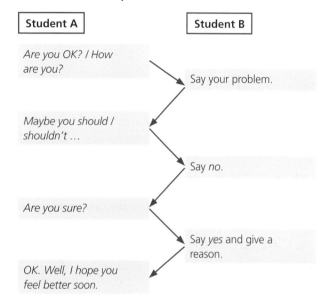

| Student A | Student B |
|---|---|
| Are you OK? / How are you? | Say your problem. |
| Maybe you should / shouldn't … | Say *no*. |
| Are you sure? | Say *yes* and give a reason. |
| OK. Well, I hope you feel better soon. | |

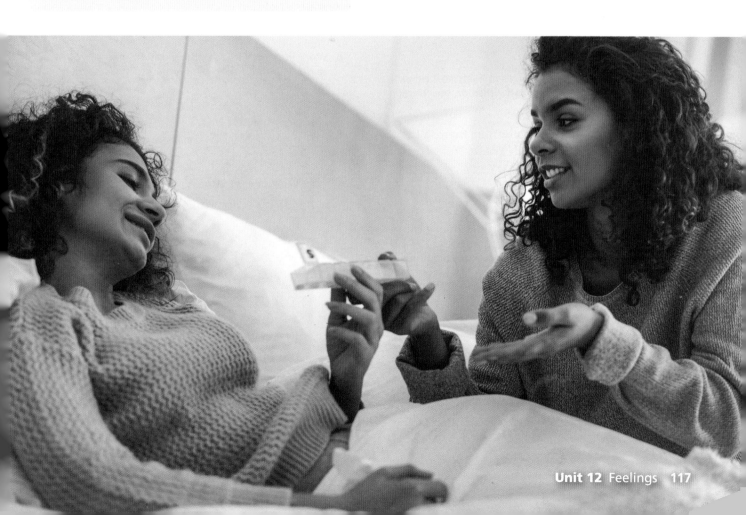

# Good news, bad news

**IN THIS LESSON, YOU:**
- explain what happened in a news story
- discuss what kind of news you watch / read – and how
- describe some good and bad news
- read some news stories

## SPEAKING

**1 Work in groups. Discuss the questions.**

1 How often do you read / listen to / watch the news?

2 Where do you get your news from? Why?

3 How do you feel about these different kinds of news? What kind do you read most?

| | | | |
|---|---|---|---|
| business | crime | entertainment | foreign |
| politics | science | sports | weather |

## VOCABULARY In the news

**2 Match the first part of sentences 1–4 with the second parts (a–d). Then match 5–8 with e–h.**

1 A plane **landed**

2 The new airport has finally

3 The government has **agreed**

4 It's going to be harder for children

5 The government is planning

6 The economy is **growing**

7 Local police are **continuing** to

8 An accident in a factory

a on a plan to help the banks. *3*

b to use social media because of a new **law**. *4*

c on the sea this morning. *1*

d **opened** after a long delay. *2*

e look for a **missing** dog. *7*

f **killed** three people. *8*

g very quickly. *6*

h to **plant** two million new trees this year. *5*

**3 Work in pairs. Which sentences in Exercise 2 do you think describe good news and which do you think describe bad news? Why?**

**4 Work in groups. Use five words from Exercise 2 to say true things about where you live.**

*A big new shopping centre opened here last year.*

## READING

**5 Read four short possible news articles from local newspapers on page 119. Match the articles (1–4) with these headlines (a–e). There is one extra headline.**

**a** New Law Needed for Dangerous Drivers

**b** Price Agreed for Star Player

**c** FOUR STILL MISSING AFTER ACCIDENT

**d** New Show Opens

**e** TOWN'S OLDEST WOMAN CONTINUES TO PLANT

**6 Read the articles again and choose the correct answers to the questions.**

1 Which sentence best describes Joyce Parkin?

  a She travels a lot.

  b She loves cooking.

  c She stays busy.

2 How is the theatre manager feeling?

  a They're worried about the building.

  b They're happy because tickets are selling very well.

  c They're excited because some famous stars are in the musical.

3 How do people feel about Pete Guthrie?

  a They like him and want him to do well.

  b They're angry because he's leaving.

  c They're happy because the club made a lot of money.

4 Why were people angry?

  a The police didn't arrive.

  b The driver didn't stay to help people who were hurt.

  c The hospital was very crowded.

**7 Work in groups. Discuss the questions.**

1 Have you heard any similar local news stories?

2 Which article is most interesting to you? Why?

3 Do you know any local news from your area / town?

## SPEAKING

**8 Work in pairs. Choose which option (a or b) you want to do. Plan how to explain your story. Use a dictionary if you need to.**

a Think of a news story you both know that made you feel happy, worried or angry.

b Choose one of these headlines and make a news story for it.

**New research shows angry people die younger**

**Police find missing dog**

**NUMBER OF PEOPLE LOOKING FOR WORK CONTINUES TO GROW**

**Birthday of world's oldest person**

**9 M Work with another pair and share your stories. How do they make you feel? Do you all feel the same way about the stories?**

## 1  e

Everyone always wants to know what they need to do to live a long and happy life. Well, Joyce Parkin says the answer is to spend as much time outside as you can. The 102-year-old lives alone in the same house she was born in – and goes for a walk in the park every morning. The rest of the time, she's in her garden. Joyce grows most of what she needs to eat – and is already planning for next year.

## 2  d

Hundreds of people went to see the musical *West Side Story* at the Crown Theatre yesterday. Excited about seeing famous stars, over 500 people bought tickets for the first night. Everyone we spoke to said it was wonderful and tickets for the next three weeks are already selling fast. The theatre was closed for six months last year after a tree fell on it. The manager is very pleased with the sales and hopes to make enough money to pay for all the repairs.

## 3  b

After eight years with local club United, 25-year-old Pete Guthrie is moving. After saying no to a first offer of £60,000, the club have said yes to a second offer and Guthrie is going to leave at the end of May. The final sale price of £70,000 is the highest United have ever earned. Lots of people in the town have really enjoyed watching Pete during his time here and we want the best for him in the future.

## 4  a

A car left the road last Saturday and hit a crowd waiting outside the cinema, hurting four people quite badly. The driver didn't stop and drove away before the police arrived. Two people are still in hospital after the accident, and the other two are now back home. Many people are angry and are asking the government to do more to stop things like this from happening again.

# Happy days

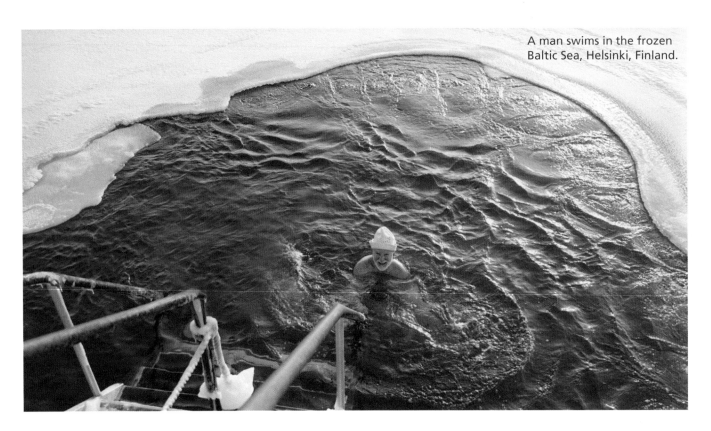

A man swims in the frozen Baltic Sea, Helsinki, Finland.

## SPEAKING

**1** Work in groups. Discuss the questions.

1 What kinds of things make you happy?

2 What makes you unhappy?

3 Do you usually feel happier at some special times of the day / year? Why?

4 Do you think governments can improve how happy people are? If yes, how?

## VOCABULARY Feelings

**2** Complete the sentences with these pairs of words.

| | | |
|---|---|---|
| apologize / angry | crazy about / upset | excited / can't wait |
| hate / stressed | lucky / surprised | pleased / successful |

1 The boss said she's very _____ with everyone's work and that we've had a very _____ year.

2 I was very _____ to find a hotel and I was _____ at how cheap it was.

3 Her son is _____ dancing. He does classes every week and gets _____ if she can't take him.

4 I should _____ to her, really. I was tired and got very _____ . I feel bad about it now.

5 I _____ working this hard. I have so much to do this week. I'm feeling very _____ .

6 We're going to Majorca for a week in October. I'm really _____ because it's our first time away without the children. I _____ !

**3** Work in pairs. Use the words from Exercise 2 to describe how you might feel in these situations.

1 You're going to see your favourite singer in concert.

2 You're working from nine to five every day and then studying in the evening.

3 Someone tells you you're wrong when you know you're not.

4 You go to another city for work and see your old teacher on the bus.

5 As a birthday present, someone pays for you to go for a ride in a helicopter.

6 You find some money in the street.

**4** Work in groups. Discuss the questions.

1 What kind of things do people do when they feel stressed?

2 Can you think of three things people might be crazy about?

3 How do you know if someone is upset?

4 Can you think of two things you might need to apologize for?

5 Can you think of two different things you might be pleased with – or pleased to hear?

6 Can you think of two different times people might feel very lucky?

**5** Work in pairs. Choose three of the words from Exercise 2 to say true things about your life.

*I found out how old a friend of mine is. I was really surprised!*

*I nearly had a car accident last week. I was lucky the other car didn't hit me.*

## LISTENING

**6** ▶ **Listen to the first part of a podcast about being happy. Number these things in the order you hear them.**

a Costa Rica

b friends and family

c Sweden and Norway

d children

e work

f Singapore

g women in Texas

h the United Nations

**7** ▶ **Work in pairs. Compare your answers. Can you remember why the woman talked about each thing? Then listen again and check your ideas.**

**8** [FS] ▶ **In fast speech, the word *was* often sounds like /wəz/. Listen to nine phrases from the second part of the podcast. Which include *was*?**

**9** ▶ **Listen to the speaker talking about what they did yesterday. For each of the nine things she talks about, choose how she felt.**

1 tired / happy

2 upset / angry

3 stressed / excited

4 happy / bored

5 stressed / pleased

6 bored / surprised

7 very worried / unhappy

8 quite excited / really tired

9 really tired / really bored

**10** ▶ **Work in pairs. Why did she have each feeling? How many of the reasons for the different feelings can you remember? Then listen again and check your ideas.**

## GRAMMAR

### *Because, so, before* and *after*

We use *because*, *so*, *before* and *after* to join two parts of a sentence.

*Because* shows why something happens.
*I was lucky **because** I got a seat.*

*So* shows the result.
*The bus was full, **so** I couldn't sit and read.*

The phrases following *because* and *so* always have a verb.

*Before* and *after* show when things happen.
*I felt terrible **before** I took the medicine.*
***After** dinner, I watched the news on TV.*

*Before* and *after* can both start a phrase that only has a noun and no verb.

**11 Join the pairs of sentences using the words in brackets. You might need to change the order of the sentences.**

1 I'm really pleased. I passed all my exams. (so)
   *I passed all my exams, so I'm really pleased.*

2 I'm going to go on holiday next month. I'm excited. (because)

3 They had a big argument. He sat on the sofa and cried. (after)

4 I'm very stressed. I have a really important exam tomorrow. (because)

5 I moved to London. Then I met my wife. (after)

6 I always go for a run in the morning. Then I go to work. (before)

7 He's quite upset. He didn't get the job he wanted. (so)

8 I had a really nice lunch with her. Then she had her accident. (before)

**12 Work in pairs. Think of five things you've done this week. Tell your partner. Say what you did, where you went and who you met. Describe your feelings.**

[G] See Grammar reference 12C. »»

## SPEAKING TASK

**13 When the United Nations does research to find out how happy people are, it asks about different things. These include some of the things in the list (a–f). For each thing in the list, decide what mark you would give your country, from 1 (very bad) to 10 (very good).**

a how close people are to friends and family

b how long people live

c how much the government helps people

d how the economy is doing

e how kind people are to others

f how much free time people have

**14** [M] **Work in groups. Compare your ideas. Explain your choices. If you come from the same country, how similar are you? How do you explain any differences?**

## ■ MY OUTCOMES ■

**Work in pairs. Discuss the questions.**

1 What speaking activities did you enjoy doing?

2 What new things can you talk about in English?

3 Can you think of three things you learned about other students?

4 When are you going to practise English this week? How?

# WRITING 6

# Emailing a friend

**IN THIS LESSON, YOU:**
- write an email to a friend recommending places to visit
- talk about visiting people and recommending places
- use different phrases in friendly emails
- recommend things to do in your country

## SPEAKING

**1  Work in groups. Discuss the questions.**

1  Do you have any friends or relatives in other towns, cities or countries?

2  Where do they live? What do they do there?

3  Have you ever visited them? If yes, when? How long for? Did you have a good time?

## WRITING

**2  Read the email. Answer these questions.**

1  What do you think is Dietmar's relationship to Tanya?

2  Where does Dietmar live?

3  Why is she writing to him now?

---

**To:** d.cremers@shoemail.de

**Subject:** Visiting Germany!

---

Hi Dietmar,

How are you? Thanks for the message on my birthday. Sorry I haven't written recently. I've been very busy with work.

Anyway, are you going to be in Hamburg in May? I'm finally going to take a holiday and I'm planning to visit Germany. I'd like to come to Hamburg and see you and Jean-Paul when I'm there. Also, where else do you think I should go while I'm in Germany? I'm going to stay for about three weeks. Let me know what you think.

Thanks,

Tanya

---

**3  Work in pairs. Imagine Tanya is visiting you in your country. Tell your partner how you would answer the email and what places you would recommend.**

**4  Read Dietmar's reply. Match the photos (a–d) with places in Dietmar's email.**

---

**To:** t.tucker@shoemail.gb

**Subject:** Re: Visiting Germany!

¹ ~~Hi~~ Tanya,

Great to ² **hear** from you. I'm ³ **fine**, thanks. Yes, we'll be here in May – come and stay with us when you're in Hamburg! We have a new apartment near the station.

So, if you haven't been to Berlin before, you should definitely go there. It's a cool city that never sleeps. If you want to go out at night, I'd try Hackescher Markt. It has eight different areas of bars, restaurants and lots of shops.

If you prefer the countryside, you should go to the Allgäu. there are lots of rivers and lakes and it's lovely for walking. If you're interested in history, there are also lots of old castles there. I'd definitely go to Neuschwanstein Castle. It's beautiful.

⁴ **Anyway**, let me know when exactly you want to come.

⁵ **all** the best,

Dietmar

---

**5  Which place sounds better to you – Berlin or the Allgäu? Why?**

## USEFUL LANGUAGE

### Writing friendly emails

We usually write emails to people we know in a similar way to how we talk. And we often reply like it's part of a conversation.

*Hi* Frank,

*How are you?*

*I'm fine, thanks.*

*Sorry I haven't written recently.*

*Great to hear from you.*

We usually finish the email with a phrases like this:

*Anyway, are you going to be in Frankfurt in May?*

*Thanks / All the best*

**6** Complete Dietmar's email with one word in each gap.

**7** Which phrases in Dietmar's email could you replace with these words and phrases (l–5)?

1  Take care
2  Hey
3  Anyway, it'll be lovely to see you.
4  I've been very busy too.
5  I was so glad to get your email.

## Recommending

We often recommend things using the pattern *If you … , you should (definitely) … / I'd (definitely) … .*

**If you** *haven't been to Berlin,* **you should definitely** *go there.*

**If you** *prefer the countryside,* **you should** *go to the Allgäu.*

**If you**'*re interested in history,* **I'd definitely** *go to Schloss Neuschwanstein.*

**8** Answer the questions.

1  What verb forms are used after *if*?
2  What's the full form of *I'd*?
3  Which is stronger: *you should go* or *you should definitely go*?

**9** Match the sentence beginnings (1–6) with the endings (a–f).

1  If you like sport, e
2  If you haven't been to Los Dinamos National Park, f
3  If you like the sea, c
4  If you want to go shopping, b
5  If you're interested in education and history, a
6  If you've never tried skiing, d

a  you should go to the Komenský Museum.
b  I'd go to Wangfujing Street. That's where the big department stores are.
c  I'd definitely go to Brittany. It has some great beaches.
d  you should go to Nagano. There are lots of places there which are good for beginners.
e  you should visit the Maracanã Stadium.
f  you should definitely go. It's a lovely place to walk in the forest.

**10** Write three similar sentences about your country.

1  If you _____ , you should definitely _____ .
2  If you _____ , you should _____ .
3  If you _____ , I'd _____ .

## PRACTICE

**11** Work in pairs. Read this email. Discuss how to answer it. Decide:

- how to start the email.
- if you are going to be home.
- where you recommend visiting in November.
- how to end the email.

Hi,

How are you? Are you going to be at home in November? I'm planning to come to your country on holiday. It would be great to see you when I'm there. Also, can you recommend some places to visit? Anyway, let me know what you think.

Love,
Amy

**12** Write your email. Write 50–80 words.

**13** Work in pairs. Read your partner's email. Discuss the questions.

1  Does your partner's email start and end correctly?
2  Does the email answer Amy's questions?
3  Can you suggest one way to improve your partner's email?

## VIDEO Out and about

**1 Work in groups. Discuss the questions.**

1 What's the best place to stay in your town or city?

2 Where's the best place to go out?

3 Where's the best place to go shopping?

4 Where's the best place to get some exercise?

### Understanding accents

Some accents add an /e/ sound when a word starts with an /st/ or /sp/ sound, so *stop* /stɒp/ may sound more like *estop* /estɒp/.

**2** 📹 **Watch five people answer the same questions. How much can you remember about what they said? Then work in pairs. Did anyone suggest similar places to you?**

**3** 📹 **Watch again. Match one or two sentences with each speaker.**

a I live in the north of the country.

b I live in the west of the country.

c The best place to stay is the area I live in.

d There are streets without any cars in the centre.

e I'm learning to do something.

f My favourite place is open late at night.

g My favourite place is a tall building with lights.

h I don't like modern shopping centres so much.

**4 Tell your partner about four places you know. Explain what they are like.**

1 a place in the north or west of your country

2 a place that is open very late

3 a place you can learn to swim or dive

4 a tall tower or building

5 a traditional market

## VIDEO Developing conversations

**5** 📹 **You're going to watch two people talking about not sleeping well. Watch and take notes.**

**6** 📹 **Work in pairs. Compare what you understood. Watch again if you need to.**

**7** FS 📹 **Watch again. Complete the sentences with two or three words in each gap.**

1 You're very quiet this morning and you _____ anything.

2 You should lie down if _____ feeling very well.

3 I think my bed is not _____ comfortable.

4 _____ sleep badly?

5 Maybe I'm also _____ about the talk I'm doing today.

6 My mum always says you _____ too much in the evenings.

7 _____ for a walk by the beach?

8 I'm going to _____ at my notes and then at 10 o'clock we can go.

## CONVERSATION PRACTICE

**8 Work in pairs. You're going to practise a conversation.**

1 Choose a Conversation practice from either Lesson 11A or Lesson 12A.

2 Look at the language in that lesson.

3 Check the meaning of anything you don't remember with your partner.

4 Have the conversation. Try to do it better than the last time you did

# Grammar and Vocabulary

## GRAMMAR

**1 Complete the conversation with one word in each gap.**

A: Why do you want to move?

B: There's too ¹_____ traffic round here. I'm worried about my kids ²_____ they don't get ³_____ fresh air living here.

A: I know! The government ⁴_____ do something about the pollution. It's bad for people's health.

B: True, but I can't wait for them. ⁵_____ easiest thing to do is move to the countryside.

A: That's terrible! People should ⁶_____ have to move because of traffic.

**2 Choose the correct option to complete the sentences.**

1 My hand hurt a lot, but it felt better *after / before / so* I put ice on it.

2 There are too *many / much / enough* accidents at work.

3 I think you *shouldn't / should / don't* go out tonight. You're too tired.

4 I had a headache *because / so / after* the match.

5 I think I felt ill because I didn't drink *too much / too many / enough* water.

6 There was an accident on the motorway *so / because / after* there were big delays.

7 The *very / most / more* interesting place to see here is the castle.

8 It's one of our *older / oldest / most old* buildings.

**3 Correct the underlined mistake in each sentence.**

1 I don't like cycling in my city. There are too <u>much</u> cars.

2 It's also bad because there <u>are</u> enough safe roads where kids can cycle.

3 Let's take a taxi. It's <u>quicker way to get there</u>.

4 You <u>shouldn't</u> read her books. She's a fantastic writer.

5 A lot of people didn't like the film and they left <u>after</u> the end.

6 The <u>easyest</u> way to contact me is by text.

**4 ▶ Listen and write the six sentences you hear. Include these words.**

1 our / artist

2 sick / cake

3 there / travelling

4 tell / stressed

5 men / world

6 I / pay / pounds

## VOCABULARY

**5 Match the two parts of the phrases.**

| | | | |
|---|---|---|---|
| 1 | touch | a | a tree / some flowers in the garden |
| 2 | change | b | on a new plan / to work together |
| 3 | come back | c | trains in Oxford / buses |
| 4 | enter | d | the old town / through the main gate |
| 5 | agree | e | to look for someone / her education |
| 6 | plant | f | later today / tomorrow |
| 7 | open | g | the screen / your card on the machine |
| 8 | continue | h | a new factory / after a delay |

**6 Decide if these words and phrases are about travel, health problems, or history and news. There are five items in each group.**

| | | | | |
|---|---|---|---|---|
| artist | century | cold | direct | fire |
| first-class | get off at | killed | knee | lie down |
| medicine | missing | platform | return | sick |

**7 Choose the correct option to complete the sentences.**

1 The government has a new *law / play* to help the environment.

2 You can see some beautiful *artists / paintings* in that museum.

3 What's the *matter / stop*? Are you feeling sick?

4 I had a stomach ache last night, but I'm feeling *badly / alright* now.

5 There was a *delay / cut* on the train, so I was late.

6 I apologized to them because I got quite *upset / pleased*.

7 She said she was *surprised / angry* that her book was successful.

**8 Complete the texts with one word in each gap. The first letters are given.**

A few years ago, I was on a plane which had a problem, so it had to ¹la_____ quickly. We were ²lu_____ because there was an airport near, so we didn't have an ³ac_____ and no-one was ⁴hu_____ , but now I really ⁵ha_____ flying and I always get very ⁶st_____ if I have to take a plane.

The architect Frank Gehry ⁷de_____ the Guggenheim museum in Bilbao, Spain. It is an ⁸un_____ building because the ⁹ro_____ and walls are all different shapes. It became famous around the world when it ¹⁰op_____ in 1997. It has a great ¹¹co_____ of modern art. It's €15 to ¹²en_____ for adults, but you can get a discount with a student ¹³ca_____ .

# 13 Nature

## IN THIS UNIT, YOU:

- have conversations about the weather and make plans
- talk about living in the countryside
- do a class survey about people's pets and opinions about animals

## SPEAKING

1 **Work in groups. Don't use a dictionary. How many words about the photo can you write in one minute?**

2 **The group with the most words should tell the class what they wrote. Does the class agree with the words? How many other words did the class think of?**

3 **Work in pairs. Discuss the questions.**

1 What do you think of the job in the photo? Which of these sentences do you agree with? What else can you say?
- You can earn a lot of money.
- It's exciting.
- It's healthy to be outside.
- You work long hours.
- You have to work at night.
- It's nice if it's sunny.

2 Do you know anyone who works outside? What do they do? Do they like it?

A photographer taking a photo of a baby penguin in Antarctica.

# There might be a storm

**IN THIS LESSON, YOU:**
- have conversations about the weather and make plans
- practise listening to conversations where people make plans
- say what is certain and uncertain about the weather and plans
- ask short questions

## SPEAKING

1 ▶ **Work in pairs. Listen to the conversation. Then say it.**

A: What do you want to do on **Saturday**?

B: I don't know. What's the weather going to be like?

A: It's going to be **wet**. They said **there might be a storm**.

B: Really? Well then, maybe we should go to **a museum** or something?

A: Oh, we could do. Which one?

B: Why don't we go to **the science museum**? **We haven't been there for a long time**.

A: OK. Let's do that.

2 **Change the words in purple. Use a dictionary if you need to. Then practise your new conversation with your partner. Exchange roles and repeat.**

## VOCABULARY  Weather

3 **Complete the sentences (1–10) with these words.**

| | | | |
|---|---|---|---|
| autumn | clouds | grey | sky 7 |
| snow | spring 6 | stars | storms |
| sunny 2 | temperature 4 | warm | windy 3 |

1 There are a lot of black **clouds** over there. It looks like there might be a storm.

2 It's been hot and **sunny** and they say it's going to stay dry for the next two weeks.

3 It was sunny, but it was also very **windy**, so it wasn't nice to lie on the beach.

4 They say the **temperature** is going to fall to minus twenty tomorrow, so we should stay at home and keep warm.

5 It's not going to **snow**, but there might be some ice on the roads.

6 **Spring** is a good time to visit the country because you can see the flowers on the trees.

7 The **sky** was really clear at night there and you could see thousands of ~~grey~~ **stars**

8 The sky was very **grey** most of the week, but it didn't actually rain.

9 They said it's going to rain and there might be one or two **storms** over the next few days.

10 In **autumn** you can wear a T-shirt during the day because it's still quite **warm**, but the temperature really starts to fall at night.

4 **Work in groups. Discuss the questions.**

1 What's the weather going to be like today? Tomorrow? The rest of the week?

2 Do you have different seasons in your country? What's the weather like in each? Which do you like most?

3 Which parts of your country have the best / worst weather? Why?

4 Which are the best months for people to visit your area?

## LISTENING

5 ▶ **Listen to three conversations. What's the weather going to be like in each?**

*Rain*
*1. ~~...~~ – 30 Degres – not so hot*
*2. cloudy in morning, Dry afternoon*
*3. Cold, might snow*

The beginning of a storm over Redcliffe, Australia.

**6** ▶ Listen again. Complete the sentences with three or four words in each gap.

1 Why don't we go _to the swimming pool_ , then.
2 The café there does a nice lunch _which is quite cheap_
3 Why don't we _relax this morning_ and then go for a walk.
4 How about _taking the car_ and going to the hills.
5 We should _go shopping one day_, though.
6 Can we be back before _the football starts_ ?

## GRAMMAR

### Be going to and might

We use *be* (*not*) + *going to* + verb and *might* (*not*) + verb to talk about the future.

*Be going to* shows we're sure. *Might* shows something is possible, but we aren't sure.

What's the weather **going to be** like?

They said it **might rain** this morning, but it**'s going to be** dry this afternoon.

It**'s not going to** rain, but it **might not be** a good day for the beach.

We don't usually use *might* in questions (*Might it rain?*).

**7** Complete the conversations (1–5) with *might* or the correct form of *be going to*.

1 A: Do you have any plans for later?
   B: I **might** go shopping, but I'm not sure.
2 A: What's happening with those empty offices?
   B: They **going to** change them into flats. The plans look quite nice.
3 A: What **are** you **going to** do when you leave school?
   B: I'd like to continue studying, but I **might** have to get a job. My family needs the money.

4 A: What **is** the weather **going to** be like tomorrow?
   B: They said it **might** be cold – like minus four – and it **might** possibly snow.
5 A: I'm afraid they said it **isn't going to be** very nice tomorrow and it might rain. So we **might not** be able to have a picnic, unfortunately. But let's wait and see.
   B: OK, let me know what you think tomorrow.

**8** Write four things you might (not) do in the next week, month or year. Think about why they are just possibilities. Is it because of the weather, money, other people or some other reason?

**9** Work in groups. Explain your ideas to each other.

**G** See Grammar reference 13A.

## DEVELOPING CONVERSATIONS

### Short questions

In conversation, we often use short questions without verbs.

A: Why don't we go to the swimming pool?
B: We could do. **Which one?**
A: The one in the sports centre.

**10** Choose the best short question to complete each conversation.

1 A: Why don't we go and see *Air*? It's on at King Cinema.
   B: Yeah, maybe. *Where? / What film? / What time?*
   A: 6 o'clock and 8:40.
2 A: I might go for a walk later.
   B: Oh, OK. *Who with? / When exactly? / Where?*
   A: Just around town. Would you like to come?
3 A: I'm tired. Why don't we take a break?
   B: *How long for? / When? / Where?*
   A: I don't know – half an hour?
4 A: Why don't you invite some friends for dinner?
   B: *Who? / Why? / When?*
   A: Do you need a reason? It's just a nice thing to do!
5 A: It's nice and sunny. Why don't we go to the beach?
   B: Yeah. We could do. *Which one? / What time? / How?*
   A: I can borrow my friend's car.

**11** Work with a new partner.

Student A: Say the first line of each conversation in Exercise 10.

Student B: Ask a different short question.

Student A: Give an answer.

## CONVERSATION PRACTICE

**12** You're going to have similar conversations to the one in Exercise 1. Work in pairs. Start the conversation like this and continue. Make a plan. Take turns to start.

A: What do you want to do tomorrow?
B: What's the weather going to be like?

# Country life

## SPEAKING

1 Work in pairs. For each of the categories, decide two things for the city and two things for the countryside.

   1 the most common animals

   2 the most common jobs

   3 the main entertainment / free-time activity outside the home

   4 things people are often afraid of

   5 things people often complain about

2 Compare your ideas with another pair. Did they have the same ideas as you?

## READING

3 You are going to read a post on a blog called *Six reasons not to …* . Read the introduction on page 131. Complete the title of the blog post.

4 Work in pairs. What do you think the six reasons might be?

5 Read the rest of the blog post and match these headings (a–f) with the paragraphs (1–6). Decide what the writer doesn't like about each thing.

   a The jobs **6**

   b The smell **1**

   c The shops **3**

   d The animals **4 2**

   e The views **5**

   f The clothes **4**

6 Work in pairs. Match the words in bold in the blog post with these meanings (1–11). Don't use a dictionary.

   1 impossible *No chance* ✓

   2 a small mountain *hills* ✓

   3 use time or money badly *choices* ✓

   4 what farmers plant each year to sell *crops*

   5 things you can choose *chemicals*

   6 bad chemicals in the air or water

   7 something used to help plants grow more quickly *scary*

   8 something that joins to another thing

   9 near to things you need; easy and quick

   10 describing something that you are afraid of

   11 an area on a farm for plants or animals, often with a wall / fence around it

7 Read the blog post again. Are these statements are true (T) or false (F)?

   1 Everything in the countryside is natural. F

   2 A cow once hurt the writer. F

   3 The shops aren't open in the evening. T

   4 It's difficult to keep your clothes clean. T

   5 Most of the countryside in the writer's country looks the same. T

   6 It's easy to use the internet. F

8 Ⓜ Work in pairs. What do you think of each of the six reasons not to live in the countryside? Do you agree or disagree with them? Use these adjectives to help you.

| funny | sad | strange | stupid | true | wrong |
|-------|-----|---------|--------|------|-------|

9 Work in pairs. Without looking at the blog post, can you remember what the writer said using these words and phrases?

| chemicals | choices | connection | convenient |
|-----------|---------|------------|------------|
| crops | field | hills | no chance |
| pollution | scary | waste | |

10 Read again and see if you were right.

## SPEAKING

11 Work in groups. Choose one of these sets of questions to answer for where you live.

**If you live in the city:**

   1 What's the countryside like around your city?

   2 Do you go there much? Why? / Why not?

   3 What's your favourite place in the countryside? Why?

   4 Do you know anyone who lives in the countryside? Where? Do they like it? What problems do they have?

   5 Would you like to move to the countryside? Why? / Why not?

**If you live in the countryside:**

   1 What's it like where you live?

   2 Do you ever go to other parts of the countryside? Why? / Why not?

   3 What's your favourite place? Why?

   4 Do you know anyone who lives in a city? Where? Do they like it? What problems do they have?

   5 Would you like to move to the city? Why? / Why not?

# Six reasons not to ~~move to the countryside~~

I saw a programme on TV yesterday about a couple building their perfect house. It cost over a million pounds and they built it in the country. They said they wanted to leave the city with its **pollution** and crime. They wanted fresh air and 'a safe environment for their children'. I shouted at the TV, 'Are you crazy? Don't **waste** all that money – don't move to the *countryside*!!'

**1** People say the countryside has fresh air, but you have to hold your nose most of the time because it's full of dirty farm animals that go to the toilet anywhere they like. You also have to smell the horrible **chemicals** that farmers use to kill insects and help their **crops** grow faster.

**2** When I was growing up, my parents took me on a walk round a farm. In one **field**, a group of cows started following us. I didn't like them following me and looking at me with their big eyes. My parents said I shouldn't worry, but I didn't believe them. I ran and then climbed on top of the wall at the end of the field, and the cows came and looked at me with their big **scary** eyes while I sat there crying. I recently found out that four or five people are killed by cows each year in the UK, so maybe I was right to be afraid! I still hate cows.

**3** The countryside might be full of cows, but can you buy milk at eight o'clock in the evening? **No chance**! And if you want to buy anything during the day, you have to travel half an hour by car to get it! The countryside is just not a **convenient** place to live.

**4** You don't have people going round cleaning the streets at night in the countryside and often there aren't any paths to clean either! If you want to walk somewhere, you have to cross a field or go along a dirty road. That's why no-one wears nice clothes in the countryside – just big boots, old coats and jeans. That's no good for me. I love fashion.

**5** I like **hills** and high mountains. I don't like climbing them, but I like looking at them. But the problem is, there aren't enough of them in our countryside and it's nearly all farms. When you travel between cities by train, you look out of the window and what do you see? A field, another field and another field, a small forest, a field, a farmer in a field, field, a field with cows (*No!!!*), field, field. It's all just very, very boring!

**6** And how do you earn money in the country? You really don't have many **choices** – be a farmer, work in a forest, work with cows (no thank you!). I know you can work online, but there are no cafés with nice cappuccinos and wi-fi. And I don't want to have my meetings in a field because it's the only place I can get a **connection** on my phone.

Look at them! They're scary!

There's a reason people don't wear smart clothes in the countryside.

It's impossible to get a signal.

# They're lovely animals

**IN THIS LESSON, YOU:**
- do a class survey about people's pets and opinions about animals
- talk about pets and animals
- practise listening to three conversations about pets and animals
- explain how long you've had or done something for

## VOCABULARY Animals

**V** See Vocabulary reference 13C.

**1** Work in groups. Don't use a dictionary. How many animals can you name in one minute?

**2** Work in pairs. Check you understand the words in bold. For each sentence, think of one animal the sentence might describe.

1 They're good **pets** because they're friendly and you can do a lot with them. *→ dog*

2 You can't **keep** them in the house. They need to stay outside. *→ seep*

3 You shouldn't keep them as pets. They're **wild** animals.

4 They're dirty. They leave **hairs** everywhere.

5 You can't have them with young children because they often **bite**.

6 You can pick them up if you're **careful**.

7 They make a lot of noise. It's **annoying** if you're trying to work or sleep.

8 You can't do much with them, but they look very **pretty**.

9 There are too many of them. They're **causing** problems.

10 They need a lot of **space** to run around and get exercise.

11 It doesn't cost a lot to **feed** them. They can eat small leaves or vegetables.

12 They're **huge**. They're too big to be in a zoo.

**3** **P** **▶** Listen to the words from Exercise 2 and practise saying them on their own and in a phrase. Which words / phrases do you find hard to say? Practise saying them again.

**4** Work in pairs. Answer the questions.

1 Do you have a pet? What's it like? What do you feed it?

2 What animal do you think is the best pet (except yours)? Why?

3 Tell your partner about a pet that you know that is:
- pretty.
- huge.
- annoying.

## LISTENING

**5** **FS** **▶** In fast speech, the main verb of a question usually has a strong sound and the grammar part (e.g. *do you, did you, have you*, etc.) is often said quickly and can be less clear. Listen and complete these questions (1–8).

*did 1* ~~tell~~ you? ~~do~~ *tell*

2 How long _____ there? *have they been*

~~Do they~~ problems? ~~did~~ *calls*

_____ to come inside? *they ever tried*

5 How long *have you had* _____ him? ~~if you have~~

6 ~~Did tell~~ *Did* you? *I tell*

7 How long *have you had* them? ~~if you have~~

8 What *are you* ~~went~~ *going to do*

**6** **▶** Listen to three conversations about animals. Answer the questions.

1 What animal is each conversation about?

2 Why are they talking about these animals?

**7** **▶** Work in pairs. Which conversation (1–3) did these phrases come from? Explain your decisions. Then listen again and check your answers.

a We need to pay someone to come in .. *3*

b Scary! *2*

c How annoying! *3*

d I found it outside the next day. *2*

e He's huge! ~~1~~ *2*

f I see them quite a lot. ~~3~~ *1*

g I think they're a bit scared of her. ~~3~~ *1*

h We have more space now. *2*

i I worry they'll bite the kids one day. ~~1~~ *3*

**8** Work in groups. Tell each other about good / bad experiences you've had with animals. For example:

- a wild animal you've been close to
- an animal that bit you or was scary
- animals in your house that you didn't want

A cat and a fox face each other in a UK garden.

## GRAMMAR

### Present perfect and *how long*

We use the present perfect – *have* + past participle – to ask and explain 'how long'. This shows we are talking about now and the time before now.

How long **have** they **been** there?

We'**ve been** here a year now.

She **hasn't had** any problems for a long time.

We often use time phrases to explain how long up to now.

*all day, all my life, (for) a year, (for) six months, (for) a few weeks, (for) a long time, (for) ages*

**9** Complete the questions using the present perfect form of the verbs in brackets.
1 How long _has he lived_ there? (he / live)
2 How long _have they been_ together? (they / be)
3 How long _have you been_ married? (you / be)
4 How long _have you know_ her? (you / know)
5 How long _have you had_ it? (you / have)
6 How long _has she worked_ there? (she / work)

**10** Which *how long* question from Exercise 9 can you use to respond to these comments? Match the comments (a–f) with the questions (1–6).
a I have a dog. 5
b My mum works for a bank in the city. 6
c I heard they're going to get married. 2
d I'm going to visit my brother in Hong Kong. 1
e We're having a party for our wedding anniversary. 3
f That's my best friend, Clover. 4

**11** ▶ Listen and check your answers. Write the answers you hear to the *how long* questions.

**12** Work in groups. Find out:
1 who has had a pet the longest.
2 who has known their best friend the longest.
3 who has lived in their home the longest.
4 if anyone knows a couple who have been together for fifty years or more.

**G** See Grammar reference 13C.

## SPEAKING TASK

**13** **M** Work in groups. Do the task.
1 Write six questions to find out about the pets people have and their opinions about animals.

   *Do you have a pet?*

   *Are you afraid of any animals?*

   *Should we keep animals in zoos?*

2 Ask your questions to different people in the class.
3 Work in your group again. Write six sentences saying what the most common answer to your question is.

   *Most people in the class don't have a pet.*

   *The most common pet in the class is a dog.*

   *Most people in the class think …*

## ■ MY OUTCOMES ■

**Work in pairs. Discuss the questions.**
1 What did you like most in this unit?
2 What can you do better now?
3 Is any of the grammar / vocabulary in this unit similar in your first language?
4 What part of this unit do you want to practise?

# 14
# Opinions

## IN THIS UNIT, YOU:

- give your opinions about films, plays and musicals
- describe life in your town, city or country
- make predictions about the future

## SPEAKING

1  **Work in pairs. Look at the photo of a modern dance group by Fredrik Rydman performing Tchaikovsky's Swan Lake in Berlin. Say which of these sentences is most true for you. Explain why.**

a  I often go and see things like this.

b  I went to something like this once and really enjoyed it.

c  I went to something like this once, but I didn't really enjoy it.

d  I've never been to see anything like this, but I'd like to.

e  It's really not for me.

2  **Work in groups. Discuss the questions.**

1  When was the last time you saw:

- a film?
- a concert?
- a play?
- a musical?

2  What did you see? What did you think of it?

Dancers in a modern dance performance of *Swan Lake* in Berlin, Germany.

# What was the film like?

**IN THIS LESSON, YOU:**
- give your opinions about films, plays and musicals
- describe good and bad things about films, plays and musicals
- practise listening to two conversations about a film and a musical
- ask for descriptions of things people have seen

## SPEAKING

1 ▶ **Work in pairs. Listen to the conversation. Then say it.**

A: Have you seen *The Eight Mountains*?

B: No, I haven't. What's it like?

A: It's **brilliant, but it's very sad. I cried at the end.**

B: Oh OK. So what's it about?

A: **These two friends in Italy and the way things change between them over time, It's very beautiful.**

B: It sounds good. I'd like to try and see it.

2 **Change the words in purple. Use a dictionary if you need to. Then practise your new conversation with your partner. Exchange roles and repeat.**

## VOCABULARY

Describing films, plays and musicals

**V** See Vocabulary reference 14A.

3 **Complete the sentences with these adjectives.**

| actor | blood | brilliant | cover | end |
| 2 | 3 | 6 | 4 | 5 |
| energy | jokes | scene | stage | strange |
| 10 | 1 | 9 | 7 | 8 |

1 It's very funny. There are some really good _jokes_ in it.

2 It has my favourite _actor_ in it.

3 There was a lot of killing and a lot of _blood_ in it.

4 It wasn't easy to watch. I had to _cover_ my eyes a few times.

5 After ten minutes, you know how it's going to _end_.

6 It was _brilliant_ one of the best things I've ever seen in my life.

7 There were only two people on _stage_ the whole time.

8 It was very _strange_ I'm not really sure I understood it.

9 No-one says anything for one whole _scene_. I've never seen anything like it.

10 The show has great _energy_ and some brilliant songs as well.

4 **P** ▶ **Listen to the words from Exercise 3 and practise saying them on their own and in a phrase. Which words / phrases do you find hard to say? Practise saying them again.**

5 **Work in pairs. Which of the descriptions in Exercise 3 sound good to you and which don't? Why?**

## LISTENING 🔊

6 ▶ **Listen to two conversations, one about a film and the other about a musical. Answer the questions about each conversation.**

1 Have both people seen the film / musical?

2 If yes, do they both like it? If no, do you think the second speaker would like it? Why? / Why not?

7 ▶ **Complete the sentences (1–10) with one word in each gap. Compare your ideas with a partner. Then listen again and check your answers.**

**Conversation 1**

1 Have you ever seen a film _called_ The Lighthouse?

2 I've heard _of_ it, but I've never seen it.

_about_

The Gaumont Cinema, Paris, France.

3 What's it _like_ ?

4 It ~~very~~ terrible! → _sounds_

5 No, it's really good! _Honestly_

**Conversation 2**

6 What did you think _of_ it?

7 I enjoyed some _scenes_ , but I just didn't think the writing was very good.

8 The _dancing_ and the music were great.

9 What about the way it _ended_ ? I thought it was too much.

10 I guess we just like different _kinds_ of things, then.

**8 Work in pairs. Discuss the questions.**

1 Would you like to see *The Lighthouse* or *Hamilton*? Why? / Why not?

2 Can you think of a film or a musical that:

a has your favourite actor in it?

b is very strange?

c is definitely not for you?

d is brilliant – one of the best things you've seen?

e is very funny?

f made you cry?

## DEVELOPING CONVERSATIONS

### *What's it like?*

If we want someone to describe something or someone, we often ask *What is / was … like?*

A: *I've never seen it.* **What's it like?**

B: *It's brilliant. It's got one of my favourite actors in.*

**9 Match the questions (1–8) with the answers (a–h).**

1 What was the film like?

2 What was the band like?

3 What was your holiday like?

4 What was the weather like?

5 What's the food like there?

6 What are your parents like?

7 What's your new job like?

8 What's your boss like?

a It's good. The money's OK and I like the people I work with. 7

b She's brilliant. She's very easy to talk to. ~~8~~ 8

c Terrible. It was really windy and it rained the whole time we were there. 4

d OK. It started well, but I didn't like the way it ended. 1

e Oh, it was wonderful. It was very relaxing and we were lucky with the weather. ~~8~~ 3

f Great. They played for two hours and did all their most famous songs. 2

g My mum's great, but I'm not very close to my dad. 6

h Amazing! They do a delicious garlic chicken! 5

**10 Work in pairs.**

**Student A:** Ask the questions in Exercise 9.

**Student B:** Answer the questions using the answers in Exercise 9 or your own ideas.

**Exchange roles and repeat.**

**11 Write three** *What is / was … like?* **questions. Then ask other students in the class your questions.**

## CONVERSATION PRACTICE

**12 Make a list of films, plays or musicals you've seen in the last few months.**

**13 M Work in pairs. Take turns to ask about the things on your list. Follow this model. Continue the conversations for as long as you can.**

A: *Have you seen …?*

B: *No, I haven't. What's it like? / Yes. I quite enjoyed it. What did you think of it?*

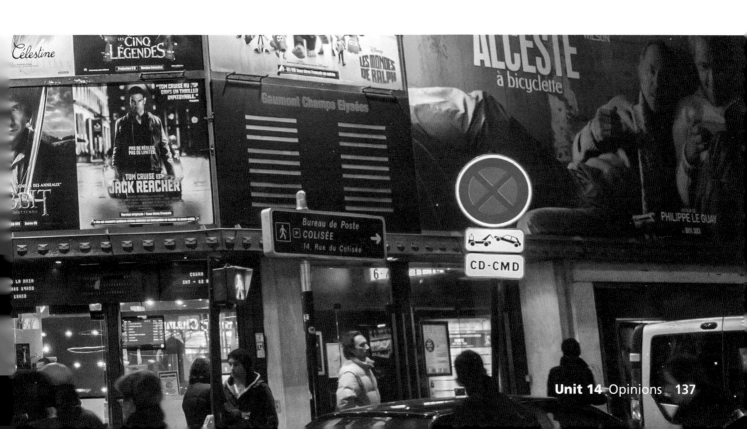

# 14B

# A better life

**IN THIS LESSON, YOU:**
- describe life in your town, city or country
- discuss what's good and bad about life in different places
- read about people who have moved to different countries
- say how you feel about different situations

## VOCABULARY  Life in different places

**1** Check you understand the words in bold. Then choose the example (a or b) that best matches each sentence (1–5).

1 The economy's doing very well at the moment.
   (a) It's easy to find work and you can earn good money.
   b People are worried and are spending **less** in the shops.

2 It's a very **safe** place.
   a There was a **war** here, so now people have guns.
   (b) You can go out at night **without** any problems.

3 The people are very friendly.
   (a) Everyone's really **helpful** and easy to talk to.
   b Everyone's very **polite**, but they don't talk to you much.

4 The weather's very good.
   a It's often very **cloudy** and we get a lot of snow.
   (b) The temperature is very **pleasant** all year.

5 People are unhappy about the **health system**.
   (a) Everyone complains about the long **waiting lists**. ✓
   (b) It's free and the doctors and **nurses** are brilliant. ✓

**2** Work in pairs. Write one more example for sentences 1–5 in Exercise 1.

**3** Work in groups. Read your sentences. Can the rest of the group guess what each sentence is about?

## READING

**4** Work in pairs. Read the introduction to the article on page 139. Discuss these questions.

1 Do many people from your country go to live in other countries? Why? In which countries?

2 Do you know anyone who has moved to another country or city? Why did they move?

3 What other reasons are there to move to another place?

**5** Work in groups of four: two As and two Bs.

**Student As:** Read about Maja.
**Student Bs:** Read about Adnan.

Work with the partner who read about the same person as you. Would you like to live in the place you read about? Why?

**6** With your partner, decide how the writer of your story (Maja / Adnan) would answer these questions.

1 How long have you lived here?
2 Why did you move here?
3 Do you like it here?
4 What do you think of the people?
5 What's the weather like?
6 What do you think of the health system?
7 Do you feel safe here?
8 Do you think you'll ever go back home?

**7** Work with a new partner who read about the other person. Ask and answer the questions in Exercise 6 to find out about your partner's story.

**8** With your partner, discuss which of the two writers you think has a better life. Why?

## GRAMMAR

### *It's* + adjective + *to* + verb

To say how we feel about situations, we often use the pattern *It's* + adjective + *to* + verb.

To form the negative, we use *It isn't / It's not*. To form questions, we use *Is / Isn't it*.

***It's** really **easy to get** a job in computing.*

***It isn't safe to go** out at night.*

***Is it hard to find** a place to live there?*

**9** Complete the sentences using *it's* + adjective + verb and these words.

| easy / pass | important / study | nice / meet |
|---|---|---|
| not cheap / get | not difficult / find | safe / travel |

1 *It's important to study* at home if you want to remember the language from class.

It isn't difficult to find work here, but the money's often really bad.

Is it safe to travel there at the moment or is it still dangerous?

It's nice to meet new people and try new things.

Is it easy to pass the driving test in your country?

It isn't cheap to get tickets for the big concerts because everyone wants to go.

**10** Complete these sentences about the place you live or work.

1 It's easy to find a job in my country
2 It's important to study English to find job
3 It's nice to meet different cultures
4 It's not cheap to get a car
5 It's sometimes difficult to live without work

G  See Grammar reference 14B.

## SPEAKING

**11** You're going to describe what life is like where you live. You might want to talk about some of these things.

| the economy | the health system | how safe it is |
|---|---|---|
| the people | the weather | work |

**12** **M** Work in groups. Share your ideas. What do you think people from other places most like about where you live? Which things might be a problem? Why?

138

# A NEW LIFE

Over 280 million people around the world have moved from one country to another – for all kinds of different reasons. They all have their own stories. Here, we talk to two people who are living in new countries. We find out why they moved and how their new lives are going.

## MAJA ▼

I came here to work. It's really easy to get a job in computing because there are so many tech companies here and the money is really good. I've lived here for five years now and I really love it.

I don't miss very much about my country. The people here are really nice and friendly and I have great neighbours too. They're always very helpful. We don't get long, dark, cold winters here – it's warm all year round. But if I want snow, I can go to the mountains and I can still watch winter sports like ice hockey here. The only problem is, it's difficult to find time to do those things because I work long hours.

Before I came here, people told me that it wasn't very safe, but I haven't had any problems. In big cities, it can sometimes be dangerous to walk around at night and some people have guns, but in my small town I've never seen anything like that. I often leave my bike outside without anyone taking it. I also heard the health system was expensive – and it is, but my company pays for me, so I've had no problems when I've needed to see a doctor or go to hospital.

## ADNAN ▼

I came here two years ago because of the war in my country. It was dangerous to live there. Of course, there are problems here – someone stole my bike once – but it's not dangerous.

People here complain about the health system, but for me it's been great. I was hurt in the war and when I came here, I went to hospital. The doctors who helped me were very kind – and it was free. People here are polite, but it's difficult to really know them. In my country, our home was always open. There were always lots of friends and family sharing food, talking and laughing. I really miss that. My friends here are all from other countries. We play football in the park every Sunday.

I've found cleaning and building work here. It's not what I want to do, but the money's OK, so I can send money home to my family. One day, I hope I'll go back home and do something else. When I go, I'd also like to take the weather with me! I know it rains a lot here, but back home, it's too hot and there's not enough water.

The start of a journey to a new life abroad.

# 14C

# What do you think will happen?

**IN THIS LESSON, YOU:**
- make predictions about the future
- talk about what's in the news at the moment
- practise listening to news stories
- listen to predictions about different news stories

## LISTENING

**1  Work in groups. Discuss the questions.**

1  What are the big news stories at the moment connected to each of these areas?

> business news (2)  entertainment news (4)  international news (3)
> national news (1)  sports news (5)  the weather

2  What do you think about each story? Why?

**2  ▶ Listen to five news stories. Which type of news from Exercise 1 is each story about?**

**3  ▶ Listen again. For each news story, choose the sentence (a–c) that is true.**

**Story 1**

a  People are choosing a new government today. ✗

b  Most people think one of the two main parties will win.

c  The final result is going to be sometime on Monday. T

**Story 2**

a  The company lost nearly four hundred million dollars last year. T

b  They're planning to close two factories and cut 500 jobs.

c  The factories are in the south of the country.

**Story 3**

a  The talks start next week.

b  Both sides are hoping for a good result. T

c  The two sides agree on how people can live and work in their different countries.

**Story 4**

a  Myleene won a TV show last year. T

b  Myleene has been together with her boyfriend for a long time.

c  Her boyfriend is a singer.

**Story 5**

a  Williams hurt herself in the match yesterday.

b  She's a very important part of the team. T

c  She's definitely going to miss the rest of the World Cup.

**4  FS ▶ In fast speech, will often sounds like /(ə)l/ and sometimes you don't really hear it at all. Listen to six opinions. Which one doesn't include will?**

**5  ▶ Listen to five comments about the news stories you heard in Exercise 2. Match each comment (a–e) with one of the stories (1–5).**

**6  Choose one of these stories to talk about. Decide if you think the story was a good thing or a bad thing – and why. Spend a few minutes preparing what you want to say.**

1  a new government

2  a company with big problems

3  talks between different countries

4  a couple getting married

5  a player who got hurt

**7  Work in groups. Share your stories. Discuss your thoughts and feelings about them.**

## GRAMMAR

### Will / Won't for predictions

We can use will / won't + verb to say what we think is sure or likely in the future. Note that we often use contractions with will ('ll = will and won't = will not).

I'm sure they**'ll solve** the problems they're having.

It's now possible that she **won't play** in the next two or three games.

What do you think **will happen**?

**8  Complete the sentences with will / 'll or won't.**

1  I probably _won't_ come out with you tonight. I need to finish some work.

2  You can try and talk to her if you want, but she _won't_ ~~will~~ change.

3  I like her a lot. I think she ~~will~~ 'll be a very good president.

4  They don't have a very good team. They ~~will~~ won't win the game.

5  The new law might help a bit, but it ~~'ll~~ won't completely solve the problem.

6  I don't think I ~~won't~~ 'll pass the exam. I haven't studied much.

7  We 'll probably arrive sometime in the evening. It depends on the traffic.

8  The company lost a lot of money this year. I hope we _won't_ lose our jobs.

9  The economy's doing well, so I think it ~~will~~ 'll be easy for you to find work here.

10  It's a very strange film. I don't think you ~~will~~ 'll like it.

Members of parliament vote in Kyiv, Ukraine.

**9** Work in pairs. Ask and answer these questions. Use the answers below and explain why.

1 Do you think you'll ever speak really good English?
2 Do you think you'll live to be 100?
3 Do you think your country will ever win the World Cup?
4 Do you think you'll ever live or work in another country?
5 Do you think you'll ever be really rich or famous?
6 Do you think we'll find life on other planets?
7 Do you think computers will ever be cleverer than people?
8 Do you think we'll ever learn how to look after the environment?

*Yes, definitely.*
*Yes, probably.*
*Maybe.*
*No.*

**G** See Grammar reference 14C. »

## SPEAKING TASK

**10** Write two predictions about what you think will / won't happen in the future. You might want to think about these areas.

| | | |
|---|---|---|
| holidays | politics | sport |
| technology | the weather | work |

**11** **M** Work in groups. Share your ideas and explain your opinions. Number the ideas in the order you think they are most likely to happen (1 = the most likely).

## ■ MY OUTCOMES ■

**Work in pairs. Discuss the questions.**

1 What activities did you enjoy doing in the unit?
2 What useful language have you learned?
3 How are you feeling about your reading in English now?
4 Do you read anything in English outside of the class? What?

# Writing social media posts

IN THIS LESSON, YOU:
- write two social media posts about photos
- discuss how you use social media
- describe what you can see in different photos
- make comments on other people's posts

## SPEAKING

**1  Work in groups. Discuss the questions.**

- Do you use social media? If yes, what kind?
- Do you ever post photos online? If yes, what of?
- Do you usually write things about any photos you post?
- Do you ever write comments about other people's photos?

## WRITING

**2  Work in pairs. Look at the photos (a–f). Say what you see.**

**3  Read four social media posts. Match the posts (1–4) with the photos (a–f). There are two extra photos.**

**1**  Kendall

It's a sad day in our house today because we said goodbye to this one at the weekend. Rocky was the best pet we've ever had! He was with us for fourteen years and we're all going to miss him – not the hair everywhere, of course, or the biting of furniture, but the walks, the fun, the love … all of that. RIP, our boy.

**2**  Ralph  6

This wasn't my idea. Really! The kids missed Rocky a lot, so I made the mistake of asking them if they wanted another pet. This was the last thing I expected! They've called him Basil. Don't ask me why. We're keeping him in a glass box downstairs. I've told them to be careful and said that *they* need to feed him – not me. They're fine with that, so …

**3**  Eduardo  C

It's our first day here and the weather's not great, as you can see. There was a big storm last night and so our flight in wasn't much fun! I wanted to go for a walk in the hills today, but there's no chance of that. It's wet and windy and the sky is dark and grey. They say it's going to get better tomorrow so maybe we can go out and enjoy the countryside more then.

**4**  Mary  ♪

I had a great weekend. On Saturday, I finally saw the new Marvel film. Some scenes were very strange and the way it ended was a surprise, but it was great. If you haven't seen it, you should. Then yesterday, we went to a concert in the park. It was brilliant – there were four different bands on stage, all of them full of energy. The weather was amazing too – hot and sunny.

**4  Match these comments (a–h) with the posts (1–4).**

- a  Lucky you. Not had time to see it yet. Hoping to see it this weekend.  4
- b  Ha ha. It's lovely and sunny here. Sorry!  3
- c  That's very … unusual! One good thing – you don't need to take it for a walk!  3
- d  That's a great photo. Hope the weather improves soon.  3
- e  Sorry to hear about this. Hope the family are OK.  1
- f  How awful! I can't even look at a photo of that thing.  2
- g  Lovely photo. He had a good, long life, anyway.  1
- h  That sounds great. Live music is the best thing!  4

a

b

c

**5** Work in pairs. Which comment do you like the most? Why? Write one extra comment for each post.

## USEFUL LANGUAGE

### As you can see

When writing about a photo – or something in a photo – we often use the phrase *as you can see*.

This shows that we think the person reading can see that what we say is true by looking at the photo.

*The weather's not great,* **as you can see***.*

*****As you can see***, I've had a haircut. What do you think of it?*

**6** Look at the six photos again. Write a sentence using *as you can see* for each one.

*As you can see, the theatre was outside.*

**7** Work in pairs. Compare your sentences. Did your partner have any similar ideas?

### Say and tell

We often use the verbs *say* and *tell* when writing social media posts about photos.

We use *say* + what someone said.

*We* **said goodbye** *to this one at the weekend.*

*They* **say it's going to get better tomorrow***.*

We use *tell* + person + what someone said.

*I* **told them I loved them***.*

*A friend of mine* **told me it was great***.*

**8** Choose the correct option to complete the sentences.

1 I *said* / told them I wanted to get a dog, but they didn't listen.
2 I wanted to *say* / tell hello, but I just didn't have a chance.
3 Don't say / *tell* me how the film ends. I don't want to know.
4 They offered me the job – and I told / *said* yes.
5 My sister *said* / told me they're a great live band and that's why I went to see them.
6 As I'm sure I've told / *said* before, it's my favourite restaurant in the world.
7 The boss said / *told* everyone to go, so we all went.
8 Mika *said* / told to *say* / tell 'thank you' for the present.

**9** Work in pairs. What kind of photo do you think each sentence in Exercise 8 is about? What kind of things might you see in each one?

## PRACTICE

**10** You're going to write two social media posts to go with two photos. Choose which photos you're going to write about. You can:
- choose the two photos from a–f you didn't need in Exercise 3.
- choose two photos you've already posted on social media.
- choose two photos on your phone.
- choose two photos from Units 13 and 14 and imagine you took them.

**11** Write two posts telling a story connected to the photos or saying something about what they show and why you're posting them. Write 50–80 words.

**12** **M** Work in pairs. Exchange your posts. Write two comments for each one.

## VIDEO Out and about

**1 Work in groups. Discuss the questions.**

1  When's a good time of year to visit your country? Why?

2  Do you prefer the countryside or the city? Why?

### Understanding accents

Some accents use an /iː/ sound instead of an /ɪ/ sound, so *his* /hɪz/ may sound more like *he's* /hiːz/.

**2 📹 Watch five people answer the same questions. Then work in pairs. How much can you remember about what each person said? Which answers were most similar to yours?**

**3 📹 Watch again. Match one or two sentences with each speaker. There is one extra sentence.**

a  I've always lived in the city, but sometimes it's good to get out.

b  December is a good time to visit because there are lots of different things to do.

c  It usually gets really cold in the winter.

d  I prefer cities, but my partner prefers the countryside.

e  I like April and May because I can just wear trousers and a T-shirt.

f  Cities are too loud for me – it's nice and quiet in the countryside.

g  I'm from Daegu and it's the hottest city in my country.

h  You can go out for dinner or go bowling in the city.

**4 Work in groups. Discuss the questions.**

1  Do you have a favourite month or time of year? Why?

2  What different things can you do where you live at different times of year?

3  What kind of countryside do you like most?

4  Do you generally prefer hot weather or cold weather? Why?

## VIDEO Developing conversations

**5 📹 You're going to watch two people talking about films and things on TV. Watch and take notes on what they say.**

**6 📹 Work in pairs. Compare what you understood. Watch again if you need to.**

**7 FS 📹 Watch again. Complete the sentences with two words in each gap.**

1  Can you recommend a film to _____ ?

2  Have you seen any good _____ ?

3  These two people meet for the first time and they _____ .

4  They get to know _____ .

5  It's very long and we couldn't _____ .

6  It's all about men and that's a _____ .

7  What _____ – the film or the book – for you?

8  OK. Let's _____ .

## CONVERSATION PRACTICE

**8 Work in pairs. You're going to practise a conversation.**

1  Choose a Conversation practice from either Lesson 13A or Lesson 14A.

2  Look at the language in that lesson.

3  Check the meaning of anything you don't remember with your partner.

4  Have the conversation. Try to do it better than the last time you did it.

# Grammar and Vocabulary

## GRAMMAR

**1** Complete the sentences with one word in each gap. Contractions (*hasn't*, *can't*, etc.) count as one word.

A: What's the weather going to be like tomorrow?

B: They said it's ¹_____ to continue raining.

A: Oh no! When do you think it ²_____ stop?

B: It's difficult ³_____ say. It can sometimes rain for days. When are you going ⁴_____ go home?

A: I don't know now. I ⁵_____ go back early. It's horrible to ⁶_____ sightseeing in the rain.

B: No! Stay. You haven't ⁷_____ here very long – and I'm sure it ⁸_____ rain for the whole weekend.

**2** Put the words in brackets in the correct place in the sentence.

1  They said it might be very hot this weekend. (not)
2  They said it's going to be very cold and it snow tonight. (might)
3  How long you worked here? (have)
4  It's easy to find. (not)
5  I've had a cough a few days now. (for)
6  I think things will get any worse. (don't)
7  I haven't known him long. (very)
8  Do you think you'll move? (ever)

**3** Rewrite the sentences as positive statements (+), negatives (–) or questions (?).

1  They'll do it before Friday. (–)
2  Is it easy to find work there? (+)
3  I might go to the party. (–)
4  I don't think they'll miss her. (+)
5  It's good to be scared at times like that. (–)
6  I think they'll win. (?)

**4** ▶ Listen and write the six sentences you hear. Include these words.

1  lived / life
2  how / known / other
3  difficult / worry / what
4  try / change
5  economy / stronger
6  said / hot / storm

## VOCABULARY

**5** Match the two parts of the phrases.

| | | | |
|---|---|---|---|
| 1 | keep | a | my eyes / the exercise |
| 2 | snow | b | very pretty / a bit strange |
| 3 | cover | c | lots of problems / an accident |
| 4 | bite | d | them twice a day / it vegetables |
| 5 | cause | e | less / a lot of money |
| 6 | feed | f | the dog in the garden / it in the house |
| 7 | spend | g | every winter / a lot this week |
| 8 | look | h | you if you're not careful / the kids |

**6** Decide if these words and phrases are about entertainment, the weather or animals. There are five items in each group.

| | | | |
|---|---|---|---|
| actor | cloud | hair | how it ends |
| huge | joke | a lot of space | on stage |
| pet | scene | storm | sunny |
| warm | wild | windy | |

**7** Choose the correct option to complete the sentences.

1  It was *brilliant* / *pretty* – one of the best films I've seen for ages.
2  There were no clouds in the sky, so we could see lots of *space* / *stars*.
3  Their dog makes a lot of noise. It's very *annoying* / *pleasant*.
4  The sky's very *blue* / *grey*. I think it'll rain later.
5  They said the *temperature* / *weather* is going to fall to minus ten tonight.

**8** Complete the text with one word in each gap. The first letters are given.

I left my country because of the ¹w_____ there. It's killed a lot of people and no one knows when it will ²e_____ . I wanted to take my kids to a place that was ³s_____ – so here we are. We had to leave very quickly and we travelled here ⁴wi_____ anything. We arrived in the ⁵sp_____ , so the weather was OK – and our neighbours were very ⁶he_____ . I've been here for six years now and I love it. It has great ⁷en_____ and I'm surprised by how ⁸po_____ most people are too. I work in the health ⁹sy_____ now – doing the same thing I did in my country. I love being a ¹⁰n_____ and I don't mind seeing ¹¹bl_____ . It's nothing new for me. The ¹²w_____ lists here are still too long, but I like helping people. The only thing I don't like here is this time of year. The ¹³a_____ is always very grey. It's ¹⁴cl_____ today and quite cold. I still hate this kind of weather!

# 15
# Technology

**IN THIS UNIT, YOU:**

- find people to give you information / advice
- discuss the use of technology in society
- do a survey about people's opinions and experiences of technology

## SPEAKING

**1 Work in pairs. Discuss the questions.**

1 Look at the photo. Would you go to a fair like this? Why? / Why not?

2 Have you ever been to a fair / show where you can see new products? Where? What did you see / like?

**2 Work with a new partner. Do you agree or disagree with these statements? Why? / Why not?**

1 You can't live life without technology.

2 New technology is the main reason that society changes.

3 A lot of new technology is not necessary.

4 I'm happiest in a place in the countryside with no technology.

5 Technology is a good thing, but the way we use it is often bad.

**3 Work in groups. Decide which statement you most agree with.**

A woman tries a virtual-reality product at the VIVA Technology Trade Show, France.

# Can you recommend anything?

## SPEAKING

**1** ▶ **Work in pairs. Listen to the conversation. Then say it.**

A: Do you have **a laptop**?

B: Yeah. In fact, I recently bought a new one. Why?

A: I'm thinking of getting one. Where did you get yours?

B: I bought it online from **computers.com**.

A: Do you know much about **laptops**? Can you recommend anything?

B: Not really. It depends what you want.

A: How did you choose yours?

B: **I talked to a friend about it and she recommended a couple of different ones**.

**2** **Change the words in purple. Use a dictionary if you need to. Then practise your new conversation with your partner. Exchange roles and repeat.**

## DEVELOPING CONVERSATIONS

### Saying emails, websites and passwords

If an email, website or password uses a word or name we know, we say it as a whole word. If we don't know the word, we say the letters and numbers. We also use 'at' (@) and 'dot' (.).

*andrew@pets.co.irl* = 'andrew at pets dot co dot I-R-L'

We can use 'double' when there are two numbers or letters together.

*rr* = 'double R'

*33* = 'double three'

We can also say if a letter is a capital or a small letter, or if two words are written together.

*MT* = 'capital M, capital T'

*buenosaires* = 'Buenos Aires – all small letters, all one word'

**3** ▶ **Listen to each group of letters which share the same vowel sound. Repeat them.**

| | |
|---|---|
| 1 | b c d e g p t v |
| 2 | f l m n s x z |
| 3 | a h j k |
| 4 | q u w |
| 5 | i y |
| 6 | o |
| 7 | r |

**4** ▶ **Listen and write the information.**

1  a website address

2  an email address

3  a wi-fi password

**5** **Write a website address, an email address and a wi-fi password. Then work in pairs. Say the information for your partner to write down.**

## LISTENING

**6** ▶ **Listen to two conversations where people ask for advice about buying things. Note anything you hear about:**

1  what they want to buy.

2  advice.

3  useful contacts or websites.

**7** M ▶ **Work in groups. Are these statements true (T) or false (F)? Use your notes from Exercise 6 to help you. Then listen again and check your answers.**

**Conversation 1**

1  The woman recommends buying a used phone.

2  You might lose your money if the phone breaks quickly.

3  The woman bought her phone from a website.

4  The website is called usedtec.co.eu.

**Conversation 2**

5  The woman wants an electric bike to go to work.

6  She has to go up a hill on the journey.

7  The man borrows his bike from a friend.

8  The email of his friend is jmorgan@terri33.com.

## VOCABULARY  Choosing a phone

**8** **Complete the sentences with these words.**

| | | | | |
|---|---|---|---|---|
| design | dropped | latest | light | memory |
| model | recommended | reviews | used | |

1  A friend _____ it because he had one and was very happy with it.

2  I just liked the _____ – it looks cool!

3  I wanted something _____ and I don't need one with a big screen.

4  I read some _____ and they said it was the best one to get.

5  I always get the latest _____ when it becomes available.

6  I do a lot of gaming, so I wanted one with a lot of _____ and a big screen.

7  Getting a _____ phone is better for the environment than always buying the _____ model.

8  I was happy with the one I had, but I _____ it down some stairs and it was cheaper to buy a new one than repair it.

A saleswoman in a tech store, Stockholm, Sweden.

**9** Work in pairs. Have you ever bought anything for one of these reasons? What did you buy?

1 You liked the design.

2 Someone recommended it.

3 It was light.

4 You read good reviews.

5 It was the latest model.

6 It's better for the environment.

7 You broke the one you had.

8 It was big or had more memory.

## GRAMMAR

### Be thinking of

To talk about plans that we aren't 100% sure about, we often use *be* + *thinking of* + *-ing* form of the verb.

I'**m thinking of getting** another phone.

She'**s thinking of buying** an electric bike.

They'**re not thinking of getting** anything very expensive.

What **are** you **thinking of getting**?

**10** Complete the sentences with the correct form of *be thinking of* and the verb in brackets.

1 I _____ the mobile phone company I use. (change)

2 My parents _____ a new car. (buy)

3 My sister _____ engineering at university. (study)

4 I _____ my dad some new clothes. (get)

5 My brother _____ an English course next year. (do)

6 We _____ to the cinema later. (go)

7 They _____ somewhere near here. (stay)

8 I _____ a pet for my younger sister. (get)

9 How much _____ ? (you / spend)

10 I _____ it immediately. (not / do)

**11** Work in pairs. Take turns to start.

**Student A:** Say one of the sentences from 1–8 in Exercise 10. Then ask *Can you recommend anything / anywhere?*

**Student B:** Make recommendations. You might also want to ask questions like these:

*Why are you think of changing?*

*How much are thinking of spending?*

*What are you thinking of using it for?*

G   See Grammar reference 15A.

## CONVERSATION PRACTICE

**12** Decide on two things you're thinking of buying / doing. Think of a reason why. Choose one of these questions to ask for each one.

*Do you know anything about …?*

*Do you have a …?*

*Have you ever …?*

**13** Ask different people one of your questions from Exercise 12. If they say no, ask your other question or ask someone else. If they answer yes, continue the conversation as in Exercise 1 and see if they can do one or more of the following:

• recommend what to buy and why.

• recommend where to buy or where to get information.

• give an email / website address for help.

# It's a good solution

**IN THIS LESSON, YOU:**
- discuss the use of technology in society
- explain what a type of technology does
- read a newsletter with stories about three technologies

## SPEAKING

**1** **Work in groups. Which of these things do you think has changed society the most? Why?**

- cars
- fridges
- washing machines
- medicines
- robots
- mobile phones

## VOCABULARY  What technology does

**2** **Match the first part of sentences 1–4 with the second parts (a–d). Then match 5–8 with e–h.**

1  It allows you to **produce**
2  It allows you to **notice**
3  It **means**
4  It could be a **solution**

a  you can do more things.
b  any changes in your health.
c  to a lot of our problems
d  electricity at home.

5  It allows you to **develop**
6  They could **replace**
7  It could help protect
8  It saves

e  **energy** because it doesn't use much electricity.
f  the **planet**.
g  your English without a teacher.
h  doctors or nurses in the future.

**3**  **P ▶** **Listen to the words from Exercise 2 and practise saying them on their own and in a phrase. Which words / phrases do you find hard to say? Practise saying them again.**

**4** **Work in pairs. Discuss what types of technology might do the different things in Exercise 2.**

## READING

**5** **Work in pairs. You are going to read a newsletter describing three types of technology. Before you read, look at the photos on page 151 and answer these questions.**

1  What do you think the technology is?
2  What might it allow people to do?

**6** **Read the newsletter and find the answers to the questions in Exercise 5.**

**7** **Work in pairs. Say which names and phrases (a–l) are about each technology (1–3) and why. Then read again to check your ideas.**

1  Grätzel cells
2  Indoor farms
3  Robot 'nurses'

a  Estíbaliz Arzoz Fernández
b  transport costs
c  improved the design
d  Michael Grätzel
e  protect the planet
f  produced rice
g  shapes and colours
h  take their medicine
i  in a similar way
j  NASA
k  younger people
l  feel alone

**8** **Work in pairs. These sentences describe possible problems for the types of technology in the newsletter. Which technology do you think each sentence is about? Why?**

1  They need a lot of electricity.
2  They don't work well at high or low temperatures.
3  They can't move very easily.
4  Buildings in cities are very expensive.
5  At the moment, there's a cheaper way to get the same result.
6  They might not notice how someone is feeling.

**9** **Work in pairs. Do you agree or disagree with these statements? Why?**

1  I like reading stories like this.
2  I feel better about the future after reading about this technology.
3  I don't think these are the most important types of technology that are being developed.
4  These technologies may help society a bit, but we need other solutions.
5  We should help more people produce their electricity from solar power.
6  I wouldn't like to eat food from an indoor farm.
7  I wouldn't like a robot to look after me when I'm older.

## SPEAKING

**10** **Think of a piece of technology for four of these categories. Think of reasons for your choice.**

1  They have recently developed it.
2  The government is spending a lot of money on it.
3  It has changed society a lot.
4  It might cause problems for society.
5  It might solve a big problem we have now.
6  We don't really need it – we can live without it.

**11** **Work in groups. Explain your choices. How many people had the same ideas?**

# Bright Ideas

# DEVELOPING TECHNOLOGY

Technology might not be the solution to all our problems, but it can certainly solve some of them. Here at *Bright Ideas*, we think you probably don't need any more bad news about the world, so every week, we like to bring you some positive stories about developing technology that can save the planet or just make life a bit more comfortable. This week, we look at ways to get more energy from the sun, grow more food in the city, and give more support to older people.

## More energy from the sun ▼

Over 30 years ago, scientists Michael Grätzel and Brian O'Regan developed a new way to produce electricity from light. The Grätzel cell, as it is often called, works in a similar way to how plants produce energy in their leaves from the power of the sun. Recently, Grätzel and his colleagues improved the design so it produces more electricity than before. Grätzel cells have already been used in buildings such as the SwissTech Convention Centre at the university where Grätzel works, and in the future they could be in many more buildings and products. That's because you can see through a Grätzel cell and make them in all kinds of shapes and colours.

Cincinnati, US.

Tübingen, Germany.

## More food in the city ▲

A lot of technology for indoor farms was first developed by NASA to feed people in space, but the idea of indoor farms to feed people on our planet is becoming popular. We're now seeing the first huge indoor farms, such as the Emirates Crop One farm in Dubai. And in Singapore an indoor farm recently produced rice for the first time. At the moment, most indoor farms grow salad plants. Farmers use special lights to grow the plants on shelves instead of in big fields. This allows farms to be in cities, so transport costs are lower. The plants also need much less water than normal farm crops and farmers don't need chemicals to kill insects, so indoor farms can help protect the planet. Indoor farmers and scientists are now trying to develop ways to save energy and grow more crops like rice or potatoes.

## More help for older people ▶

In the future, there are going to be many more older people and there probably won't be enough younger people to look after them. As a solution to this problem, scientists in Europe and Japan are developing robot 'nurses' which could replace human carers and allow people to live in their own homes for longer. The robots can do things like tell an older person to take their medicine, help them call friends or family, or read books to them. Estíbaliz Arzoz Fernández, one of the leaders of the project, said that older people who used the robot 'didn't feel alone'.

Hangzhou, China.

# My tech

**IN THIS LESSON, YOU:**
- do a survey about people's opinions and experiences of technology
- talk about things that go wrong with technology
- practise listening to four people answering questions about technology
- understand how we add information to verbs with an adverb

Nobody talks to each other anymore!

## VOCABULARY  Technology going wrong

1  **Work in pairs. Say what you think the phrases in bold (in 1–8) mean or decide how to translate them into your first language.**

1  I did a **search** online, but I couldn't find what I was looking for.

2  I wrote an email, but sent it to the wrong person **by mistake**.

3  I couldn't find the **file** on my computer, but I'm sure I **saved** it.

4  I had several files open and I **deleted** the wrong one.

5  I've called someone to come and fix the **printer**, but I've just **realized** it's not connected to the computer!

6  I **downloaded** the file from a message and opened it. I **immediately** realized I had made a mistake.

7  My computer **suddenly** stopped working. When I move the **mouse** now, nothing happens.

8  I completed the form for the job online, but I **obviously** didn't **click** 'send' because they said they didn't get it.

2  **Work in pairs. Discuss what you might say to each person in Exercise 1.**

1  *Maybe you should change the words in your search?*

2  *Oh dear. I've done that. What was in the email?*

3  *That's annoying. What was in the file?*

3  **Change partners. Take turns to read out a sentence from Exercise 1. Your partner should respond. Continue the conversation if you can.**

## LISTENING

**4** **Work in pairs. Discuss the questions.**

a How much do you use email?

b How often do you look at your phone?

c How many items of technology do you usually carry around with you?

d How often do you pay for things with your phone?

e How well can you use technology?

f Have you ever had a virus on your computer or phone?

g Have you ever sent an email to the wrong person?

**5** **FS** ▶ **It can be difficult to understand simple phrases used with adverbs because the adverbs are sometimes said fast. Listen to these phrases and write down the missing adverbs.**

1 I had two weeks' holiday

2 I realized

3 this is terrible

4 the phone started

5 it's difficult

6 I wear headphones

7 I use an app

**6** ▶ **Listen to four people answering questions about technology. Match each speaker (1–4) with a question from Exercise 4 (a–g).**

**7** ▶ **Listen again. Answer the questions.**

1 What does speaker 1 really like doing?

2 How do they pay for things?

3 What was waiting for speaker 2 when they returned from holiday?

4 Does their brother have an email account?

5 Where did speaker 3 recently go?

6 Did they change their behaviour when they came back?

7 Where does speaker 4 work?

8 What did their friend's message say?

**8** **Work in pairs. Were the speakers' answers to the questions in Exercise 4 similar or different to yours? In what way?**

## GRAMMAR

### Descriptive adverbs

Adverbs can describe the way you do something.

*I wrote the email quite **quickly**.*

*I didn't check it very **carefully** for mistakes.*

*You can't change your behaviour **easily**.*

*Does he speak English **well**?*

**9** **Look at the examples in the Grammar box. Choose the correct word to complete the rules (1–3).**

1 Adverbs that describe the way you do something usually go *before / after* the verb phrase (verb + noun).

2 The most common way to make a descriptive adverb is to add *-ly* to the end of a *noun / adjective*. Some adverbs are irregular, e.g. *well*.

3 We *can / can't* add words like *quite* or *very* to descriptive adverbs.

**10** **Put the adverbs in brackets in the correct place in the sentences.**

1 If I have a problem with technology, I can usually find a solution. (quite easily)

2 I always read the instructions for technology. (very carefully)

3 I can use Microsoft Word, but I don't know much about other software. (well)

4 Our country is changing. I don't like it. (quickly)

5 I only understand what people say in English if they speak. (slowly)

6 I don't write because I don't often write with a pen. (very clearly)

7 Our local sports team is playing at the moment. They've lost most of their games. (really badly)

**11** **Work in pairs. Are the sentences in Exercise 10 true for you? Why? / Why not?**

**G** See Grammar reference 15C.

## SPEAKING TASK

**12** **M** **You're going to find out about people's experiences with technology and how they feel about it. Follow the instructions.**

1 Work in pairs. Write three more pairs of questions like these to find out about people's experiences with technology and how they feel about it.

   *1 Have you ever lost work you've done on a computer? How?*

   *2 How many TVs do you have at home? Which rooms are they in?*

   *3 How much time you spend looking at a screen? Are you worried about it?*

2 Ask the example questions in 1 and the ones you wrote to people in the class.

3 Now work in groups of four or five. Write sentences saying six things you found out about your class.

   *1 Most people haven't lost work on a computer.*

   *2 The average number of TVs is two. One person didn't have a TV at all.*

   *3 The most time someone spent looking at a screen was 10 hours a day.*

## ■ MY OUTCOMES ■

**Work in pairs. Discuss the questions.**

1 What did you enjoy talking about in class?

2 What new things can you now say about technology?

3 What do you remember from the reading?

4 How will you practise language from this unit?

# 16
# Love

## IN THIS UNIT, YOU:

- share news about relationships
- write poems about promises
- tell a personal story

## SPEAKING

**1 Work in groups. Discuss the questions.**

1 Look at the photo. Do you know anyone who loves the same kind of things?

2 Why do you think people love things like this?

3 Do you love anything that other people think is unusual?

4 What other ways of showing love can you think of?

**2 Work in pairs. Choose four things from this list and tell each other as much as you can about them. Explain why you feel the way you do.**

- a place you love
- a dish or a drink you love
- a film you love
- a song you love
- a person you love
- an animal you love
- a thing you love
- a book you love

**3 Work with a new partner. Think of someone you know and two things from Exercise 2 that you know they love. Tell your partner as much as you can about them.**

A woman who loves being out in nature.

# 16A

# Did I tell you my news?

**IN THIS LESSON, YOU:**
- share news about relationships
- describe different events in relationships
- practise listening to four conversations about relationships
- introduce news you want to give

## SPEAKING

**1** ▶ **Work in pairs. Listen to the conversation. Then say it.**

A: Did I tell you **my sister**'s getting married?

B: No. That's great! When's the wedding?

A: Sometime in May, I think.

B: That'll be lovely. So what's **her** partner like?

A: He's nice, actually. Very friendly and easy to talk to.

B: Well, that's **good**. Say congratulations from me.

A: Thanks. I will.

**2** **Change the words in purple. Use a dictionary if you need to. Then practise your new conversation with your partner. Exchange roles and repeat.**

## VOCABULARY Love and relationships

**3** **Complete the sentences with these pairs of words.**

| | |
|---|---|
| broken up / argued | couple / shame |
| date / guy | fell in love / romantic |
| left / relationship | marriage / achievement |
| pregnant / congratulations | |

1 They _____ the first time they saw each other. It was very _____ .

2 You're _____ ? Wow! That's amazing! _____ !

3 His partner _____ him last year, so he doesn't want to be in a _____ at the moment.

4 I have a _____ on Friday with this _____ from work. I've liked him for ages.

5 Wow! You've been together a long time! Fifty years of _____ is a real _____ .

6 Sorry, but I'm a bit upset. Toni has _____ with me! We _____ quite a lot and now he's met someone else.

7 They were a lovely _____ . It's a real _____ they're not together anymore.

**4** **P** ▶ **Listen to the words from Exercise 3 and practise saying them on their own and in a phrase. Which words / phrases do you find hard to say? Practise saying them again.**

**5** **Choose three or four sentences from Exercise 3 and imagine you are talking to the people who said them. Write a comment and / or question in response.**

*A: They fell in love the first time they saw each other. It was very romantic.*

*B: That's a lovely story. So where did they meet?*

**6** **Work in pairs. Say your conversations from Exercise 5 together. Try to continue each conversation.**

## LISTENING

**7** ▶ **Listen to four short conversations where someone gives news about a relationship. Match each conversation (1–4) with one of these sentences (a–d).**

a A relationship has ended.

b There's going to be a wedding.

c A new relationship might start soon.

d Someone's going to have a baby.

**8** ▶ **Listen again. Answer the questions (1–9).**

**Conversation 1**

1 How long has Owen been together with his girlfriend?

2 What's she like?

**Conversation 2**

3 Do the couple have a date for the birth yet?

4 Do they know if it's a boy or a girl?

**Conversation 3**

5 Why have Imke and Thorsten broken up?

6 How long were they together?

A couple at their wedding in Baghdad, Iraq.

**Conversation 4**

7 Who was the woman's date with?

8 What's he like?

9 What did they do on the date?

**9 Work in groups. Discuss the questions.**

1 Do you know any couples who got married after only being together for a short time?

2 Why do you think some people choose not to find out if their baby is going to be a boy or a girl?

3 Have you heard of any couples breaking up recently? Do you know what happened?

4 Do you think karaoke is a good thing for a first date? Why? / Why not? What might be better?

## DEVELOPING CONVERSATIONS

### Did I tell you …?

We often introduce news we want to give by asking *Did I tell you (that) …?* The news might be about the future, past or present, so we use different verb forms.

**Did I tell you** *(that) my brother's wife* **is** *pregnant?* (present simple)

**Did I tell you** *(that) I* **had** *a date on Friday?* (past simple)

**Did I tell you** *(that) Imke and Thorsten* **have broken up**? (present perfect)

**Did I tell you** *(that) Owen* **is going to get** *married?* (future)

**10 Complete the questions with the correct form of the verb in brackets.**

1 A: Did I tell you Mena and I _____ travelling next year? (go)

   B: Really? That's exciting. Where are you thinking of going?

2 A: Did I tell you Rebecca _____ a new boyfriend? (have)

   B: No. Have you met him yet?

3 A: Did I tell you that I _____ Martin's parents last week? (meet)

   B: No. How did it go?

4 A: Did I tell you that Lucia and Marc _____? (break up)

   B: No, but I'm not surprised. When did that happen?

5 A: Did I tell you we _____ finally _____ a flat? (find)

   B: No. That's great! Where is it?

6 A: Did I tell you that we _____ a big party to celebrate ten years of marriage? (have)

   B: No! Is that an invitation?

**11 Work in pairs. Practise saying the conversations in Exercise 10. Take turns to be A and B. Continue the conversations by answering B's questions.**

## CONVERSATION PRACTICE

**12 Write a piece of news about a relationship starting *Did I tell you (that) …?* Your news can be true or invented.**

**13 Ask different students your question starting *Did I tell you (that) …?* Your partners should ask questions to continue the conversation.**

## 16B

# I promise

## VOCABULARY Promises

**1 Work in groups. Check you understand the words in bold. Use a dictionary if you need to. Do you agree with the statements? Why? / Why not?**

1 I don't usually **make promises** to anyone.

2 You shouldn't **promise to buy** your kids things 'if they're good'.

3 Everybody **breaks a promise** sometimes. You shouldn't feel bad about it.

4 I always **expect** people to do what they've promised.

5 If a promise sounds too good to be true, I don't **believe** it.

6 I never believe any promises that **politicians** make.

7 You should always **keep your promises**.

8 It's better to be **honest** about when you can do something than to promise too much.

## GRAMMAR

### Will / Won't for promises

To make promises, we often use *will / won't* (+ verb). We sometimes add *I promise*.

*I'm too busy today.* I**'ll take** *you next week.* (**I promise.**)

*We* **won't forget.** *Don't worry.*

**Will** *you* **come** *to the party? Please say yes.*

We often promise something by using *will / won't* as a short response.

*A: Call me later.*     *B:* **I will.**

*A: Don't be late.*     *B:* **We won't.**

**2 Work in pairs. Make promises using *will / won't* and these ideas.**

1 promise to call me later

   *I'll call you later.*

2 promise not to tell anyone

3 promise to try harder

4 promise not to be late

5 promise not to get angry

6 promise to tell me when you hear more news

**3 Work in pairs. Take turns to say and respond to the sentences. Respond using *I will / I won't* (+ *I promise*).**

1 Don't start before I get back.

   *I won't. I promise.*

2 You need to pay me back tomorrow.

3 Remember to go to the bank.

4 Don't forget to call your mum later.

5 Be careful.

6 I don't want you to miss the train.

**G** See Grammar reference 16B.

## READING

**4 Work in groups. Discuss the questions.**

1 Do you know the names of any famous poems? Can you remember any parts of them?

2 Who are the most famous poets in your country?

3 Do / Did you study them at school? Do / Did you like them?

4 Do you read poems now? If yes, by which poets?

5 Have you ever written a poem? When? What about?

**5 Read the poems on page 159 (1–4) and match them with these titles (a–d). Then work in pairs and check your ideas.**

a In memory

b Your first day

c Breaking up

d No more time

**6 With your partner, decide who is making the promises in each poem – and who to.**

**7 Match the words in bold in the poems with these meanings. Use a dictionary to help you.**

1 stop holding something

2 twice as much

3 help someone do well by saying nice things

4 become less strong (of a colour, sound or memory)

5 plants that you don't want in your garden

6 stay

7 believe someone is honest

8 problems

**8** **M** **Work in groups. Discuss the questions.**

1 Which poem do you like most? Why?

2 Were there any parts you didn't understand? Can anyone in your group explain them?

## SPEAKING

**9 Work in pairs. Think of promises that these people might make.**

1 two people who are in love

2 a child to a parent

3 a student to a teacher

4 a teacher

5 a boss

6 a politician

**10 With your partner, choose one of the people in Exercise 9 – or use your own ideas – and write a short poem. Follow the pattern of one of the poems on page 159.**

**11 Work in groups. Say your poems. Can you guess which person in Exercise 9 each poem is about?**

1 _____

This I promise.
I'll try to be a person that you're happy to love.
I'll try to **encourage** and not to complain –
Try to ask, not to tell.
I'll look after you, be there to hold you,
But I promise I won't hold you too long –
I'll let you grow and then **let go**.

2 _____

I'm sorry for what I did.
*How could you?*
I'll change.
I'll be better; I'll be stronger.
*How can I be sure?*
I'll be here; I won't fail or fall.
*How can I **trust** you?*
Because I'll love you.
*And you didn't before?*

3 _____

I'll look after your garden.
I'll remove any **weeds** that might grow in it.
I'll plant new flowers when others die.
I won't let it **fade**.
I'll keep it alive.
And you'll **remain** –
In my heart.

4 _____

I'll pay you back.
*I've asked before.*
I'll pay you **double**.
*I've given you chances,*
*said there'd be **trouble**.*
I'll do what you want.
*I've waited,*
*but I'll wait no more.*

# Love at first sight

## SPEAKING

**1  Work in groups. Discuss the questions.**

1  What do you think *love at first sight* means?

2  Have you ever heard any stories about love at first sight? Do you believe them?

3  Do you think it's possible to fall in love with things or places – as well as people – at first sight? If yes, can you give examples?

## LISTENING

**2  Work in pairs. Look at the photos. How do you think each photo might connect to the idea of love at first sight?**

**3  ▶ Listen to three people talking about their experiences of love at first sight. Match each person (1–3) with a photo (a–c). Were your ideas from Exercise 2 correct?**

**4  FS ▶ In fast speech, when a word that ends with the letter *s* joins a word that starts with a vowel sound, you often hear a /z/ sound. Write down the eight phrases that you hear.**

**5  ▶ Listen again. Tick (✓) the sentences (1–9) that are true.**

**Speaker 1**

1  They needed to move house quickly because they planned to start a family.

2  They didn't have an appointment to visit the house they bought.

3  They offered the owners a lower price.

**Speaker 2**

4  She wasn't interested in music until she was twelve.

5  Her first guitar was a present.

6  She now makes money playing music.

**Speaker 3**

7   She met her future husband through an online dating site.

8   She was single when she started playing online games a lot.

9   She isn't actually married yet.

**6   Work in pairs. Discuss the questions.**

1   Where would your dream house be? What would it be like?

2   Can you play any musical instruments? How well?

3   Which people have had a big effect on you?

4   Do you know anyone who plays online games a lot?

5   What do you think is good / bad about meeting a partner in an online game?

# GRAMMAR

## Past continuous

To make the past continuous, we use *was / were* (+ *not*) + *-ing* form.

He **was playing** in a band at the time.

Things **weren't going** very well.

What **were** you **doing** there?

We often use the past continuous and the past simple in the same sentence. We use the past continuous to show one thing started and was in progress at the time that a past simple thing happened.

I **was playing** one of my favourite games when I **met** my future husband.

We **were arguing** all the time, so I **started** spending more and more time online.

**7   Choose the correct options to complete the sentences.**

1   We *were both studying / both studied* English when we first *met / were meeting*.

2   I *wasn't looking / didn't look,* so I *walked / was walking* into him. That's how we met!

3   I *worked / was working* in a restaurant and one day she *came / was coming* in with some friends of hers.

4   My mum *was travelling / travelled* round Europe with a friend and *met / was meeting* my dad on a train one night.

5   I *worked / was working* all night, so I *was missing / missed* your call. Sorry.

6   What *did you do / were you doing* when you *heard / were hearing* the news?

**8   Complete the sentences (1–10) with the correct past continuous form of these verbs.**

| do | have | listen | not look | not plan |
|----|------|--------|----------|----------|
| stay | take | try | walk | watch |

1   We _____ dinner in a restaurant when she came in and sat at the next table.

2   She _____ in a hotel in Singapore when one day he got in the same lift as her.

3   I _____ the bus across town when she got on and sat opposite me.

4   He _____ for a new relationship, but when he saw her, it was love at first sight.

5   I _____ through a street market one day when I saw it on a table.

6   They _____ to move, but then she got pregnant, so they had to.

7   I _____ some shopping in town when I saw it in one of the shops. It was love at first sight!

8   I _____ to the radio one day when this song came on and I just fell in love with it.

9   So where _____ you _____ to get to when she stopped and gave you a lift?

10   I _____ TV one night when an advert for it came on and I just thought it looked amazing.

**G**   See Grammar reference 16C.

## SPEAKING TASK

**9   Choose one of these things to talk about. Use the questions to help you plan your story. Use a dictionary if you need to.**

1   Something you saw / heard and fell in love with
   • What was it?
   • Where were you?
   • What were you doing?

2   A famous person you've met / seen
   • When did you see / meet them?
   • Where were you?
   • What were you doing there?

3   How and when you first met your best friend(s)
   • When was it?
   • Where were you?
   • What were you doing?

4   How and when a couple you know first met
   • When was it?
   • Where were they?
   • What were they doing?

**10   M   Work in groups. Do the following:**

1   Tell your stories to each other.

2   Ask questions to find out more details.

3   Together, decide which story is the most interesting.

4   Choose someone in the group to re-tell this story to the class.

## MY OUTCOMES

**Work in pairs. Discuss the questions.**

1   What have you enjoyed most about this course?

2   What are three things you can do better in English now?

3   Which was your favourite unit? Why?

4   What are you going to do next to improve your English?

# Writing short stories

**IN THIS LESSON, YOU:**
- write a short story about some pictures
- talk about stories you like and what makes a good story
- read four short stories and decide what's good / less good about them
- join different actions and situations in one sentence

*k*

## SPEAKING

**1 Work in groups. Discuss the questions.**

1 Do you read or listen to stories much? Do you have any favourite ones?

2 Have you ever written a story? When? What about?

3 Think about what makes a good story for you. Which of these statements do you agree with?

 a They include some kind of problem.

 b They have a lot of descriptions.

 c They show an unusual experience.

 d They're about people who are different to me.

 e You don't know what's going to happen.

 f They have a happy ending.

 g They make you feel something.

## WRITING

**2 Work in pairs. Look at pictures a–c. Answer the questions about each picture.**

1 Who are the people? Where are they? What are they doing? What are they going to do? What's the weather like? Is there a problem? How are they feeling? What are they saying or thinking?

2 Where are they now? Is there anyone else there? Who? What's happening? Is there a (new) problem? How are they feeling? What are they saying or thinking?

3 Where are the people now? What are they doing? What's happened since the last picture? Did they solve their problem? How are they feeling? What are they saying or thinking?

**3 Now read the short stories (1–4). Answer the questions.**

1 Which story is about the pictures?

2 Were your ideas in Exercise 2 similar to the story?

3 Which story do you prefer? Why?

**1** b  3

A girl went to the park with her dad. She played in the playground and had fun. The next day was her birthday. Her parents bought her a dog. She was very happy and took the dog for a walk in the park.

**2** a

Gina was going to the park to meet her best friend in the park. Gina forgot to charge her phone before she left. On the way to the park, she suddenly realized her phone wasn't working. When she arrived, the park was very crowded because there was a running race. She couldn't find her friend, so she had to go home without meeting her.  3

**3** c

Mario was taking his daughter Paula to the park to spend some time together. Paula was annoyed she had to go with him. She wanted to play video games. On the way home, they saw a poster in a shop for a beautiful little dog that needed a home. Paula immediately fell in love with it. Her Dad wasn't sure, but Paula promised to look after it. They got the dog and now Mario has to take it to the park every day!

4 out of 5

**4** C

An old man was in the park with his dog. It was a lovely, sunny day. He sat on a seat. He saw a small bag next to him. There was no-one else there. When he looked in the bag, he found an address. He took the bag to the address. The old lady who answered the door was very happy. She offered to make him tea to say thanks. He said yes.

**4** Read the stories again. Give each one two marks between 1 (= bad) and 5 (= good):

1 for the story.

2 for the language it uses.

**5** Work in pairs. Compare your marks. Which is the best story? Why?

## USEFUL LANGUAGE

### On the way / When

We use *on the way* and *when* to show the time of another action / situation in the same sentence.

We use *on the way* + *to* [place] / *home* / *there*.

**On the way to the park**, *she suddenly realized her phone wasn't working.*

**On the way home**, *they saw a poster in a shop.*

We use *when* + subject + verb.

**When she arrived**, *the park was very crowded.*

**When he looked** *in the bag, he found an address.*

**6** Complete the sentences with *on the way* or *when*.

1 _When_ she got home, she asked her dad to buy the dog.

2 _on the way_ there, she was complaining a lot.

3 _on the way_ to work, he had an accident.

4 _When_ they opened the box, they realized the computer was broken.

5 His parents were angry _when_ he told them.

6 They didn't say anything _on the way_ home.

**7** Complete the sentences with your own ideas.

1 When he saw her, _he talked to her_

2 _on the way to London_, they were really happy.

3 On the way to the wedding, _he had an_ accident.

4 _on the way to the park_, she met a friend of hers.

### Had to and couldn't

*Had to* is the past simple form of *have to*. *Couldn't* is the past simple form of *can't*.

*She was annoyed she* **had to** *go with him.*

*She* **couldn't** *find her friend, so she had to go home.*

**8** Match the start of the sentences (1–3) with two possible endings (a–f).

1 He forgot his passport,

2 It was very, very hot,

3 The card wasn't working,

a so he couldn't get on the plane. 1

b so she had to stay inside. 2

c so she couldn't pay. 3

d so he had to get some cash. 3

e so they couldn't go to the playground. 2

f so they all had to drive back to get it. 1

**9** Complete the sentences with *had to* / *couldn't* + verb.

1 He lost his phone, so …

2 She hurt her leg, so …

## PRACTICE

**10** Work in pairs. Look at pictures d–f. Answer the questions in Exercise 2 about these pictures.

**11** Write a short story about the pictures. Write 50–80 words. You can give the people names if you want to.

**12** Work with a new partner. Read your partner's story. Discuss the questions.

1 Does the story match the pictures?

2 What good language does it have?

3 Can you add or change one thing to improve the story?

d

e

f

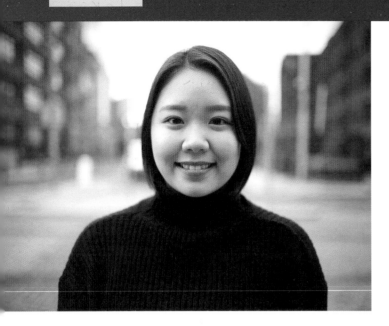

## VIDEO Out and about

**1** **Work in groups. Discuss the questions.**

1 Have you had any good news recently?

2 When / How did you meet your best friend?

### Understanding accents

Some accents use a /b/ sound instead of a /v/ sound, so *very* /veri/ may sound more like *berry* /beri/.

**2** 🎥 **Watch six people answer the same questions. How much can you remember about what they said? Then work in pairs. Did anyone have similar experiences to you?**

**3** 🎥 **Watch again. Match one or two sentences with each speaker.**

a I'm planning to go to see someone in another country.

b I heard someone is going to get married.

c I can travel more easily to the UK now.

d I'm going to change my class.

e I know someone who's had a baby.

f My best friend was my colleague.

g My best friend has the same name as me.

h My best friend played sport with me at school.

i My best friend is the brother of my brother's friend.

**4** **Tell your partner about four of these different people. Give examples.**

1 someone you have done sport with or who was in the same team as you

2 someone who has the same name as you

3 someone who's getting married or having a baby

4 someone who has a friend or family who lives abroad

5 someone who is a friend of a friend

## VIDEO Developing conversations

**5** 🎥 **You're going to watch two people talking about relationships and people they know. Watch and take notes.**

**6** 🎥 **Work in pairs. Compare what you understood. Watch again if you need to.**

**7** FS 🎥 **Watch again. Complete the sentences with three to five words in each gap.**

1 I saw her on the high street _____ , shopping.

2 She was coming _____ very specific shop.

3 Don't say anything though. _____ told her parents yet.

4 So Mary, _____ , she met her boyfriend eight months ago.

5 You know _____ together for a very long time.

6 A bit jealous – decided they _____ married too, maybe.

7 Izzy's boyfriend came to meet them _____ approval for the wedding.

8 I'm going to text Patsy _____ .

## CONVERSATION PRACTICE

**8** **Work in pairs. You're going to practise a conversation.**

1 Choose a Conversation practice from either Lesson 15A or Lesson 16A.

2 Look at the language in that lesson.

3 Check the meaning of anything you don't remember with your partner.

4 Have the conversation. Try to do it better than the last time you did it.

# Grammar and Vocabulary

## GRAMMAR

**1 Complete the conversation with one word in each gap.**

A: What [1]_____ you doing last night? I called you, but you didn't answer.

B: Yeah. I was [2]_____ a romantic dinner with Paula.

A: Oh yes, I forgot. Did it go [3]_____ ?

B: Yes, [4]_____ well. We're going to get married!

A: Fantastic! That's great news! When are [5]_____ thinking of having the wedding?

B: We [6]_____ thinking of having it in August next year, but I [7]_____ let you know! Obviously, you're invited!

A: Great. I promise I'll [8]_____ there.

**2 Complete the sentences with the correct form of be.**

1 I _____ thinking of going to the cinema later.

2 I broke my leg when I _____ skiing.

3 We met when we _____ working for a local company.

4 They _____ thinking of moving house. They want somewhere smaller.

5 What _____ you thinking of doing this evening?

6 I saw Dua Lipa once when she _____ coming out of a hotel.

**3 Put the adverb form of the adjectives in brackets in the correct place in the sentences.**

1 I can't run very because I have a bad leg. (quick)

2 I can't swim unfortunately. (good)

3 It only worked for a few months. (successful)

4 She hurt her leg in the accident. (bad)

5 He had a game yesterday and won. (easy)

6 I didn't understand because he wasn't speaking. (clear)

**4 ▶ Listen and write the six sentences you hear. Include these words.**

1 met / Germany

2 asking / me

3 anything / first

4 when / New York

5 accident / fast

6 tell / news

## VOCABULARY

**5 Match the two parts of the phrases.**

| | | | |
|---|---|---|---|
| 1 produce | a | congratulations / sorry |
| 2 notice | b | 'send' / on the link |
| 3 save | c | a lot / with my girlfriend |
| 4 download | d | oil / electricity from the sun |
| 5 click | e | energy / the file in a folder |
| 6 fall | f | in love / asleep |
| 7 say | g | any changes / if there's a problem |
| 8 argue | h | the software / the file from our website |

**6 Decide if these words and phrases are about technology, love and relationships, or promises. There are five items in each group.**

| | | | | |
|---|---|---|---|---|
| break | break up | couple | date | delete |
| honest | keep | make | marriage | memory |
| mouse | politician | pregnant | printer | search |

**7 Choose the correct option to complete the sentences.**

1 I like my laptop. It is very *light / heavy* to carry around.

2 I read a few *reviews / designs* before I bought it.

3 I bought this one because a friend *promised / recommended* it.

4 I *dropped / fell* my laptop and broke the screen.

5 I was doing my homework, when my laptop *obviously / suddenly* stopped working.

**8 Complete the two texts with one word in each gap. The first letters are given.**

For some people it doesn't matter if their 'old' phone still works well or the [1]de_____ of a new one is very similar, each year they [2]re_____ their phone with the [3]la_____ model. This can be bad for the [4]pl_____ because it [5]me_____ we waste a lot of [6]en_____ and things to make them. That's why I always buy [7]us_____ phones which have been repaired well, and keep them for as long as possible.

Three years ago, I started an English class. When the lesson began, I [8]re_____ I might be in the wrong class because I didn't understand what the teacher was saying. I asked the [9]gu_____ next to me If this was for beginners. He said, 'No, it's Advanced.' I [10]im_____ got up and left. In the break, I saw the man from the Advanced class. We started chatting in our first language. He was really nice. 'What a [11]sh_____ we're not in the same class,' he said. Well, that man is now my husband. We always tell people we met by [12]mi_____ !

# Grammar reference

## 1 PEOPLE AND PLACES

### PRESENT SIMPLE *BE*

*Be* has three forms in the present simple (*am, is, are*).

| I | am |
|---|---|
| he she it | is |
| you we they | are |

We usually use the short forms *I'm, you're, he's, they're*, etc. in spoken English and in informal writing.

*Hello.* **I'm** *Bruce.* (= I am)
**You're** *late!* (= You are)
**She's** *a doctor.* (= She is)
**He's** *21.* (= He is)
**It's** *cold today.* (= It is)
**We're** *from Venezuela.* (= We are)
**They're** *our friends.* (= They are)
*The office* **is** *over there.*
*My parents* **are** *teachers.*

### Negatives

We add *not* to form the negative.
**I'm not** *hungry.* (= I am not)
**You're not** *in the right class.* (= You are not)
**He's not** *French.* (= He is not)
**She's not** *very interesting.* (= She is not)
**It's not** *cheap.* (= It is not)
**We're not** *happy about it.* (= We are not)
**They're not** *married.* (= They are not)

We also use the negative forms *isn't* and *aren't*. There is no difference in meaning or use between the two negative forms.
*He* **isn't** *French.*                      *It* **isn't** *cheap.*
*We* **aren't** *happy about it.*      *They* **aren't** *married.*

### Questions

To form a question, we put *am / is / are* before the subject. Note that question words or phrases (*when, who, what time*, etc.) go before *is / are*.
**Am I** *next?*                      *Where* **am I** *on the map?*
**Are you** *OK?*                      *How* **are you**?
**Is he** *happy here?*      *Where* **is he** *from?*
**Is she** *ill today?*          *Who* **is she**?
**Is it** *cold outside?*      *What time* **is it**?
**Are we** *late?*                *Why* **are we** *here?*
**Are they** *good?*            *What* **are their names**?

### Exercise 1

**Complete the conversation with the correct form of *be*.**

A: Hi. Come in. Sit down. How ¹_____ you?
B: Fine, thanks.
A: I ²_____ Joanna. What ³_____ your name?
B: Miguel Hernández.
A: And where ⁴_____ you from, Miguel? Spain?

B: No. I ⁵_____ from Mexico.
A: Which part?
B: Chihuahua. It ⁶_____ a city in the north.
A: ⁷_____ it nice?
B: Yeah. Some things ⁸_____ nice.
A: ⁹_____ it hot?
B: Now? No, it ¹⁰_____ not hot at the moment. But in the summer, it ¹¹_____ very hot.
A: OK. And what do you do? What ¹²_____ your job?
B: Oh, I ¹³_____ a police officer.
A: Really? You ¹⁴_____ a police officer?
B: Yes.
A: Interesting.

### DID YOU KNOW?

When we answer *Are you / Is it ... ?* questions, we often only say *yes* or *no*. Sometimes, we add *I am / it is / he isn't*, etc.
*Are you from here?*          *Yes,* **I am**.      or      *No,* **I'm not**
*Is it cold outside?*            *Yes,* **it is**.      or      *No,* **it isn't**.

There is further practice of this in Unit 7 when you look at short answers.

### Exercise 2

**Write the sentences as negatives. Write both negative forms where this is possible.**

1  It's interesting.
   *It's not interesting. / It isn't interesting.*
2  She's from Germany.
3  They're students.
4  I'm hungry.
5  You're late.
6  It's boring.

### Exercise 3

**Put the words in the questions and answers in the correct order.**

1  A: where / from / you / are ?
   B: from / Italy / I'm .
2  A: 's / your / job / what ?
   B: teacher / a / French / I'm .
3  A: it / time / is / what ?
   B: half / past / 12 / it's .
4  A: are / grandparents / old / how / your ?
   B: not / I'm / sure .
5  A: winter / it / is / cold / in ?
   B: yes, / very / cold / it's .
6  A: hungry / you / are ?
   B: no, / not / I'm .

### Exercise 4

**Write your own answers to the questions in Exercise 3.**

## 1B  *THERE IS ... / THERE ARE ...*

### Use

We use *there is / there are* to say that something exists or to say where something is. We often use it to say what things a place has or doesn't have.

**There's** *a supermarket in South Street.*
**There are** *some cafés near the river.*

## Form

We use *there is* with singular nouns and *there are* with plural nouns.

**With singular nouns**

| There | 's | a / an | cinema. museum. park. |
|---|---|---|---|
| | isn't | | |
| Is | there | | café? airport? |

**With plural nouns**

| There | are | two some a lot of | cinemas. parks. shops. |
|---|---|---|---|
| | aren't | any a lot of | places for kids. bars. |
| Are | there | any a lot of | shops? people? |

With plural nouns, in positive sentences we usually say how many there are (e.g. *two cinemas*) or we use *some* (e.g. *some parks*). In negative sentences, we often use *any*.

We also use *there is some / a lot of …* and *there isn't any / a lot of …* with uncountable nouns.

**There isn't any traffic.**
**There's some sugar** on the table.

There is more practice of uncountable nouns in Unit 2, when you look at countable and uncountable nouns.

### Exercise 1

**Choose the correct option to complete the sentences.**

1  *Is there / Are there* a cinema in the town?
2  It's a lovely area. *There's / There are* a lot of trees and parks.
3  *There isn't / There aren't* a bank near here.
4  *Is there / Are there* a bridge over the river near here?
5  *Is there / Are there* any nice restaurants near here?
6  It's a nice city, but *there's / there are* a lot of cars!
7  *There's / There are* some small shops here, but *there isn't / there aren't* a big supermarket.
8  *There's / There are* a great beach and *there's / there are* a few cafés.

### Exercise 2

**Correct the mistake in each sentence.**

1  There not are any jobs here.
2  Is a car park there near here?
3  There is a lot of expensive houses in this area.
4  Is there any buses after 11 p.m.?
5  Is a nice place to eat near here?
6  There is not any cheap hotels in the centre.

### Exercise 3

**Complete the sentences about where you live.**

1  There's a …
   *There's a lovely park near my house.*
2  There are some …
3  There isn't a …
4  There aren't any …
5  There are a lot of …

## 1C  PRESENT SIMPLE

### Use

We use the present simple to talk about facts and things which are usually or always true. We often use it to talk about a person's life, for example their home, job, likes and habits.
We **live** in a small apartment.
He **goes** to work by bus.
I **don't eat** meat.

### Form

***I / You / We / They***
For *I, you, we* and *they*, the present simple form is the same as the infinitive.
I **go** swimming every day.
You **drink** a lot of coffee!
We **live** in the north of the country.
They **work** at the University of Salamanca.

***It / He / She***
For *it, he* and *she*, we add *-s*.
It rain**s** a lot in the winter.
He like**s** swimming.
She work**s** in a hospital.

Note these spelling changes for *it / he / she* forms.
have – ha**s**
do – do**es**
go – go**es**
try – tr**ies**
cry – cr**ies**

### Negatives

To form the negative, we use *I / you / we / they* + *do not* + verb. In speaking and informal writing, we usually use the short form *don't* + verb.
I **don't like** the town very much. (= do not)
You **don't know** my town, I'm sure.
We **don't go** there a lot.
They **don't visit** us very often.

We use *it / he / she* + *does not* + verb. We usually use the short form *doesn't* + verb.
It **doesn't snow** here. (= does not)
He **doesn't have** any brothers or sisters.
She **doesn't** feel safe.

### DID YOU KNOW?

We usually use the full forms *do not* and *does not* in signs and notices.
**Do not** sit on the grass.
The school **does not** open on Sundays.

### Questions

To form questions, we use *do* + *I / you / we / they* + verb.
**Do you live** near here?
**Do they have** any children?
Where **do I go** now?
How **do we go** there?

We use *does* + *it / he / she* + verb.
When **does it start**?
What **does he do**?
**Does she speak** English?
Where **does she work**?

Note that a question word or question phrase (*where, when, what time*, etc. ) goes before *do / does*.

## Exercise 1

**Choose the correct option to complete the sentences.**

1 She *work / works* for a big company.
2 Does he *like / likes* his job?
3 We *get up / gets up* at five every morning.
4 What time do *you / he* finish work?
5 Where *do / does* your grandparents live?
6 He's 40 and he *live / lives* with his mum.
7 I *doesn't / don't* like pizza.
8 My sister *have / has* three children.
9 It *don't / doesn't* rain a lot there.
10 How many cars do *he / they* have?

## Exercise 2

**Complete the present simple questions.**

1 Where _____ your parents live?
2 When _____ she finish work?
3 How long _____ the journey take?
4 _____ you like rock music?
5 What _____ your father do?
6 Why _____ they like it? It's very bad!
7 _____ she speak French?
8 How often _____ you go the gym?

### DID YOU KNOW?

When we answer *Do you / Does she* … etc. questions, we often only say *yes / yeah* or *no*. Sometimes we add *I do / I don't / she doesn't*, etc.
A: *Do you enjoy your job?*   B: *Yes, **I do**. / No, **I don't**.*
A: *Does he work with you?* B: *Yes, **he does**. / No, **he doesn't**.*

There is further practice of this in Unit 7 when you look at short answers.

## Exercise 3

**Complete the questions and answers with *do, does, don't* or *doesn't*.**

1 A: What _____ you do?
  B: I'm a cleaner.
2 A: What _____ he do?
  B: I _____ know.
3 A: Where _____ your mother work?
  B: She _____ have a job at the moment.
4 A: Where _____ your parents live?
  B: Budapest.
5 A: _____ you enjoy working there?
  B: No, I _____ .
6 A: We _____ live near my office, so I take the train to work.
  B: So, what time _____ you leave home?
7 A: _____ they have any kids?
  B: Yes, they _____ . Two, I think.
8 A: _____ your school have a café?
  B: Yes, it _____ . There's a small one, but I _____ use it.

## Exercise 4

**Complete the questions with your own ideas.**

1 Do you play …
  *Do you play online games?*
2 How often do you …
3 Do you like …
4 Where do you …
5 Does your school …

---

# 2 DAILY LIFE

## 2A VERB PATTERNS (*-ING* OR INFINITIVE WITH *TO*)

When two verbs are used next to each other, the second verb is usually in the *-ing* form or uses the infinitive with *to*. There are no rules for this and you have to learn which verbs use the *-ing* form for the second verb and which verbs use the infinitive with *to*.

**Verb + *-ing***
After some verbs, we often use the *-ing* form. These verbs include *enjoy, like, love* and *hate*.
*I **love playing** tennis.*
*He really **likes swimming**.*
*I **enjoy working** on my own.*
*We **hate living** in the countryside.*

Note the spelling changes.
For verbs ending in *-e*, remove the *-e*.
*danc**e** → danc**ing**     hav**e** → hav**ing**     liv**e** → liv**ing***

For verbs ending in consonant–vowel–consonant, double the final consonant.
*cha**t** → cha**tting**     ru**n** → ru**nning**     swi**m** → swi**mming***

**Verb + infinitive with *to***
After some verbs, we often use the infinitive with *to*. These verbs include *learn, need, try* and *want*.
*I'm **learning to drive**.*
*They **need to go** now.*
***Try to use** the new words.*
*She doesn't **want to live** in an old building.*

## Exercise 1

**Complete the sentences with the correct form of the verbs in brackets.**

1 I don't like *swimming*. (swim)
2 Do you want ~~to go out~~ later? (go out)
3 I try ~~going~~ for a run every day. (go)
4 I hate ~~to dance~~ and I'm very bad at it. (dance)
5 How do you learn *to be* a teacher? (be)
6 They really enjoy *playing* music together. (play)
7 My dad loves ~~to watch~~ tennis. (watch)
8 We need ~~to choose~~ where to have lunch. (choose)

## Exercise 2

**Correct the mistake in each sentence.**

1 My brother really likes read. *ing*
2 She hates sing. She's really bad at it.
3 My parents want having more free time. → *to have*
4 I don't really enjoy to work in an office. *working*
5 I always try go to bed before 11. *to go*
6 I need finishing my homework before I go out.
7 We love go to the cinema with friends. *going*
8 I want learn French. *to learn*

## Exercise 3

**Complete the sentences with your own ideas. Use an *-ing* form or an infinitive with *to*.**

1 I love …
  *I love swimming in the sea.*
2 I want …
3 I hate …
4 I don't like …
5 I need …
6 I always try …

## 2B ADVERBS OF FREQUENCY

We use adverbs of frequency to say how often we do something or something happens.

| I<br>We<br>They | 100%<br><br><br>0% | always<br>usually<br>often<br>sometimes<br>don't /<br>doesn't often<br>never | have a coffee after lunch. |
|---|---|---|---|
| He<br>She | | | has a coffee after lunch. |

Note that the adverb of frequency usually goes before the main verb, but it goes after the verb *be*.
I **usually walk** to work.
I **never watch** TV.
She **is always** on time.

### DID YOU KNOW?
We can also use *don't / doesn't … very often* or *… but not (very) often*.
I **don't** go to the gym **very often**.
We **sometimes** go out for dinner, **but not often**.

### Questions
We use *always*, *usually*, *often* and *sometimes* in questions.
A: Do you **always** walk to work?
B: Not always, but usually.

A: Where do you **usually** go on Saturdays?
B: Usually into town, but we sometimes go to the beach.

We also use *ever* in questions.
A: Do you **ever** play computer games?
B: No, never.

### Exercise 1
**Choose the correct option to complete the sentences.**

1 I usually read books about science and nature, but I *sometimes / often* read history books.
2 I don't earn much money, so I *don't often / sometimes* go out for dinner.
3 I really like rugby, but I *never / often* go and watch matches at the stadium.
4 My mum *usually / always* finishes work at six, but she sometimes works late – until eight or nine.
5 I *never / sometimes* drink coffee. I don't like it and it's bad for your health.
6 I enjoy cooking, but I *often cook / don't cook very often*.

### Exercise 2
**Put the adverb in the correct place in each sentence.**

1 I sleep until twelve on Sundays. (often)
2 My parents do sport. (not often)
3 I don't go shopping. (very often)
4 I watch sport on TV. (never)
5 I'm late for work. (sometimes)
6 We go to a restaurant, but we don't go. (sometimes / very often)
7 A: What time do you get up? (usually)
   B: It's seven o'clock during the week. (usually)
8 A: Do you work on Saturdays? (always)
   B: Not every Saturday, but I do. (often)

### Exercise 3
**Complete the sentences to make them true for you.**

1 I never _____ .
   *I never cook at home.*
2 I always _____ .
3 I often _____ .
4 I sometimes _____ , but I usually _____ .
5 I sometimes _____ , but not very often.

## 2C COUNTABLE AND UNCOUNTABLE NOUNS

### Countable nouns
Nouns that have both a singular and plural form are called countable nouns (because we can count them, e.g. *two pencils, ten shops*).
With singular nouns, we use *a / an*.
I need **a** drink.
I don't work in **an** office.
Do you have **a** pen?

With plural nouns, we usually use:
• **some** or **a lot of** in positive sentences.
   I need **some new pens**.
   There are **a lot of cafés** near here.
• **any** and **many** in negative sentences and questions.
   They don't have **any kids**.
   There aren't **many places** to sit.
   Are there **any good places to eat** near here?
   Do you know **many people** here?

### Uncountable nouns
Some nouns have no singular or plural form. These nouns are called uncountable nouns. Note that we use the singular form of the verb with uncountable nouns (e.g. *There is … , there isn't …*).
Useful uncountable nouns include:

| | | | | | |
|---|---|---|---|---|---|
| countryside | fish | food | fruit | help | homework |
| milk | money | music | news | paper | rubbish |
| time | traffic | water | | | |

Like with countable nouns, we usually use:
• **some** or **a lot of** in positive sentences.
   I need **some water**.
   There's **a lot of traffic** today.
• **any** and **much** in negative sentences and questions.
   We don't have **any homework**.
   I don't have **much money**.
   Do you have **any paper**?
   Is there **much water**?

Note that we don't use *a / an* with uncountable nouns.

### DID YOU KNOW?
With both countable and uncountable nouns, we can use *some* in questions. This is often when the question is an offer or a request.
Do you want **some chips**?
Do you want **some help**?
Can I have **some juice**, please?

### Exercise 1
**Choose the correct option to complete the conversations (1–6). In one item, both options are possible.**

1 A: Do you have *some / a* dictionary?
   B: Yeah, here you go.
2 A: Do you need *a / some* help?
   B: No, thanks. I'm fine.

3  A: Is it a good place to live?
   B: It's great. There are *a lot of / any* parks and trees, and there's not *much / many* traffic.
4  A: Do you want to take *any / a* break?
   B: No. We don't have *much / some* time.
5  A: Do you have *any / a* paper?
   B: Yes. How *much / many* do you want?
6  A: Do you want *some / any* fruit?
   B: Yes, please. Do you have *an / any* oranges?

## Exercise 2

**Find one mistake in each conversation. Correct it.**

1  A: Do you have any pen and some paper? I need to write a shopping list.
   B: Have a look in the drawer next to the fridge.
2  A: Do you have a money with you?
   B: Sorry, I don't. I usually use a card or my phone these days.
3  A: Are there any good places for a coffee near here?
   B: Yes, there are any nice cafés on the next street.
4  A: Ah, there isn't some milk I'm afraid.
   B: That's OK. Black coffee is fine.
5  A: Do you have much homeworks this evening?
   B: Yes, I have a lot of vocabulary exercises to do.
6  A: There's many traffic round here today.
   B: Yes, I think there's a big event at the stadium later.

There is further practice of countable and uncountable nouns in:
• Unit 5, when you look at *that / this / these / those*.
• Unit 10, when you look at explaining quantity.

## 3 HOME

### 3A  PREPOSITIONS OF PLACE

We use prepositions of place to say where something is.

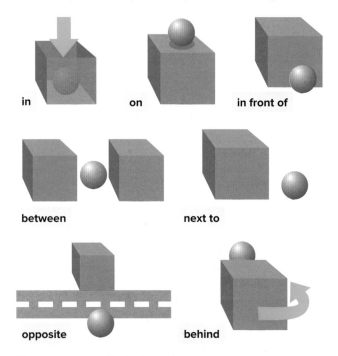

in    on    in front of

between    next to

opposite    behind

*There are some cafés **in** the main square.*
*The supermarket is **opposite** the main square.*
*The department store is **next to** the supermarket.*

*The car park is **behind** the supermarket.*
*The taxis wait **in front of** the station.*
*The clothes shop is **between** the bank and the book shop.*
*There's a flag **on** the roof of the museum.*

Note that we use *opposite* when the places are separated by a road or a river, etc.

#### On
There are some useful phrases with *on*.
*The bank is **on the left** and the book shop is **on the right**.*
*The department store is **on the corner of** Central Street **and** Station Road.*

#### In
*In* has the general meaning of inside something.
*He's **in the library**.*
*We can meet **in the café**.*
*I work **in the shopping centre**.*
*Is there a lake **in the park**?*

#### At
We use *at* to talk about a location in general.
*Wait **at the bus stop**.*
*Let's meet **at the cinema**.*
*I often see him **at the gym**.*

There are some useful phrases with *at*.
*It's **at the end of the road**.*
*She's not **at home**. She's **at work**.*

**DID YOU KNOW?**
We use both *on* and *in* to say the street or road for a place. There is no difference in meaning.
*There's a supermarket **on Green Road**. / There's a supermarket **in Green Road**.*
*I live **on North Street**. / I live **in North Street**.*

#### Exercise 1

**Complete the sentences with one word in each gap.**

1  There's a big car park _____ the end of this road.
2  He spends a lot of time _____ his room.
3  My house is number 52. It's _____ the left.
4  There's a new supermarket _____ the corner of Station Road and Queens Road.
5  We live _____ a park. It's on the other side of the road to our house.
6  My office is _____ to the big bank in town. It's the building _____ the right.
7  There's a good café _____ this road. It's next _____ the music shop over there.
8  There are lots of places to eat _____ the area, especially _____ the main square.
9  The shop is _____ two restaurants – a fast food place on one side and a Vietnamese place on the other.
10 The car park is _____ the supermarket. You can't see it from the road. You need to drive down the side of the supermarket to get to it. But if you go by bus, there's a bus stop in _____ of the supermarket.

## Exercise 2

**Look at the map and write sentences using the notes and prepositions of place.**

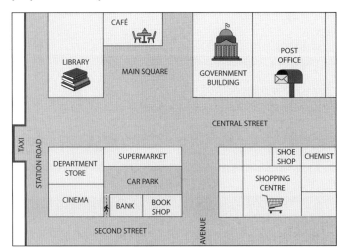

1 The cinema / corner / Second Street / Station Road
2 The library / next / the main square / left
3 The book shop / end / Second Street
4 The bank / the cinema / the book shop
5 The café / the main square
6 The department store / the library
7 The government building / Central Street
8 The entrance to the car park / Second Street

## Exercise 3

**Choose five places on the map in Exercise 2 and write sentences beginning *Let's meet* ...**

*Let's meet at the café.*
*Let's meet outside the cinema.*

## 3B POSSESSIVES

We show possession (who or what something belongs to) in three main ways: using person + *'s*, using a possessive adjective (*my, their*, etc.) or using a possessive pronoun (*mine, theirs*, etc.).

### Person + *'s*

We add *'s* (also known as possessive *'s*) to the person.
*Maria**'s** family are great.*
*This is my dad**'s** car.*

Note that for people and for some places and things, we do not usually use *the … of*.
*~~The family of Maria are great.~~*
*~~This is the car of my dad.~~*

If there are two or more people, we usually put the *'s* after the final person.
*This photo is from Luke and Ricardo**'s** party.*
NOT *~~This photo is from Luke's and Ricardo's party.~~*

For plural nouns that end in -*s*, we just add *'* (without *s*).
*This is my friends**'** house*
*We met at his parents**'** wedding.*

### DID YOU KNOW?

We also use time phrases, animals and some places and things with *'s*.
*Good luck in tomorrow**'s** exam.*
*This is the dog**'s** bowl.*
*It's the school**'s** problem.*

## Possessive adjectives and possessive pronouns

We can also use possessive adjectives and possessive pronouns to talk about possession.

| Subject | Possessive adjective | Possessive pronoun |
|---------|---------------------|--------------------|
| I | my | mine |
| you | your | yours |
| he | his | his |
| she | her | hers |
| it | its | – |
| we | our | ours |
| they | their | theirs |

We use a possessive adjective before a noun.
*Do you like **my jacket**? It's new.*
***Our house** is very near here.*
*This isn't **her car**.*

We use a possessive pronoun instead of repeating a possessive form + noun.
*That isn't my jacket. This one is **mine**. (= my jacket)*
*I'm not sure, but I think this house is **hers**. (= her house)*
*There's a phone on the table. Is it **yours**?  (= your phone)*

### Common mistakes

- *Is this ~~your's~~ your car?*
- *This house is ~~their's~~ theirs.*

Do not use *'s* with possessive adjectives and possessive pronouns.

### DID YOU KNOW?

To talk about our friends, a useful phrase is *a friend of mine*.
*Freddie's **an old friend of mine**.*
*Do you know Lara? She's **a good friend of mine**.*

## Exercise 1

**Choose the correct option to complete the sentences.**

1 *Your / Yours* house is really nice.
2 *Their / Theirs* house is next to the sea.
3 *Jakub's pizzas / The pizzas of Jakub* are usually OK, but I prefer *my / mine*.
4 This coat isn't *my / mine*. Is it *your / yours*?
5 *My parents' car / The car of my parents* is very old.
6 I really like *the flat of Andrew / Andrew's flat*.
7 The woman in the photo is my aunt. She's my *mum's / mums'* sister.
8 This isn't *my / mine* car. It's my *parents' / parents's*.

## Exercise 2

**Correct the mistakes in the sentences.**

1 Where do yours parents live?
2 My dads' family are from Malta.
3 Is this bag your? Or is it Alex's?
4 The sister of my boyfriend lives with us.
5 It's not my money. It's of Valentin.
6 I don't like the government new ideas.
7 Don't forget about tomorrow meeting!
8 My grandparents's house is really big.
9 This is Ana's and Olga's apartment.
10 Olivier is a good friend of me.

## 3C  CAN / CAN'T

### Use

We use can and can't to talk about possibility. Two ways we use can and can't are:

- to ask if something is possible or to ask someone to do something.

  **Can** we **eat** out tonight?
  **Can** I **stay** here?
  **Can** you **give** me a lift to the station?
  **Can** you **open** the window?

- to say something is possible or not possible.

  I **can drive** you to the station.
  You **can sit** where you want.
  I **can't do** this exercise.
  I'm afraid I **can't come** to class tomorrow.

### Form

Can and can't have the same form for all persons. We use can / can't + verb.

I / you / he / she / it / we / they **can help** them.
I / you / he / she / it / we / they **can't wait** here.
Can I / you / he / she / it / we / they wait here?

NOT ~~She can to help them.~~   ~~You can't to wait here.~~
~~Can we to wait here?~~

### DID YOU KNOW?

We can make questions using can't. This is often when the speaker thinks something is not possible.
**Can't** we watch TV this evening?
**Can't** I sit here? Why not?

### Useful answers

Look at these common answers to questions with can.

| + | – |
|---|---|
| Yeah, of course. | No. Sorry. |
| Yeah, sure. | I'm afraid not. |
| Go ahead. | Sorry, that's / it's not possible. |

A: Can I open the window?     B: **Yeah, sure.**

A: Can I sit here?     B: **Sure. Go ahead.**

A: Can I sit here?     B: **No. Sorry. It's taken.**

### Exercise 1

**Write questions with Can I ...? or Can you ...? and the words in brackets.**

1  A: I can't see the TV. (move it)
   *Can you move it?*
   B: Yeah, of course. There. Is that better?
2  A: I need to do some shopping. (take me in the car)
   B: I'm afraid not. I'm busy.
3  A: I can't speak now. (phone you back later)
   B: Yes, of course. Call me after six.
4  A: Dinner's ready. (tell the others)
   B: Sure.
5  A: I'm hot. (open the window)
   B: Yes, of course. Go ahead.
6  A: I need to eat something. (make a sandwich)
   B: Sorry, but we don't have any bread.
7  A: There's something wrong with my bike. (look at it)
   B: Sure. Just a moment.
8  A: The cake is delicious. (have some more)
   B: Yeah, of course.

### Exercise 2

**Complete the sentences with can or can't and these verbs.**

| eat | go | park | smoke | use | wait |
|---|---|---|---|---|---|

1  You _____ on the road or in the car park behind the building.
2  You _____ in here. It's no-smoking area.
3  Sorry, but you _____ your mobile phone in here. You need to go outside.
4  We _____ in through that door. It says 'Staff only'. Maybe we need the door over there.
5  We _____ over there. Look, there's a picnic area and some tables.
6  You _____ here or come back later if you want to.

## 4 TIME OFF

### 4A PAST SIMPLE POSITIVE

### Use

We use the past simple to talk about something that is finished in the past.
I **watched** TV last night.
I **bought** a new phone yesterday.
We **lived** in Italy for three years.

### Form

**Be**

Be has two past simple forms: was and were.

| I / He / She / It | was | late. |
|---|---|---|
| You / We / They | were | here. |

| There | was | a lot of traffic. |
|---|---|---|
| | were | a lot of people. |

### Regular verbs

We usually add -ed to the verb.
I **played** tennis and really **loved** it.
I **cooked** dinner and then **watched** TV.
I **stayed** with a friend. She **showed** me the town.

Note these spellings:

- For verbs ending in e, add -d.
- like + -d – like**d**
- For verbs ending in y, remove the y and add -ied.
  try + -ied – tr**ied**
- For verbs ending in consonant–vowel–consonant, we usually double the final letter: chat + t + -ed – cha**tted**
  stop + p + -ed – sto**pped**

### Irregular verbs

A lot of verbs are irregular. They have different forms and you need to learn the past simple forms. Common and useful irregular verbs include:

| buy – bought | come – came | do – did | feel – felt |
|---|---|---|---|
| get – got | go – went | have – had | make – made |
| meet – met | read – read | see – saw | sleep – slept |
| spend – spent | swim – swam | take – took | tell – told |

I **went** to bed at midnight.
We **had** pizza for lunch today.
I **did** some homework last night.
I **met** some interesting people at the party.

For a more complete list of irregular verbs, see page 190.

## Time phrases often used with the past simple

We often use the past simple with a phrase of finished time. The time phrase usually goes at the end of the sentence. These include:

| | | |
|---|---|---|
| yesterday | yesterday morning | last night |
| in March | two days ago | last week |
| a few weeks ago | in 2022 | last year |
| five years ago | when I was 16 | on / last Saturday |

I saw Jeremiah **yesterday**.
They got married **last month**.
I went to the cinema **on Saturday**.

### Exercise 1
**Find the irregular past forms and write the verb at the end of the sentence.**

1 I <u>felt</u> ill so I <u>went</u> home. *feel, go*
2 I went shopping and got some new boots.
3 I was lucky. I found €20 on the pavement.
4 I slept badly because I drank too much coffee.
5 We met at school. I sat next to her in class.
6 I spent three years in Japan. I taught English there.
7 I saw her yesterday and she said hello to you.
8 My son made dinner for us yesterday. It wasn't great, but I ate it.
9 She told me she swam five miles last Saturday.
10 We were very busy at work today. I had a quick lunch in my office.

### Exercise 2
**Complete the story with the past simple form of the verbs in brackets.**

Last weekend, I ¹_____ (go) to the beach with some friends and we ²_____ (make) a fire. We ³_____ (sit) round the fire all night and ⁴_____ (eat) lots of food, ⁵_____ (talk), ⁶_____ (tell) jokes and ⁷_____ (laugh) a lot. At six in the morning, we ⁸_____ (watch) the sun coming up. It ⁹_____ (be) beautiful. We really ¹⁰_____ (love) it. Then we ¹¹_____ (swim) in the sea. We ¹²_____ (be) very cold afterwards! I ¹³_____ (get) home at nine o'clock in the morning. I ¹⁴_____ (have) breakfast and then I ¹⁵_____ (sleep) until five in the afternoon!

### Exercise 3
**Complete the sentences to make them true for you.**

1 I went …
  *I went shopping on Saturday.*
2 I saw …
3 I bought …
4 I met …
5 I ate …
6 I had …

## 4B PAST SIMPLE NEGATIVE

### Be
*Be* has two past simple negative forms: *wasn't* and *weren't*.

| I / He / She / It | wasn't | on time. |
|---|---|---|
| You / We / They | weren't | happy about it. |

| There | wasn't | time to do it. |
|---|---|---|
| There | weren't | many cars on the road. |

## Other verbs
We form the past simple negative of other verbs with *didn't* + verb.
I **didn't go** out last night.
You **didn't try** very hard.
He **didn't do** the work.
She **didn't arrive**.
It **didn't rain**.
We **didn't find** my phone.
They **didn't talk** about it.

### DID YOU KNOW?
In more formal writing, we sometimes use the full forms *was / were not* and *did not*.
I **was not** at the meeting.
The company **did not** reply to my emails.

### Exercise 1
**Complete the sentences with *didn't*, *wasn't* or *weren't*.**

1 Sorry, I *didn't* hear you. Can you say it again?
2 I *didn't* do my homework. I was busy.
3 Petra *wasn't* in class today. Do you know why?
4 Sorry to hear you *weren't* well last week. Are you OK now?
5 I *didn't* call them yesterday. I forgot.
6 I'm sorry that there *wasn't* anyone to meet you at the airport.
7 I *didn't* see Dina at the party. I *wasn't / wasn't* there for long and I left early.
8 I *didn't* have lunch today. I *wasn't* hungry.
9 There *weren't* many people at the party. I *didn't* enjoy it.
10 I'm sorry I *wasn't* at the meeting. I *didn't* know about it.

### Exercise 2
**Correct the mistake in each sentence.**

1 There wasn't any cheap hotels in the old town, so we stayed outside the city. *weren't*
2 I was only in Cairo for two days, so I not have time to see much. *didn't*
3 We went to their apartment, but they wasn't there. *weren't*
4 I was very tired, so I didn't went out last night. *go*
5 I not do anything on Sunday. I just stayed at home and relaxed. *didn't*
6 We stayed in the mountains and we weren't see another person all weekend. *didn't*
7 I looked in ten different shops, but I didn't found what I wanted. *find*
8 I just had a very quick lunch because I didn't hungry. *wasn't*

### Exercise 3
**Rewrite the sentence using a negative verb and the word in brackets.**

1 The hotel was a long way from the sea. (near)
  *The hotel wasn't near the sea.*
2 We went to bed early. (late)
3 The hotel was expensive. (cheap)
4 I had a quiet weekend. (busy)
5 People were unfriendly. (friendly)
6 We stayed for a short time. (long)
7 My parents were upset. (happy)
8 We arrived late. (on time)

## 4C PAST SIMPLE QUESTIONS

*Be*

We form a question with *was / were* + subject.
**Was she** OK?
**Was the film** interesting?
**Were they** OK?
**Were you** there?
How **was your holiday**?
What time **was the flight**?
Who **were they** with?

**Other verbs**

We form a question with *did* + subject + verb.
**Did he talk** to you?
**Did you ask** him?
**Did she enjoy** the film?
**Did it rain**?

Who **did you go** with?
How much **did it cost**?
What time **did you get** home?

Note that a question word or question phrase (*when, who, what time,* etc.) goes before *was / were* and *did.*

### Exercise 1

**Put the words in the correct order to make questions.**

1  did / what / last / do / you / night ?
2  see / you / what / did / film ?
3  it / good / was ?
4  did / go / who / with / you ?
5  where / you / your / buy / shoes / did ?
6  they / very / were / expensive ?
7  get / did / you / else / anything ?
8  there / you / do / usually / go / shopping ?

### DID YOU KNOW?

When we answer *Were you …?* and *Did you …?* questions, we often only say *yes / yeah* or *no*. Sometimes we add *I was / I wasn't* and *I did / I didn't.*

A: *Were you there?*     B: *Yes,* **I was**. / *No,* **I wasn't**.
A: *Did you enjoy it?*     B: *Yes,* **I did**. / *No,* **I didn't**.

### Exercise 2

**Match the answers (a–h) to the questions in Exercise 1.**

a  *Don't Look Up.* It was an interesting film.
b  No, not really. They were €50.
c  No, I didn't have any more money.
d  Yes, it was. It was really good.
e  No, I don't. That was the first time.
f  I went to the cinema.
g  I went with a friend of mine, actually.
h  In Jeffer's, the department store in town.

### Exercise 3

**Complete the questions using *you* and the past simple form of these verbs.**

| be̶ | be | do | do | go̶ | ha̶v̶e̶ | start |
|---|---|---|---|---|---|---|

1  What *did you do* at the weekend?
2  What *did you have* for dinner last night?
3  *Did you start* any sport or exercise yesterday?
4  When *did you start* learning English?
5  *Did you go* away on holiday last summer?
6  Where *Were* at 8:30 this morning? *Were* at home?

### Exercise 4

**Write your answers to the questions in Exercise 3.**

*1  I met some friends and went shopping on Saturday. We had lunch in the city centre.*

## 5 SHOPPING

## 5A *THIS / THESE / THAT / THOSE*

We generally use *this* and *these* for things that are near to us (for example, things that we're wearing or holding or things that are next to us) and we use *that* and *those* for things that are further away from us (for example, when we point at things). We use *this* and *that* with singular and uncountable nouns. We use *these* and *those* with plural nouns.

| Singular and uncountable nouns | | Plural nouns | |
|---|---|---|---|
| This | is OK. orange is very sweet. music is good. one is nice. | These | are fine. jeans feel good. ones are quite cheap. |
| That | 's my book! T-shirt looks good. coffee was nice. one, please. | Those | are my shoes! people bought a lot. ones look OK. |

### Exercise 1

**Choose the correct word.**

1  *That / Those* jacket is nice. I love the colour.
2  Do you like *this / these* dress?
3  How much *is / are* those jeans? The black ones at the back.
4  *This / These* colour is fine for me. Thanks.
5  These *is / are* too big. Do you have them in a smaller size?
6  Can you pass me *this / that* pen on the table?
7  Did you know all *these / those* people at the party?
8  Come and listen to *this / that* song. I love it.

### DID YOU KNOW?

To avoid repeating a noun, after *this / these / that / those*, we often replace the noun with *one* or *ones*.
A: *Which shirt did you buy?*
B: *I got* **this one**, *look.* (= this shirt)

A: *Which cakes do you want?* **These ones**?
B: *No,* **those** small **ones** over there.

A: *Do you prefer* **these ones** or **those ones**?
B: *The blue ones, I think.*

### Exercise 2

**Replace the nouns in the conversations (1–5) with *one / ones*, where possible.**

1  A: Which cake do you want?
    B: That cake. The one with the pink sweets on top.
2  A: Those jeans look OK, but I prefer those other jeans you tried on before.
    B: Mmm, OK. What about these black jeans?
    A: Yeah – they're nice as well. Which jeans are cheaper?
3  A: How much are the apples?
    B: These apples here are five euros a kilo and those apples are 4.50.
4  A: Excuse me. Do you have these jumpers in an extra-large?
    B: No. Sorry. We only have this jumper in small, medium and large, I think.

5 A: I can't decide whether to get this bag or that bag. What do you think?

B: Well, I like this bag. I think it's a nicer colour. And that bag's a bit too big, I think.

## 5B PRESENT CONTINUOUS

### Use

We use the present continuous to talk about an action or situation that started but is not finished.

### Form

The present continuous is a present form of *be* (*am* / *is* / *are*) + *-ing* form. We usually use the short forms – *I'm* / *she's* / *they're*, etc.

I**'m working** very hard.

She**'s working** at home this week.

They**'re building** a new supermarket.

We form negatives with *am* / *is* / *are* + *not* + *-ing* form. We usually use the short forms *aren't* and *isn't*.

*I'm not working today.*

*Sales aren't improving.*

*It **isn't raining** at the moment.*

We form questions with *am* / *is* / *are* + subject + *-ing* form.

**Is** Sami **working** today?

**Are** any shops in town **having** a sale at the moment?

*What **are** you **looking** for?*

Note these spelling changes.

- For verbs ending in *-e*, remove the *-e*.

  giv**e** – givi**ng**     hav**e** – havi**ng**     improv**e** – improvi**ng**
  leav**e** – leavi**ng**

- For verbs ending in consonant–vowel–consonant, double the final consonant.

  get – ge**tt**ing     set – se**tt**ing     shop – sho**pp**ing
  run – ru**nn**ing

### DID YOU KNOW?

We often use the present continuous with time phrases such as *at the moment, now, just now, today, this week, this month*, etc.

*I'm not working **today**.*

*We're selling a lot of these **at the moment**.*

### Exercise 1

**Make present continuous sentences using the notes.**

1 Can you come back later? I / make / dinner / at the moment.
2 He's not ready. He / change / his clothes.
3 They / build / a new shopping centre near my house.
4 She / not work / today. She / visit / her grandparents.
5 I / not go / to the shop just now. It / rain.
6 A: What / you / make?
   B: I / make / a cake.
7 A: you / look for / something?
   B: Yes. I / look for / my bag.
8 A: Where / he / go?
   B: He / go / to the supermarket.

### Future meaning

We also use the present continuous to talk about an action or situation in the future. This is because we have this plan now.

I**'m getting** a new phone soon.

*Dani and Silvia **are coming** for dinner this evening.*

*The shop **is having** a sale next week.*

### Exercise 2

**Complete the conversations with the present continuous form of these groups of verbs.**

| come / make   do / try / not work   look / read   meet / go / play |
| --- |

1 A: Andrea _____ for dinner this evening.
  B: Nice. What _____ you _____ ?
2 A: I _____ Ollie and Freda later. Do you want to join us?
  B: I can't. I _____ to a concert. My brother _____ in it.
3 A: Can you help me? I _____ for something for a teenager who's interested in sport.
  B: How about this book here, *100 Great Sporting Moments*? I _____ it myself at the moment. It's great.
4 A: What _____ you _____ ?
  B: I _____ to order something online, but the website _____ very well.

### Exercise 3

**Complete the sentences to make them true for you. Use the present continuous.**

1 I _____ at the moment.
   *I'm reading a great book at the moment.*
2 I _____ today.
3 I _____ later.
4 I _____ at the weekend.

## 5C A, AN AND THE

### A / An

We use *a* / *an* + noun when we are talking about one thing, but it's not important which exact one.

*Is there **an exit** near here?*

*Do you want **a drink**?*

*I bought **a new phone**.*

We also use *a* / *an* + adjective + noun, when we are talking about an exact or specific thing, but when we are adding a description to it.

*That's **a really nice dress**. Is it new?*

*Thanks, that's **a great suggestion**.*

*That was **an easy exam**.*

### The

We use *the* + noun when we are referring to an exact thing or things and it is clear which exact thing / things we are talking about.

**The lift** is over there.

*Can I try **the black ones**?*

*Travel books are on **the third floor**.*

### Exercise 1

**Choose the correct options to complete the sentences (1–9).**

1 I need to buy *a* / *the* new pair of shoes for Joanna's party at *a* / *the* weekend.
2 Is there *a* / *the* good sports shop in *a* / *the* town centre?
3 *A* / *The* laptop I bought last week has got a problem. I need to take it back to *a* / *the* shop.
4 I had *an* / *the* amazing meal at that new place on *a* / *the* High Street.
5 I need to get *a* / *the* new phone card. Is there *a* / *the* shop that sells them near here?
6 My friend works at *a* / *the* department store, so she gets *a* / *the* discount on everything.
7 I'm going to *a* / *the* bookstore. I ordered *a* / *the* book last week and I need to collect it.

8  Thanks for telling me about that café. It's *a / the* great place and I really like *an / the* area it's in.

9  *A / The* magazine I bought isn't here – I think maybe I left it on *a / the* bus.

## Exercise 2
**Complete the text with *a*, *an* or *the*.**

My town's shopping centre is ¹___a___ big place with lots of different shops and places to eat. Inside ²___the___ shopping centre, you can find ³___a___ variety of shops selling food, clothes, mobile phones, books, sports equipment and much more. There is also ⁴___a___ chemist. ⁵___the___ shopping centre has three floors. On ⁶___the___ top floor, there's ⁷___a___ cinema and there are also restaurants and cafés where you can have something to eat or drink. It's ⁸___a.___ busy place, especially at weekends. It's ⁹___a___ great place to meet friends and hang out.

## 6 EDUCATION

### 6B  COMPARATIVES

**Use**

We use a comparative adjective to compare things. We use *than* when we say the thing we are comparing with.
*This week's class was **better**.*
*Today's exam was **more difficult.***
*I think English is **easier than** Polish.*
*Bilingual people are **more creative than** other people.*
*I think history is **more interesting than** geography.*

**Form**

*-er*

- For one-syllable adjectives, we add *-er*.
  *hard – hard**er***
  *cheap – cheap**er***
  *tall – tall**er***
  *late – lat**er***

- For adjectives ending in e, we just add *-r*.
  *nice – nice**r***
  *strange – strange**r***

- For adjectives ending vowel–consonant, we double the final letter and add *-er*.
  *big – bi**gg**er*
  *hot – ho**tt**er*

*-ier*

For adjectives ending in *-y*, we change *-y* to *-ier*.
*easy – eas**ier***
*lazy – laz**ier***
*friendly – friendl**ier***

*More*

For longer adjectives (two or more syllables), we use *more*.
*boring – **more** boring*
*interesting – **more** interesting*
*expensive – **more** expensive*
*popular – **more** popular*

**Irregular comparatives**
*Good* and *bad* have irregular comparative forms.
*good – **better***
*bad – **worse***

## Exercise 1
**Complete the sentences with the comparative form of the adjectives in brackets.**

1  Basketball is _____ than tennis in my country. (popular)

2  My brother's a bit _____ than me. (short)

3  Some of my classmates always get _____ grades than me. (high)

4  They say that people in the south are _____ than people in the north. (friendly)

5  It's _____ today than yesterday. It's _____ and _____ . (nice, warm, sunny)

6  The weather is _____ in my country than it is here. It's _____ and _____ . (bad, cold, rainy)

7  The TV is _____ here. The programmes are _____ . (good, interesting)

8  It's _____ to pass exams now. It was _____ in the past. (difficult, easy)

## Exercise 2
**Write sentences to compare these things. Use the adjective in brackets.**

1  Thailand / Japan    (big)
   *Thailand is bigger than Japan.*

2  Spain / Germany    (hot)

3  weekends / weekdays    (relaxing)

4  football / rugby    (popular)

5  going by train / going by bus    (fast)

6  a sensible diet / eating lots of fast food    (good)

7  the weather in October / the weather in June    (bad)

8  chatting with friends today / it was twenty years ago    (easy)

## Exercise 3
**Complete the sentences with your own ideas.**

1  _____ older than _____ .
   *I'm older than my sister.*

2  _____ more popular than _____ .

3  _____ easier than _____ .

4  _____ more interesting than _____ .

5  _____ healthier than _____ .

6  _____ more expensive than _____ .

### 6C  MODIFIERS

Modifiers go before adjectives to make the adjective 'stronger' or 'weaker'.
- ***Very*** and ***really*** make an adjective stronger.
- ***Quite*** makes an adjective weaker.
- ***Not very*** makes an adjective weaker than *quite*.

*very / really*                ↑   (= make the adjective stronger)

*quite*

*not very*                      ↓   (= make the adjective weaker)

*Today's class was **really good**.*
*The book is **very interesting**. I'm really enjoying it.*
*The exam was **quite difficult**. But I think I did OK.*
*My school is**n't very far** from where I live. It's only a five-minute walk.*

**DID YOU KNOW?**
We can also use *a bit* with some adjectives. We usually use it with negative ideas.
*He's **a bit** unfriendly.*
*It's **a bit** expensive.*

## Exercise 1

**Put the modifier in brackets in the correct place.**

1  It's cold in here. Can we turn on the heating? (quite)
2  Thanks for inviting us. We had a great time. (really)
3  It's interesting. We always do the same things. (not very)
4  He's OK, I guess, but he's strange! (a bit)
5  She's good at sciences. She always gets A grades. (really)
6  My teachers were helpful, so that made the course easier. (very)
7  I'm hungry, but I can wait for lunch. (quite)
8  I'm good at maths. I'm better at subjects like history and geography. (not very)

## Exercise 2

**Choose the correct option to complete the sentences.**

1  The history class is *not very / very* interesting. The teacher makes it really fun and we learn a lot.
2  My classmates are *really / not very* friendly. And they always help when I have questions.
3  The teacher explained the lesson *very / a bit* clearly. I understood everything.
4  The food in the school cafeteria is *quite / very* good. But it could be better.
5  I'm *a bit / really / not very* interested in art. I love visiting galleries and museums.
6  I'm *really / quite / not very* interested in studying for this subject. It's boring.
7  The English test was *quite / not very / really* easy. I finished early and got 100%.
8  The class was *quite / very / not very* interesting, but I got *a bit / very / not very* bored a few times.

## Exercise 3

**Complete the sentences so they are true for you.**

1  I'm quite good at …
   *I'm quite good at maths.*
2  I'm not very good at …
3  I'm really interested in …
4  … is very kind.

## 7 PEOPLE I KNOW

## 7A  SHORT ANSWERS

When we answer a *yes/no* question, we can sometimes answer with just *yes, yeah* or *no*.
A: Are you hungry?       B: **Yeah**.

A: Are they here?        B: **No**.

However, we often use *yes / yeah / no* + subject + auxiliary verb (e.g. *be, do, can*).

| | |
|---|---|
| **Are** you over 18? | Yes, I **am**. / No, I**'m not**. |
| **Is** he staying with you? | Yes, he **is**. / No, he **isn't**. |
| **Did** they go with you? | Yes, they **did**. / No, they **didn't**. |
| **Do** you live near here? | Yes, I **do**. / No, I **don't**. |
| **Does** she live with you? | Yes, she **does**. / No, she **doesn't**. |
| **Did** you get the tickets? | Yes, I **did**. / No, I **didn't**. |
| **Can** you see the board? | Yes, I **can**. / No, I **can't**. |

Note that for the negative of *is* or *are*, we can usually use two different contractions.
A: Is she coming too?
B: No, she**'s not**. / No, she **isn't**.

A: Are they here?
B: No, they**'re not**. / No, they **aren't**.

### DID YOU KNOW?
We can also put the *yes / yeah / no* after the subject + auxiliary.
*Are they here?*       *They're not, **no**.*
*Do you like it?*      *I do, **yes**.*

## Exercise 1

**Choose the correct option to complete the conversations.**

1  A: Can you take me to the airport later?
   B: I'm sorry, but I *can / can't*. I'm busy.
2  A: Did you see the film on Channel Six last night?
   B: Yes, I *was / did*. It was really good.
3  A: Do you two like baseball?
   B: I *did / do*, yes, but Jack doesn't.
4  A: Are you feeling OK?
   B: No, I *aren't / I'm not*, actually. I've got a bad headache.
5  A: Do your children still live at home with you?
   B: Two of them *does / do*, but my son left home last year.
6  A: Did you stay till the end of the party.
   B: I *don't / didn't*, no. I had to leave to get my bus.
7  A: Can we park here?
   B: We *can / do*, yeah. But it says only for 30 minutes.
8  A: What's her new apartment like? Is it nice?
   B: It *is / isn't*, yeah – and a great location.

## Exercise 2

**Complete the replies with the correct subject pronoun and the correct form of *be, do* or *can*.**

1  A: Is Russ from New Zealand?
   B: Yes, _____ . But he left when he was a kid.
2  A: Do you know what she's doing these days?
   B: No, _____ . No idea.
3  A: Did we see that film together?
   B: Yeah, _____ . When it first came out, remember?
4  A: Can I leave my bike here?
   B: No, _____ , I'm afraid. But you can over there.
5  A: Are you ready?
   B: Yes, _____ . Just give me a few seconds.
6  A: Did you put the milk back in the fridge?
   B: Yes, _____ . Is it not there now?

## Exercise 3

**Give short answer replies that are true for you. Add more information.**

1  Are you a student?
   *No, I'm not. I work.*
2  Did you go out last night?
3  Do you do any sports?
4  Can you drive?
5  Do you live alone?

## 7B  *HAVE TO*

*Have to / Has to* + verb has a similar meaning to *need(s) to*. It shows that something is necessary.
*All the kids have jobs in the house. For example, I **have to empty** the dishwasher.*
*My mum **has to work** in the office three days a week. The other two days, she works at home.*

*Don't have to / Doesn't have to* + verb has a similar meaning to *don't / doesn't need to*. It shows that something is not necessary. However, sometimes we can choose to do the thing if we want to.
*My friends **don't have to do** jobs in the home, but they sometimes help.*
*There are lots of buses, so she **doesn't have to drive** the kids to school.*

We form a question with *do / does* + subject + *have to* + verb.
*What time **do we have to leave**?*
***Does he have to wear** a uniform at school?*

## Exercise 1
**Choose the correct option to complete the sentences.**
1 Alexa can't come to the cinema with us. She *has to / doesn't have to* collect her brother from school.
2 Our dog has a lot of energy, so we *have to / don't have to* take it for a lot of walks.
3 My dad sometimes *has to / doesn't have to* work really long hours.
4 I tidied the kitchen last time. You *have to / don't have to* do it this time. And I'll do it next time.
5 Tell Yarik he *has to / doesn't have to* pick me up. I got a taxi.
6 I can't repair it, I'm afraid. You *have to / don't have to* take it to a shop.
7 We *have to / don't have to* play computer games if you don't want to. We can do something else.
8 You *have to / don't have to* leave now. You can stay a bit longer if you like.

## Exercise 2
**Complete the sentences with the correct form of (*don't*) *have to* and these verbs.**

| do | go | have | leave | wait | work |
|----|----|------|-------|------|------|

1 It's late. I _____ now. I don't want to miss my bus.
2 Please, start eating. You _____ for me.
3 My son _____ a lot of homework this year. Much more than last year.
4 Tomorrow is a public holiday, but our boss said we all _____ . We're not happy about it!
5 She _____ to school tomorrow. It's a public holiday.
6 _____ we _____ pasta again tonight? We had it last night!

## Exercise 3
**Write three sentences about what you have to do or don't have to do at home. You can use some of these ideas to help you.**

| buy my own food | cook a meal every day |
|-----------------|----------------------|
| do my own washing | help with the cleaning |
| keep the house tidy | pay the bills |

*I don't have to buy my own food.*

## 8 PLANS

## 8A GOING TO

### Use
We use *be going to* to talk about the future. We especially use it to talk about the plans we have.
***I'm going to see** my sister at the weekend.*
***We're going to watch** a film this evening.*

### Form
We use *be* + *going to* + verb.
***I'm going to arrive** tomorrow night.*
***Daniel's going to start** his new job next week.*
***It's going to take** a long time.*
***We're going to stay** in a hotel.*

We form the negative with *not*.
***I'm not going to get** a new phone.*
*She **isn't going to study** fashion. She's going to study history of art.*
*They**'re not going to wait** for us.*

Note that we usually use contractions: *I'm, you're, she's, it's, we're, they're*, etc.
We can also use the negatives *aren't / isn't*.

### Questions
To form a question, we put *be* before the subject.
***Am** I **going to see** you later?*
***Are** you **going to speak** to him?*
***Is** it **going to start** soon?*
***Is** Alex **going to come** with us?*
***Are** we **going to stay** here?*
***Is** someone **going to meet** us?*
*What time **is** he **going to book** the table for?*

### Time phrases with *going to*
We often use future time words and phrases with *going to*. These include:

| in a minute | soon | tonight | this evening |
|-------------|------|---------|--------------|
| next week | in an hour | later | tomorrow |
| this afternoon | next year | | |

## Exercise 1
**Match the questions (1–6) with the answers (a–f).**
1 What are you going to do later?
2 What time are you going to leave?
3 Are they going to stay with you?
4 Are you going to go by train?
5 How long are you going to stay?
6 Why aren't you going to come?

a No, I think we're going to get the bus.
b Nothing. I'm going to go to bed early. I'm very tired.
c Three weeks. I'm going to come back on the 30th.
d No, they're going to stay in a hotel in the city centre.
e I'm not going to be here. I'm going to go to Zurich that day.
f The flight is at seven so the taxi's going to collect us at four.

## Exercise 2
**Use the notes to write sentences with the correct form of *going to*.**
1 I / get a taxi home. How / you / get home?
2 He / not / have a big party, but a few people / go out to a restaurant.
3 Maria / be here in a few minutes. You / come with us?
4 I / not / go for a run. I / go to the gym instead.
5 Where / your cousins / stay when they visit? They / stay with you or in a hotel?
6 A: Where / you / meet Abdul?
   B: He / come here and then we / get the bus into town.

## Exercise 3
**Correct each sentence by adding one word.**
1 I'm not to do anything special tonight.
2 How are you going get to the station?
3 Where they going to go on holiday this year?
4 What your sister going to study?
5 What time are you going arrive?
6 I going to have dinner with my parents tonight.

178

## Exercise 4

**Complete the sentences about your plans using *going to*.**

1 _____ this evening.
   *I'm going to watch TV this evening.*
2 _____ at the weekend.
3 _____ next week.
4 _____ soon.

## 8C   WOULD LIKE TO

We use *would like to* + verb to talk about things we want, or hope, to do. We usually say and write *would* as *'d*.
**I'd like to go** travelling for a year.
He**'d like to spend** less time working.
We**'d like to move** to a bigger house.

### DID YOU KNOW?

We can make *would like* stronger using *really*.
I'd **really** like to go travelling for a year.
We'd **really** like to visit you sometime soon.

The negative is *wouldn't like to* + verb.
I **wouldn't like to live** in a big city.
I **wouldn't like to be** famous.

The question form is *would* + subject + *like to* + verb.
**Would** you **like to live** in the US one day?

### DID YOU KNOW?

Note that we also use the question *Would you like …?* to offer something in the future or the present.
**Would** you **like to come** for dinner some time?
**Would** you **like to try** one of these?

**Time phrases with *would like to***

With *would like to*, we often use time phrases such as:
one day        sometime in the future
sometime soon        sometime in the next few years

I'd like to learn a musical instrument **one day**.
I'd like to live abroad sometime **in the next few years**.

## Exercise 1

**Complete the sentences with these pairs of verbs. Don't repeat *would like to* for the second verb.**

| join / get   learn / go   leave / get   save / buy   start / become |
|---|

1 I'd like to _Join_ a gym and _get_ fitter.
2 I'd really like to _learn_ Arabic one day and _go_ to Egypt.
3 Would you like to _start_ your own business and _become_ a successful business person?
4 I'd like to _leave_ home and _get_ my own apartment sometime soon.
5 I'd really like to _save_ some money and _buy_ a car.

## Exercise 2

**Rewrite the sentences and questions using *would like*.**

1 I really want to learn the piano one day.
2 Do you want to live in an English-speaking country one day?
3 I don't want to do the same job all my life.
4 I want to get married in my early 30s. I don't want to get married before that.
5 Do you want to do something at the weekend?
6 I really want to stop working as soon as I can.

## Exercise 3

**Complete the sentences with your own ideas using *would like to*.**

1 I _____ sometime soon.
   *I'd like to get my own place to live sometime soon.*
2 One day, I _____ .
3 I _____ really _____ .

## 9 EXPERIENCES

## 9A   PRESENT PERFECT QUESTIONS (*BEEN, TRIED*)

### Use

We use the present perfect to talk about experiences from the past to now. We ask questions using the present perfect to find out about someone's experiences.

### Form

To form a question, we use *have / has* + subject + past participle. A common use of the present perfect is the question *Have you been …?* and *Have you tried …?* Note that we use *been* as the past participle of *go*.
**Have** you **been** to the UK?
**Has** your friend **been** to London before?
A friend of mine is going to move to Santiago. **Have** you **been** there?
**Has** she **tried** Vietnamese food before?
There's a new Greek place near here. **Have** you **tried** Greek food?

### DID YOU KNOW?

We sometimes add *ever* to mean 'at any time in your life'.
Have you **ever** been to Australia?
Have you **ever** tried Thai food?
We'd like to go to Turkey on holiday this year. **Have** you **ever been** there?

### Short answers

We can answer *Have you …?* questions with just *Yes* or *No*. However, we often answer with a phrase such as *Yes, I have. / Yes, once. / No, I haven't. / No, never. / No, but I'd like to.*
A: Have you been to that new café by the river?
B: **Yes, I have**. It's pretty good.
A: Have you been to Rome?                B: **No, never**.
A: Have you ever tried snowboarding?      B: **No, but I'd like to**.

## Exercise 1

**Complete the conversations with one word in each gap.**

1 A: _____ your friend been _____ Mexico before?
   B: No, never.
2 A: Have you ever _____ to Cairo in Egypt?
   B: No, never, but I'd really _____ to one day.
3 A: Have you _____ tried German food?
   B: Yes, I _____ . Have _____ ?
   A: No. What's it like?
4 A: Have you ever _____ Mexican food?
   B: No, I _____ . Have you?
5 A: Have you _____ to Thailand before?
   B: No, never. This is my first time.

## Exercise 2

**Complete the conversations (1–6). Use the present perfect and the ideas in brackets.**

1 A: I'm going to Oxford next month. _____ ? (you / ever / there)
   B: Yes, a few times, actually.
   A: Great. Can you give me some ideas of things to do?

2 A: I'm going to go to Tokyo for work next week.

B: Wow! _____ there before? (you / go)

A: Yes, I have, actually. I went there last year on holiday. _____ there? (you / go)

B: No, but I'd like to one day.

3 A: _____ to Seoul before? (you / go)

B: No, this is my first time.

A: Ah, and _____ Korean food before? (you / try)

B: No, never. But I'm looking forward to it.

4 A: My friend Erika is planning to go to Olomouc for a few days next month.

B: Nice! _____ the city before? (she / visit)

A: No, never.

B: Well, it's a really great city. I can suggest some things to do if you like.

5 A: _____ Nepalese food? (you / ever / try)

B: No, never. You?

A: Yes, I love it. There's a great restaurant near here. Perhaps we can go some time.

6 A: My friend is going to New York for a few days. Can you give her any advice?

B: _____ there before? (she / go)

A: I don't think so.

B: Ah OK, well …

### Exercise 3

**Write short answers that are true for you.**

1 Have you ever been to Spain?

*Yes, a couple of times.*

2 Have you ever tried snowboarding?

3 Have you ever been to Iceland?

4 Have you ever been to a concert?

5 Have you ever tried Chinese food?

6 Have you ever been to Peru?

## 9B PRESENT PERFECT POSITIVE AND NEGATIVE

### Use

A common use of the present perfect is to talk about our experiences. These could be a recent experience or a past experience at some time in our life.

When we use the present perfect, we <u>do not</u> usually say when the event or situation happened.

NOT ~~I've been there last year.~~      ~~We've met two years ago.~~

To add detail, such as when the event or situation happened, we usually use the past simple.

*Yes, I've been there. I **was** there last year.*

*We've met before. We first **met** two years ago.*

### Form

To make the present perfect, we use *have / has* + past participle. We can also use the short forms *'ve* and *'s*.

*I**'ve seen** the film twice.*

*James has **lived** in a few different countries.*

*We**'ve met** a few times.*

We make the negative with *have / has not*. However, we often use the short forms *haven't* and *hasn't*.

*I **haven't seen** it.*

*He **hasn't been** to Europe.*

*We **haven't met** before.*

We sometimes form the negative with *have / has never*.

*I**'ve never been** skiing.*

*He**'s never lived** in the UK.*

### Past participles

Most past participles are regular, i.e. we add -*ed* to the verb (e.g. *played, lived, tried, travelled*).

Some past participles are irregular (e.g. *been, seen, met*) and you need to learn these. Note that for some irregular verbs, the past simple and the past participle are the same and for some irregular verbs they are different.

For a more complete list of irregular verbs, see page 190.

### Exercise 1

**Complete the sentences with the correct present perfect form of these verbs.**

| go | not go | have | never learn | live | never see | take |

1 I have taken my driving test three times.

2 I've never seen any of the *Fast and Furious* films.

3 Jacqui has had a lot of different jobs.

4 We have gone / haven't gone to Ireland, but we lived to the UK.

5 He has lived and worked all over the world, but he has never learned a foreign language.

### Exercise 2

**Complete the conversations with the correct present perfect or past simple form of the verb in brackets.**

1 A: Do you know Kamila?

B: Well, we have met (meet) a couple of times, but I don't know her very well. We first met (meet) two years ago, I think.

2 A: Have you seen (see) any good films recently?

B: Yeah. I've saw (see) *Polite Society* last week. Have you seen (see) it yet?

A: No, but I'd like to.

B: You should. It's great.

3 A: Have you lost (lose) something?

B: Yeah, my keys.

A: I haven't seen (not see) them. Sorry.

4 A: I like the sound of that new restaurant by the river. Have you been (go) there?

B: Ah, yes. I've been (go) there a few times, actually. It's really good. I've been

5 A: Where's Anna from?

B: I'm not sure. I know she has lived (live) in several different countries and I think she lived (live) in the Netherlands as a child, but I'm not sure where she was born.

6 A: A lot of people have never been (never be) outside their country. In fact, most people, I think.

B: True. And I was in my late 20s before I traveled (travel) abroad.

### Exercise 3

**Think about experiences in your life and complete the sentences to make them true for you.**

1 I've never been to USA

*I've never played volleyball.*

2 I've been to Qatar several times.

3 I've played tennis.

4 I haven't been to Italy , but I'd like to.

several

## 10B  EXPLAINING QUANTITY

We use different words and phrases to talk about quantity.
We use *a lot of*, *quite a lot of, some* and *any* with both countable nouns and uncountable nouns.
We use *many* with countable nouns.
We use *much* with uncountable nouns.

|  | Uncountable nouns | Plural nouns |
|---|---|---|
| Do you eat | **much** meat?<br>**any** fruit? | **many** chips?<br>**any** vegetables? |
| I eat | **a lot of** ice cream.<br>**quite a lot of** sugar.<br>**some** fish. | **a lot of** biscuits.<br>**quite a lot of** sweets.<br>**some** beans. |
| I don't eat | **much** rice.<br>**any** cheese. | **many** cakes.<br>**any** eggs. |

Note that *a lot of* and *much / many* have the same meaning. However, we usually use *a lot of* in positive sentences and *much / many* in negative sentences and questions.
I've got **a lot of** money.
I've eaten **a lot of** biscuits.
I haven**'t** got **much** money.
I haven**'t** eaten **many** biscuits.

We also usually use *some* in positive sentences and we use *any* in negative sentences.
I ate **some** fruit.
I did**n't** eat **any** fruit.

### Exercise 1
**Complete the sentences with *much* or *many*.**
1  I don't eat _____ sweet food.
2  Do you eat _____ fresh fruit?
3  Do you eat _____ vegetables?
4  He doesn't eat _____ meat.
5  There aren't _____ restaurants in my town.

### Exercise 2
**Complete the sentences with *some* or *any*.**
1  We haven't got _____ milk. Can you get some?
2  We had _____ lovely meals on holiday.
3  I'm about 90% vegetarian, but I eat _____ fish sometimes.
4  I don't want _____ coffee, thank you.
5  I like _____ vegetarian food, but it's often a bit boring.

### DID YOU KNOW?
*Quite a lot of* is less than *a lot of*.
I drink **a lot of** coffee, say five cups a day.
I drink **quite a lot of** coffee, say two or three cups a day.

### Exercise 3
**Choose the correct option to complete the sentences. Sometimes, both options are possible.**
1  I usually use *much / a lot of* onions when I cook.
2  I try not to eat *many / any* meat. It's better for the environment.
3  I drink *a lot of / quite a lot of* coffee!
4  I eat *quite a lot of / some* fish, but I don't eat *many / any* red meat.
5  We don't really drink *much / some* coffee – maybe just one cup a day.

6  I don't drink *any / many* soft drinks. They have *a lot of / much* sugar in them.
7  A: Do you eat *many / any* dairy products?
   B: *No, not many. / Yes, quite a lot.*
8  A: Did you use *much / many* cream in the sauce?
   B: Yeah, *some / quite a lot.*

### Exercise 4
**In each sentence, which words in italics show the bigger quantity?**
1  I use *a lot of / quite a lot of* salt in my cooking.
2  I don't put *much / any* sugar in my coffee.
3  There aren't *any / many* good restaurants near here.
4  I eat *some / a lot of* fast food.
5  I eat *quite a lot of / some* eggs.

### Exercise 5
**Complete the sentences so they are true for you.**
1  I eat a lot of …
   *I eat a lot of cheese.*
2  I eat quite a lot of …
3  I don't cook any …
4  I don't drink much …
5  I don't eat many …

## 10C  *ME TOO, ME NEITHER* AND AUXILIARIES

We can agree with someone using *me too* and *me neither*.

*Me too*
We use *me too* to agree with a positive statement.
A: *I hate tomatoes.*     B: **Me too**.

A: *I'm going to go to the cinema later.*
B: *Oh, **me too**! What are you going to see?*

A: *I've been there several times.*     B: *Yeah, **me too**. It's great.*

*Me neither*
We use *me neither* to agree with a negative statement, i.e. one with *not* or *never*.
A: *I ca**n't** decide what to eat.*
B: **Me neither.** *It all looks so delicious.*

A: *I do**n't** like beef.*     B: **Me neither**.

A: *I've **never** had Mexican food before.*
B: **Me neither**, *but this is really good, isn't it?*
A: *Yeah, it's great.*

*I do / don't* and *I did / didn't*
We can use *I do, she does, they didn't*, etc. to disagree with a statement in the present simple.
• We use a positive auxiliary (*I do, he does*, etc.) to disagree with a negative statement.
   A: *I do**n't** eat much meat.*     B: *Oh, I **do**. I have it every day.*

   A: *He does**n't** like reading.*     B: *Yes, **he does**!*
• We use a negative auxiliary (*I don't, he doesn't*, etc.) to disagree with a positive statement.
   A: *My kids love seafood.*     B: *Really? **Mine don't**.*

   A: *I work near my home.*     B: *Oh I **don't**. You're lucky!*
• We use a past auxiliary (*I did, we didn't*, etc) in the same way to disagree with a statement in the past simple.
   A: *I didn't enjoy the film.*     B: *Oh, we **did**.*

   A: *I really liked the restaurant.*
   B: *I **didn't**. I thought it was pretty terrible, to be honest.*

## Other auxiliary verbs

We sometimes use other auxiliary verbs like *have*, *would*, *can*, *be*, etc. to disagree. We use the same auxiliary verb as the one in the statement we disagree with.

| Statement | Reply – disagree |
|---|---|
| A: I **haven't** had Mexican food. | B: I **have**. It's nice. |
| A: I**'ve** been there before. | B: I **haven't**. What's it like? |
| A: I **wouldn't** like to try it. | B: Oh, I **would**! |
| A: We**'d** like to go there. | B: Really? I **wouldn't**. |
| A: I **can't** see him. | B: I **can**. He's over there. |
| A: She **can** cook quite well. | B: That's good, because he **can't**! |
| A: I**'m** not going to go. | B: Why not? We **are**. |
| A: I**'m** hungry. | B: I**'m not**. Can you wait? |

There is more practice of auxiliary verbs in Unit 7, when you look at short answers.

### Exercise 1

**Complete the conversations with a phrase for agreeing or disagreeing. Replace the words in brackets. Use *me too*, *me neither* or an auxiliary verb.**

1  A: I love cheese.
   B: (I love cheese.) What's your favourite?
2  A: I don't like seafood.
   B: (I don't like seafood.) It makes me feel ill.
3  A: I drink too much coffee.
   B: Really? (I don't drink too much coffee.) I hate coffee!
4  A: I don't drink enough water.
   B: (I drink enough water.) I always have a bottle with me.
5  A: I'd like to learn to drive.
   B: Really? (I wouldn't like to learn to drive.) It's too expensive and I prefer to cycle.
   A: (I prefer not to cycle.) It's too dangerous with all the cars on the roads!
6  A: I've never been abroad.
   B: (I've never been abroad.) I'm afraid of flying.
   A: (I'm not scared of flying.) I enjoy it.

### Exercise 2

**Complete the conversations (1–4) with one word in each gap. Contractions (*don't*, *can't*, etc.) count as one word.**

1  A: Are you going to go to Jean's birthday dinner next week?
   B: No, I can't.
   A: No, me _____ , but I want to get him something.
   B: Me _____ . Let's put our money together.
2  A: The writing's too small. I can't read the instructions.
   B: I _____ . Let me have a look.
   A: I think I need to have an eye test.
   B: Me _____ , actually! I was wrong. I can't read them either!
3  A: What are you going to have?
   B: I haven't decided.
   A: Me _____ . There's too much choice.
   C: Well, I think I'm going to have the cheese pizza.
   A: Really? I hate cheese.
   B: Oh, I _____ . I love it.
   C: Me _____ . How can anyone *not* like cheese?
   B: I don't know. I just don't.

4  A: I love that new restaurant on the square.
   B: Me _____ , but Katya _____ . She had a really bad meal there.
   A: Ah. That's a shame. Everything I've had there has been great.
   B: Yeah, same here.

### Exercise 3

**Write responses that are true for you to agree or disagree with these statements.**

1  I don't like cooking.
   *Me neither. / I do.*
2  I eat a lot of meat.
3  I've never eaten Indian food.
4  I love hot, spicy food.
5  I didn't have breakfast this morning.
6  I can't cook very well.
7  I eat in a restaurant every week.
8  I'd like to eat less meat.

## 11 TRAVEL

### 11B  *TOO MUCH, TOO MANY* AND *NOT ENOUGH*

We use *too much* and *too many* to show that there is more of something than we want or need. We use *not enough* to show there is less of something than we want or need.

*Too much*

We use *too much* with uncountable nouns.
There**'s too much crime**. The government needs to do more.
You can't ride a bike here. There**'s too much traffic**.
I ate **too much**. I don't feel so good. (= too much food)

*Too many*

We use *too many* with plural (countable) nouns.
You can't sit on the bus. There **are too many people**.
There **are too many cars**. I can't park.
Do you want a coffee? I ordered **too many**.  (= too many coffees)

*Not enough*

We use *not enough* (*isn't enough*, *haven't got enough*, *didn't have enough*, etc.) with uncountable nouns or plural nouns.
There **isn't enough help** for older people on public transport.
There **aren't enough places** to park.
I **haven't got enough room** in my bag.
I **don't eat enough** fruit and vegetables.

Remember to use *there is* with uncountable nouns and *there are* with plural nouns.

### Exercise 1

**Choose the correct option to complete the sentences.**

1  There is too *much / many* traffic on my street.
2  There are too *much / many* accidents on our roads.
3  There aren't *much / enough* cheap seats on the trains.
4  Sorry. There's *not / too* enough space for all those bags in my car.
5  There are *not / too* many people in our city. It's always crowded.
6  The government says there's not *many / enough* money to repair the roads.
7  There are too *many / much / enough* coffee shops in the town.
8  I spend too *many / much / enough* on eating out. I need to cook at home more.

## Exercise 2

**Complete the sentences with *too much*, *too many* or *enough*.**

1 There are _____ vans in city centres these days. They're everywhere!
2 Let's try the café next door. There aren't _____ seats for all of us here.
3 The local government is going to reduce some bus services because they cost _____ money.
4 We haven't got _____ time to get some lunch before the bus leaves. We can eat later.
5 It costs _____ to eat out these days, so we only go out to a restaurant once a month.
6 I don't drive into town. There's always _____ traffic and it's difficult to park. There aren't _____ parking spaces.
7 I don't get _____ exercise, but I never have _____ time! Perhaps I could start cycling to work instead of driving.

## Exercise 3

**Complete the sentences to make them true for where you live.**

1 There isn't enough …
   *There isn't enough to do in the evening.*
2 There aren't enough …
3 There are too many …
4 There's too much …
5 It costs too much to …

# 11C SUPERLATIVES

To compare more than two things, use *the* + superlative adjective.

**-est**

- For one-syllable adjectives, we add *-est*.
  *fast – fastest*
  *cheap – cheapest*
  *small – smallest*
  *late – latest*
- For adjectives ending in *-e*, we just add *-st*.
  *nice – nicest*
  *strange – strangest*
- For adjectives ending vowel–consonant, we double the final letter and add *-est*.
  *big – biggest*
  *hot – hottest*

**-iest**

For adjectives ending in *-y*, we change *-y* to *-iest*.
*early – the earliest*
*lazy – the laziest*
*busy – the busiest*

**The most + adjective**

For longer adjectives (two or more syllables), we use *the most* + adjective.
*boring – **the most** boring*
*interesting – **the most** interesting*
*popular – **the most** popular*

**Irregular superlatives**
*good – the **best***
*bad – the **worst***
*far – the **furthest***

## Exercise 1

**Choose the correct option to complete the sentences.**

1 Yesterday was *hottest / the hottest* day of the year.
2 That was the *more / most* difficult exam I've ever taken.
3 They were the *loudest / most loud* band I've ever heard!
4 I live in one of the *busyiest / busiest* streets in town.
5 It was the *worse / worst* day of my life!
6 The *easiest / most easy* way to get around is on foot.
7 They were the *most nice / nicest* people I've ever met.
8 I'm the *tallest / most tallest* person in my class.

### DID YOU KNOW?

We often use *one of the* + superlative adjective.
*That was **one of the funniest** films I've ever seen.*
*Delhi is **one of the biggest cities** in the world.*
*He's **one of the nicest** people I know.*

## Exercise 2

**Complete the sentences with a superlative form of the adjective in brackets.**

1 She's one of _____ teachers I've had. (good)
2 October is _____ time of year in Zambia. It was 38 degrees the day we left! (hot)
3 Jakarta is one of _____ cities in the world! (big)
4 Moussa is _____ of my children. He's eight years old. Mariam is _____ . She's only four. (old, young)
5 Joanna is great. She's one of _____ and _____ people I know. (nice, friendly)
6 That film was one of _____ things I've ever seen! And it felt like _____ (boring, long)

## Exercise 3

**Complete the conversations with the superlative form of these adjectives.**

| bad | beautiful | cheap | dangerous | expensive | ~~quick~~ |
|-----|-----------|-------|-----------|-----------|-----------|

1 A: What's *the quickest* way to get back to our hotel?
   B: Take the underground. It's only two stops away.
2 A: How was Vienna?
   B: Amazing. It's one of _____ cities I've ever been to.
3 A: How was your journey?
   B: It was terrible – one of _____ flights I've had.
4 A: Is the crime bad there?
   B: Yes. It's one of _____ cities in the world!
5 A: Is it an expensive hotel?
   B: Well, it's not _____ place to stay, but it's not _____ either.

## Exercise 4

**Complete the sentences to make them true for where you live.**

1 One of the oldest buildings is …
   *One of the oldest buildings is the castle.*
2 The tallest building is …
3 One of the best places to eat is …
4 The busiest part is …
5 The most popular place for visitors is …
6 The most interesting thing to do is …

## 12A *SHOULD / SHOULDN'T*

We use *should / shouldn't* + verb to give advice and to make suggestions.
*Should* shows we think it's a good idea to do something.
*She **should stop** smoking.*
*You **should take** a break.*
*They **should talk** to their boss about it.*

*Shouldn't* shows we think it's a bad idea to do something.
*You **shouldn't sit** in the sun for so long.*
*He **shouldn't work** so hard.*
*They **shouldn't** worry about it.*

### DID YOU KNOW?

We often add *maybe* or *perhaps* to make the suggestion or advice sound less strong.
***Maybe** you should look for a new job.*
***Perhaps** we should wait a little longer.*

We can also use *really* to make the suggestion or advice sound stronger.
*You **really** should try to do more exercise.*
*You **really** shouldn't eat so much fast food.*

### Exercise 1

**Complete the sentences with a pronoun (*I, you, she, we,* etc.) + *should / shouldn't*.**

1  A: I feel a bit sick.
   B: Maybe *you should* lie down.
2  A: I've eaten too much! I don't feel so good.
   B: Maybe *you shouldn't* have any more to eat today.
3  A: He says he's really stressed and very tired.
   B: Maybe *he should* take some time off work.
4  A: Hurry up! We're late.
   B: Perhaps *we should* take a taxi.
5  A: The kids are always tired in the morning.
   B: Perhaps *they shouldn't* stay up so late.
6  A: She often says her back hurts a lot.
   B: *she* really *should* go and see a doctor about it.

### Exercise 2

**Complete the sentences with *should* or *shouldn't* and these words.**

| be | cook | do | eat | get | need | spend |
|----|------|----|----|----|----|----|

1  I spend too much money eating out. I really *should cook* more.
2  I think there *should not be* better public transport to stop people driving so much.
3  I really *shouldn't eat* so much fast food. I need to eat more fresh fruit and vegetables.
4  I think the government *should do* more to improve the health service. People *shouldn't need* to wait so long for an appointment.
5  My son *shouldn't spend* so much time on the sofa in front of the TV. He *should get* out of the house and be more active.

### Exercise 3

**Complete the sentences to make them true for you.**

1  I should …
   *I should read more.*
2  I shouldn't … *sleep more*
3  I really should … *Pay some closet*
4  Maybe I should … *call my family*

## 12C *BECAUSE, SO, BEFORE* AND *AFTER*

We use *because, so, before* and *after* to join two parts of a sentence.

*Because*
*Because* shows why something happens. *Because* is followed by a phrase with a verb.
*He was upset **because his boss shouted at him**.*
*I missed lunch **because I wasn't hungry**.*
*I stayed at home last night **because I was tired**.*

*So*
*So* shows the result. *So* is followed by a phrase with a verb.
*The bus was full, **so I couldn't sit and read**.*
*I was tired, **so I stayed at home last night**.*
*I passed my driving test, **so I went out to celebrate**.*
Note that we usually use a comma (,) before *so*.

*Before* and *after*
*Before* and *after* show when something happens.
- *Before* and *after* can be followed by a phrase with a verb.
  ***After the meeting finished**, I went back to my office.*
  ***Before you leave**, close all the windows.*
  *My Dad sold his business **after he stopped working**.*
  *I did some shopping **before I went home**.*

- *Before* and *after* can also be followed by a noun phrase (that has no verb).
  ***After the meeting**, I went back to my office.*
  ***Before work**, I often go for a run.*
  *He started his business **after university**.*
  *I need to finish the report **before the end of the week**.*

### Exercise 1

**Choose the correct option to complete the sentences.**

1  Elena was smiling all day *so / because* she received some good news about work.
2  We got back home *after / before* it started raining, *so / because* we didn't get wet.
3  Sarah felt worried *so / because* she had to talk to the whole class.
4  Simon was really tired *because / after* the long drive from Scotland to London.
5  We missed the last bus, *before / so* we had to get a taxi home.
6  Where did you work *after / before* here?
7  Let's meet *after / before* my meeting. It should be finished at about 3:30.
8  The roads were busy, *because / so* we were late.

### Exercise 2

**Complete the sentences with *because, so, before* or *after*.**

1  I had a headache, _____ I went home early.
2  _____ I had lunch, I felt a bit sick. I think I ate too much.
3  She can't come with us _____ she's hurt her back.
4  Don't forget to come and say goodbye _____ you leave.
5  Our flight was delayed for hours _____ the weather was so bad.
6  They told him he's going to lose his job, _____ he's quite upset.
7  Let's get something to eat _____ the film. It starts at 7:30, _____ let's meet at six.
8  I was quite angry _____ my brother took my house keys. I couldn't get in, _____ I had to wait for him to come back.

## Exercise 3

**Complete the sentences with your own ideas.**

1  I'm tired because …
   *I'm tired because I went to bed late last night.*
2  It's raining, so …
3  I usually … before …
4  I'm going to … after …

## 13 NATURE

### 13A *BE GOING TO* AND *MIGHT*

We use both *be going to* + verb and *might* + verb to talk about the future.

We use *be (not) going to* to show that we are sure about something. We often use it to talk about plans we have.
I**'m going to stay** at home this evening. I**'m going to do** some work.
We**'re going to be** late. The traffic is terrible.
It**'s going to rain** later, so we**'re not going to go** out for a walk.
What **are** you **going to do** about your job? **Are** you **going to look** for a new one?

We use *might (not)* to show that we are not sure about something, but that it is possible.
I **might stay** at home this evening, but I **might go out**. I'm not sure.
I **might be** a bit late. It depends what time my meeting ends.
I think it **might rain** later, so we **might not go out**. Let's wait and see.
**Might** you **come** with us if we go to the beach?

Note that it is possible to use *might* in questions, but we don't often do this.

#### DID YOU KNOW?

We often use these expressions with *might*:

| | | |
|---|---|---|
| possibly | I'm not sure | I haven't decided |
| it depends | I don't know | |

I might go, but **I'm not sure**.
They might come with us, but **they haven't decided**.
We might go to the beach, but **it depends** on the weather.

### Exercise 1

**Choose the correct option to complete the sentences.**

1  She *might* / *'s going to* come with us. It depends if she can get time off work.
2  We *might* / *'re going to* be free at the weekend, but I need to check. I'll let you know.
3  I *might not* / *'m not going to* be able to join you for lunch. Sorry about that, but I have to stay at the office.
4  I *might* / *'m going to* get a new car soon. But I haven't decided.
5  I *might not* / *'m not going to* be able to join you later. It depends when I finish work.
6  We *might* / *'re going to* have a barbecue on Sunday. It's *going to* / *might* be a lovely day. Would you like to come?
7  A: I need to give this book to Dan.
   B: I can give it to him if you like. I *might* / *'m going to* see him later.
8  A: Are you going to the picnic?
   B: I'm not sure. I *might* / *'m going to* go, but I *might* / *'m going to* stay at home instead.

### Exercise 2

**Complete the sentences. Use *might* in one gap and the correct form of *be going to* in the other gap.**

1  The weather forecast says it _____ be very hot tomorrow. They say it _____ even reach 40 degrees.
2  We _____ see that new exhibition tomorrow. In fact, we _____ have an extra ticket if you'd like to go. I'll let you know.
3  I think it _____ rain later, but I'm not sure. But I _____ take a coat and umbrella just in case.
4  It _____ take at least three hours to get there at this time of day. It _____ take a lot longer if the traffic is very bad.
5  I _____ get the job. It depends how many other people also want it. But I _____ do my best, that's for sure.
6  I _____ be able to meet you later, but I'm not sure. I _____ see my parents first, so it depends how long I spend with them.

### Exercise 3

**Complete the sentence with your own ideas.**

1  I might _____ later.
   *I might go for a coffee later.*
2  I'm going to _____ later.
3  It might _____ at the weekend.
4  It's going to _____ tomorrow.
5  I'm not going to _____ .

### 13C PRESENT PERFECT AND *HOW LONG*

We can use the present perfect (*have* + past participle) to talk about or ask about how long from the past up to now.
He**'s lived** in London all his life.
They**'ve been married** for sixty years.

A: How long **has she been** there?
B: For about five years now.

A: How long **have you worked here**?
B: Ten years.

**Time phrases**
To say how long from the past to now, we can use time phrases with *for*:

| | | |
|---|---|---|
| for ten minutes | for six months | for a year |
| for a few weeks | for a long time | for ages |

I've been here **for six years**.
She's work here **for a long time.**

However, we often use these time phrases without *for*.
I've been here **six years**.

We can also use time phrases with *all*:
I've been here **all day**.
She's lived here **all her life**.
I haven't seen him **all week**.
Note that we don't usually use *for* with these phrases.

### Exercise 1

**Complete the sentences using the present perfect form of these verbs.**

| be | not eat | have | know | live | not rain |
|---|---|---|---|---|---|

1  We ~~have had~~ our dog for over ten years.
2  He ~~he's lived~~ in the same house all his life.
3  They ~~I've known~~ each other for a long time.
4  My grandparents ~~have been~~ married for 50 years, I think.
5  I ~~have't eaten~~ meat for over ten years, but I sometimes eat fish.
6  It ~~has n't~~ ~~rined~~ for months. Everywhere is very dry.

## Exercise 2

**Write questions using the present perfect.**

1  A: How long / you / have / your cat?
   B: For about five years.
2  A: you / be / together for a long time?
   B: Quite a long time. Over ten years.
3  A: How long / they / be married?
   B: I think five or six years.
4  A: they / know / each other long?
   B: Just a few months.
5  A: How long / she / work there?
   B: For about ten years, I think.
6  A: How long / he / live / here?
   B: Not long. Just a few months, I think.

## Exercise 3

**Correct the mistake in each sentence.**

1  How long you been here? *have*
2  How long you have lived here?
3  How long have you did that job? *done*
4  She has her dog for five years. *had*
5  I live here for three months now. *have*
6  I don't have had this phone very long. *haven't*

## Exercise 4

**Complete the sentences using the present perfect so they are true for you.**

1  _____ for a few years.
   *We've lived in our apartment for a few years.*
2  _____ for about a year.
3  _____ for over five years.
4  _____ for ages.
5  _____ all my life.

## 14 OPINIONS

## 14B *IT'S* + ADJECTIVE + *TO* + VERB

We can use the pattern *It's* + adjective + *to* + verb to say how we feel about something or to give our opinion about something.

*It's **important to study** hard.*
*I love my new car. **It's great to drive**.*

We form the negative with *It's not* + adjective + *to* + verb.
***It's not easy to find** work here.*
***It's not safe to walk** here at night.*

Note that we can also use *It isn't …*
***It isn't easy to find** work here.*

We form a question with *Is it* + adjective + *to* + verb.
***Is it expensive to live** here?*
***Is it easy to find** that restaurant?*

### DID YOU KNOW?

We can use *really* and *very* to make what we say stronger.
*This car is **really** great to drive.*
*It's **very** expensive to live here.*

## Exercise 1

**Match the first half of the sentences (1–6) with the second half (a–f).**

1  Is it possible
2  It's really great
3  It's strange
4  It's not easy
5  It's normal
6  Is it necessary

a  to meet you at last. I've heard a lot about you.
b  to be nervous before an exam. It's sometimes a good thing.
c  to get there by public transport. It's better to drive.
d  to park here? Or should I park somewhere else?
e  to drive on the left. It takes a lot of focus and concentration.
f  to wear a suit and tie? Or can I wear jeans and a T-shirt?

## Exercise 2

**Complete the conversations with *to* + these verbs.**

| drink | ~~find~~ | leave | meet | park | read | see | understand |
|-------|----------|-------|------|------|------|-----|-----------|

1  A: When I first arrived here, it was difficult *to find* somewhere to live.
   B: Really? Why was that?
2  A: Is it safe _____ the water here?
   B: Yes, it's totally fine. Don't worry.
3  A: It's not easy _____ the car in town.
   B: I know. They should build more car parks.
4  A: Are you ready _____ ? We mustn't be late.
   B: Yes, just give me a couple of minutes.
5  A: It's always interesting _____ the differences between countries.
   B: Yes, I agree. And it's always great _____ people from other countries and cultures.
6  A: I think it's really helpful _____ children's books when you first study a new language.
   B: Me too. They're easier _____ .

## Exercise 3

**Complete the sentences to give some advice about learning a new language.**

1  It's helpful …
   *It's helpful to watch films in that language.*
2  It's useful …
3  It's important …
4  It's not good …

## 14C *WILL / WON'T* FOR PREDICTIONS

We can use *will* + verb to make predictions about what we think is likely or sure in the future. Note that we often use the short form *'ll*.

*I think we**'ll get** there before midnight.*
*You**'ll have** a great time, I'm sure.*
*Don't worry. Everything **will be** fine.*

The negative is *will not*, but we usually use the short form *won't*.
*It's not your kind of book. You **won't like** it.*
*It **won't be** a problem. I'm sure of it.*

We make questions with *will* + subject + verb.
***Will** Oli **be** at the meeting?*
*What time **will** they **arrive**?*
*What **will** the weather **be** like?*

*Think + will*
Because we are making a prediction, we often use *I think / I don't think* with *will*.
*I think he**'ll get** the job.*
*I don't think I**'ll go**. (NOT ~~I think I won't go.~~)*

We often ask questions using *do you think*.
***Do you think** you**'ll see** her soon?*
*Who **do you think will win**?*

*Will + probably*

We often use *probably* with *will* and *won't*. Note that *probably* usually goes after *will* and before *won't*.

*We'll probably go* to Greece this summer.
*She probably won't get* the job.

### Exercise 1

**Choose the correct option to complete the sentences.**

1 They said *there'll be / there be will* snow tonight.
2 What do you think *will they / they will* say?
3 When *will the meeting start / will start the meeting*?
4 She *won't / won't not* be happy about it.
5 I'm sure they *don't will / won't* be late.
6 I don't think *you'll / you won't* pass the exam.
7 I *probably won't / won't probably* see you before then.
8 What *your parents will / will your parents* do about it?

### Exercise 2

**Put the words in the correct order to make predictions or questions.**

1 to take / you / need / I / think / will / a test .
2 offer / think / don't / will / they / me / I / the job .
3 the exam / I / will / think / difficult / be .
4 busy / the restaurant / be / this evening / won't .
5 expensive / do / it / be / you / will / think ?
6 be / doesn't / will / easy / it / think / she .
7 you / think / agree / do / he / will ?
8 they / arrive / won't / 6:30 / before .

### Exercise 3

**Complete the questions with *will* and these verbs.**

| be | go | learn | live |
| --- | --- | --- | --- |

1 Do you think you _____ shopping at the weekend?
2 Do you think you _____ another language after this?
3 Do you think you _____ famous for something one day?
4 Do you think you _____ in a different country one day?

### Exercise 4

**Write your own answers to the questions in Exercise 3. Use these words and phrases.**

| Yes, definitely. | Yes, probably. | Maybe. | Probably not. | No. |
| --- | --- | --- | --- | --- |

## 15 TECHNOLOGY

### 15A *BE THINKING OF*

We use *be thinking of* + *-ing* form of the verb to talk about plans we are not 100% sure about.

*I'm thinking of doing* a web design course next year.
*She's thinking of looking* for a new job.
*We're thinking of getting* a new car.
*We're not thinking of moving* until next year.
*Where are you thinking of going*?

### Exercise 1

**Write full sentences using *be thinking of* and these ideas (1–10).**

1 I / think / join a gym.
2 What model / you / think / buy?
3 They / think / move sometime next year.
4 he / think / leave the company?
5 Who / you / think / ask?
6 they / not / think / change the price.
7 Which university she / think / go to?

8 I / think / get a new computer.
9 Why / he / think / retire? He's only 48.
10 We / not / think / get married yet.

### DID YOU KNOW?

We often use *be thinking of* + *-ing*, and then ask for a recommendation using *Can you recommend …?*

*We're thinking of renting* a place for my son's 18th birthday party. *Can you recommend anywhere?*
*I'm thinking of getting* my car looked at. *Can you recommend a good garage?*

### Exercise 2

**Complete the sentences with *be thinking of* and these verbs.**

| buy | change | ~~do~~ | go | go | visit |
| --- | --- | --- | --- | --- | --- |

1 My brother *is thinking of doing* an English course next year. Can you recommend anywhere?
2 We _____ to the cinema later. Can you recommend anything?
3 I _____ the mobile phone company I use. Can you recommend one? Who do you use?
4 My sister _____ a new car. Something small. Can you recommend anything?
5 We _____ somewhere warm this winter. Can you recommend anywhere?
6 I _____ Cambridge for the weekend. Can you recommend a good hotel that's not too expensive?

### Exercise 3

**Match the questions in Exercise 2 (1–6) with these recommendations (a–f).**

a Well, you could try Dubai. It's always hot at that time of year – and not too expensive.
b I'm not really sure, to be honest. I haven't seen any films for ages!
c Well, I use Blue and they've always been great.
d Well, there are lots of them, but people always say the Old Star hotel is good.
e Well, I spent two years at York House and really enjoyed it. I had great teachers.
f You're asking the wrong person, I'm afraid. I can't drive, so I don't know much about it.

### Exercise 4

**Write three sentences about things you are thinking of doing.**

*I'm thinking of getting a new phone.*

### 15C DESCRIPTIVE ADVERBS

Descriptive adverbs describe the way we do something. We usually form descriptive adverbs by adding *-ly* to the adjective (*slow – slowly, quiet – quietly*, etc.). For adjectives ending in *-y* we remove the *-y* and add *-ily* (*easy – easily, happy – happily*).

*They solved the problem quickly.*
*Can you please leave quietly?*
*I always read slowly.*
*They played badly.*
*The children are playing happily.*

Note that there are some irregular adverbs that are not formed by adding *-ly* to the adjective.

*early – early     fast – fast     good – well     hard – hard     late – late*

*We left early, but we arrived late.*
*He played well.*
*She's working hard.*

## Position

Descriptive adverbs usually go after the verb phrase (verb + noun).

*I read the report* **carefully**. (NOT *I read carefully the report.*)
But they can sometimes go before the verb.
*I* **carefully** *read the report.*

## Modifiers

We can add words like *quite, very* and *really* to descriptive adjectives to describe how much.
*The economy's doing* **quite** *badly.* (= a bit badly)
*I had a problem, but the company solved it* **very / really** *quickly.*
*Things are changing* **really / very** *fast.*

### Exercise 1

**Complete the conversations using the adverb form of these adjectives.**

| bad | early | easy | good | happy | hard | late | quick | ~~slow~~ |
|-----|-------|------|------|-------|------|------|-------|------|

1  A: Can you speak *slowly*, please. I can't understand you.
   B: Oh yes, sorry. So ... what ... I ... said ... was ...
2  A: The bank has a great app. It allows you to see what you are spending really _____ .
   B: Yeah – my bank has one too. I use it all the time.
3  A: How did his exam go?
   B: Oh! Unfortunately, it went really _____ . He's not happy as he did a lot of work for it.
4  A: My son can spend all day quite _____ playing video games.
   B: Mine too.  And he always does his homework really _____ so that he can get back to the game!
5  A: I don't like their website. The search doesn't work very _____ , so it's difficult to find what you want.
   B: Yeah, I know. I stopped using it.
6  A: You look tired.
   B: I am. I went to bed _____ and had to get up _____ . And I'm also working really _____ for my exams at the moment.

### Exercise 2

**Complete the second sentence in each pair with the correct adverb. The two sentences should have the same meaning.**

1  a  They're not very good at organizing things.
   b  They don't organize things very _____ .
2  a  I didn't sleep very well last night.
   b  I slept quite _____ last night.
3  a  The app is a safe place to keep all your passwords.
   b  The app allows you to keep all your passwords _____ in one place.
4  a  He's in his 80s, but he's still a very careful driver.
   b  He's in his 80s, but he still drives very _____ .
5  a  Her instructions weren't clear.
   b  She didn't give the instructions very _____ .
6  a  The app gives you a quick and easy solution.
   b  The app solves the problem _____ and _____ .

### Exercise 3

**Complete the sentences to make them true for you. Use *very, really* or *quite* in your sentences if you want to.**

1  _____ carefully.
   *I always do my homework carefully.*
2  _____ slowly.
3  _____ quickly.
4  _____ well.
5  _____ badly.

## 16B *WILL / WON'T* FOR PROMISES

We often use *will / won't* + verb to make a promise.
*Thanks.* **I'll pay** *you back next week.*
**I'll call** *you when I can.*
**I won't tell** *anyone. Don't worry.*

We can also use *I will / I won't* in short answers.
A: *Call me later.*      B: **I will**.
A: *Don't forget.*      B: **I won't**.

To make the promise stronger, we can add *I promise* or *don't worry*.
A: *Dad, can we go to the cinema today?*
B: *Sorry. I'm too busy.* **I'll take** *you next week,* **I promise**.

**I won't tell** *anyone.* **Don't worry**.

A:  *Call me later.*
B:  **I will**. **I promise**.

### Exercise 1

**Choose the correct option to complete the sentences.**

1  *I'll / I won't* tell anyone. I promise.
2  Sorry about that. *It will / It won't* happen again. I promise.
3  Don't worry. *We'll / We won't* be there on time.
4  *I'll / I won't* bring you back a nice present. I promise.
5  *I'll / I won't* send you the photo when I have time. I promise.
6  A: Have you spoken to the bank yet?
   B: *I'll / I won't* do it as soon as possible.
7  A: I hope you're not going to do that again.
   B: *I will. / I won't.* Don't worry.
8  A: Take care.
   B: *We will. / I won't.*

### Exercise 2

**Write a promise using the words in brackets to follow these requests.**

1  Can I borrow your car? (be careful / don't worry)
   *Can I borrow your car? I'll be careful. Don't worry.*
2  Could I borrow some money? (pay back / next week)
3  Can I borrow your book? (lose / don't worry)
4  Can you wait for us? (be long)
5  Will you excuse me? (be back / few minutes)
6  Can I borrow your jacket? (look after / promise)
7  Could we stay with you? (stay long)
8  Is it OK if some friends come over tonight? (make any noise / promise)

### Exercise 3

**Write short responses. Use *I promise* or *don't worry* in your responses.**

1  Don't be late.
   *I won't. I promise.*
2  Don't forget the book.
3  Call me tomorrow.
4  Let me know when you arrive.
5  You mustn't tell anyone.
6  Remember to book the taxi.

## 16C PAST CONTINUOUS

### Use
We use the past continuous to talk about something in progress at a time in the past.

### Form
We form the past continuous with *was / were* + *-ing* form of the verb.

*I saw you when I **was driving** to work this morning.*
*We **were living** in Scotland when we got married.*
*I **was working** in a restaurant when one night I met my future husband.*

We form the negative with *wasn't / weren't* + *-ing* form of the verb.

*I **wasn't feeling** well this morning, so I stayed at home.*
*We **weren't living** there in 2020. We moved there the year after.*

We form a question with *was / were* + subject + *-ing* form of the verb.

***Was she working** when you called her?*
*Where **were you studying** before?*

### Past continuous and past simple
We often use the past continuous and the past simple in the same sentence. We use the past continuous to show one action was already in progress at the time that a past simple action happened.

*We **were** both **doing** a Spanish course when we **met**.*
*We **were walking** by the river when it **started** raining.*
*I **saw** Greta when **I was shopping** in town.*

### *When* and *so*
To link the two actions together, we often use *when*. *When* can go before the past continuous or before the past simple.

*We were both working in the same office **when** we met.*
*I saw you this morning **when** I was driving to work.*

We also link the ideas using *so*. This is when the second idea is a result of the first idea. *So* goes before the past simple.

*I wasn't feeling very well, **so** I went home and went to bed.*
*She wasn't enjoying it, **so** she decided to stop and do something else.*

### Exercise 1
**Complete the sentences. Use the past continuous and notes in italics.**

1 Sorry I didn't answer your call. *I / talk / to* someone else when you called.
2 We met when *I / work / in* a restaurant. He was a regular customer.
3 *It / not / work / very well*, so I took it back to the shop.
4 *Where / you / live / in 2021?*
5 *They / not / get on / very well*, so they decided to break up.
6 *Who / you / talk to / a few minutes ago?* Is she the new sales director?
7 I wasn't in the office last week. *I / work / from home.*
8 I saw you this morning when *I / drive / to work. You / wait / for the bus outside the park.*

### Exercise 2
**Complete the sentences with the past continuous or past simple form of the verbs in brackets.**

1 We _____ (study) at the same university when we first _____ (meet).
2 I first _____ (see) him when he _____ (work) in a café near my office.
3 It _____ (rain), so they _____ (cancel) the picnic.
4 She _____ (not feel) well, so she _____ (go) home.
5 It was a lovely surprise. Two of my friends _____ (wait) for me when I _____ (arrive) at the airport.
6 Sorry I _____ (not answer) the phone, but I _____ (have) dinner.

### Exercise 3
**What were you doing at these times? Complete the sentences to make them true for you. Use the past continuous.**

1 At 7:30 this morning, I …
  *At 7:30 this morning, I was having breakfast.*
2 At 11:30 last night, I …
3 Ten minutes ago, I …

# Irregular verbs

| Infinitive | Past simple | Past participle |
| --- | --- | --- |
| be | was / were | been |
| become | became | become |
| begin | began | begun |
| bite | bit | bitten |
| blow | blew | blown |
| break | broke | broken |
| bring | brought | brought |
| build | built | built |
| burn | burned / burnt | burned / burnt |
| buy | bought | bought |
| catch | caught | caught |
| choose | chose | chosen |
| come | came | come |
| cost | cost | cost |
| cut | cut | cut |
| do | did | done |
| draw | drew | drawn |
| dream | dreamed / dreamt | dreamed / dreamt |
| drink | drank | drunk |
| drive | drove | driven |
| eat | ate | eaten |
| fall | fell | fallen |
| feed | fed | fed |
| feel | felt | felt |
| fight | fought | fought |
| find | found | found |
| fly | flew | flown |
| forget | forgot | forgotten |
| get | got | got |
| give | gave | given |
| go | went | gone |
| grow | grew | grown |
| have | had | had |
| hear | heard | heard |
| hide | hid | hidden |
| hit | hit | hit |
| hold | held | held |
| hurt | hurt | hurt |
| keep | kept | kept |
| know | knew | known |
| lead | led | led |

| Infinitive | Past simple | Past participle |
| --- | --- | --- |
| learn | learned / learnt | learned / learnt |
| leave | left | left |
| lend | lent | lent |
| lie | lay | lain |
| light | lit | lit |
| lose | lost | lost |
| make | made | made |
| mean | meant | meant |
| meet | met | met |
| pay | paid | paid |
| put | put | put |
| read | read | read |
| ride | rode | ridden |
| ring | rang | rung |
| run | ran | run |
| say | said | said |
| see | saw | seen |
| sell | sold | sold |
| send | sent | sent |
| shake | shook | shaken |
| show | showed | shown |
| shut | shut | shut |
| sing | sang | sung |
| sit | sat | sat |
| sleep | slept | slept |
| speak | spoke | spoken |
| spend | spent | spent |
| stand | stood | stood |
| steal | stole | stolen |
| swim | swam | swum |
| take | took | taken |
| teach | taught | taught |
| tell | told | told |
| think | thought | thought |
| throw | threw | thrown |
| understand | understood | understood |
| wake | woke | woken |
| wear | wore | worn |
| win | won | won |
| write | wrote | written |

taken

# Vocabulary reference

## 1 PEOPLE AND PLACES

### 1A WHERE?

#### COUNTRIES

Australia

Chile

China

Colombia

Germany

Greece

Morocco

Nigeria

Saudi Arabia

South Korea

the UK

the US

*occasionally*

### 1C WORK

#### JOBS

builder

businessman / businesswoman

cleaner

cook / chef

dentist

farmer

hairdresser

receptionist

waiter / waitress

## 2B DAILY ACTIVITIES

### HOBBIES

do puzzles

do some cooking

do some drawing

go climbing

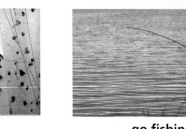

go fishing

go skateboarding

play board games

play cards

play chess

### SPORTS

go skiing

go snowboarding

play baseball

play cricket

play golf

play hockey

play rugby

play table tennis

play volleyball

## 2C IN THE CLASSROOM

### LEARNING IN CLASS

board

desk

dictionary

exam paper

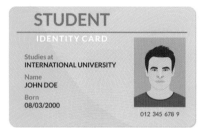
ID card

ruler

## 3 HOME

### 3B HOMES AND FAMILY

### IN THE BEDROOM / LIVING ROOM

armchair

blanket

bookcase

carpet

clock

curtain(s)

drawer

lamp

mirror

## IN THE KITCHEN

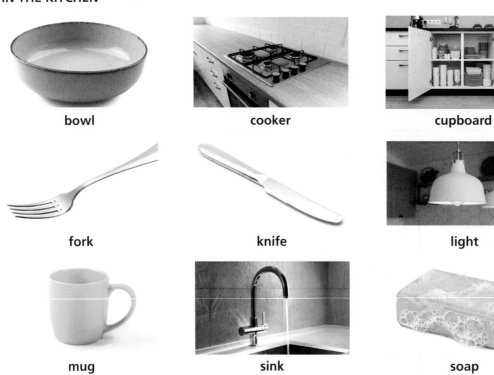

bowl

cooker

cupboard

fork

knife

light

mug

sink

soap

spoon

# 5 SHOPPING

## 5B MONEY AND SHOPPING

### CLOTHES

cap

jumper

(football) kit

pocket

raincoat

scarf

sunglasses

tie

tights

trousers

## THINGS YOU BUY

balloons

(mobile phone) case

comb

diary

kite

model (train)

postcards

snacks

toys

wallet

## 10 FOOD

### 10C FOOD

**FOOD NOUNS**

burger

cereal

grapes

honey

jam

mushrooms

omelette

salt and pepper

sauce

sweets

toast

## FOOD VERBS AND ADJECTIVES

bake

boil

fresh

fry

roast

sweet

## 11 TRAVEL

## 11A TRAVEL AND TICKETS

### GETTING AROUND

boat

coach

passenger

petrol station

(electric) scooter

seat

tram

underground

waiting room

### 12A HEALTH PROBLEMS

**BODY AND HEALTH**

(broken) arm

back

finger

head

heart problems

leg

(hurt your) neck

toe

toothache

## 13 NATURE

### 13C ANIMALS

**ANIMALS**

bear

chicken

duck

elephant

insect

lion

monkey

rabbit

rat

snake

## 14A DESCRIBING FILMS, PLAYS AND MUSICALS

### FILMS AND ENTERTAINMENT

advertisement

cartoon

clown

comic (book)

dinosaurs

king and queen

poster

(cinema) screen

### MUSIC

classical

drums

guitar

hip-hop

jazz

keyboard

piano

violin

# Information files

## FILE 1    UNIT 5

### 5C EXERCISE 12, SPEAKING TASK

**Student A: Customer (and translator)**
Roleplay these three situations with the assistant.

**Situation 1**
Choose what you want to ask about, starting with one of the phrases.

*I'm looking for **(a shop called) Jeffer's**.*

*I want to get some **shoes** / **a camera** / **a new phone**. Where can I go?*

*Is there a **café** / **cake shop** / **Jeffer's** here?*

**Situation 2**
In a shop or café, ask the assistant for some help. Use one or more of these questions.

*Where's …? / Do you have any …?*

*Can I try **these**? / Do you have **a medium size**?*

*Can I have …? / How much …? / What **is that cake** made from?*

**Situation 3**
Pay for the items. Then ask for directions to somewhere else (e.g. the toilets / buses / car park).

*Can I pay for these?*

*Thanks. Sorry. Can you tell me how to get to …?*

## FILE 2    UNIT 6

### 6C EXERCISE 12, SPEAKING TASK

**Student A**

> **CAR REPAIR COURSE   £49**
> Are you looking for a new job? In ten online lessons, this course helps beginners understand cars and do simple repairs. You can study the lessons in your own time at home. There's a test at the end of the course.

> **ART FOR EVERYONE   £499**
> Our art course is for all ages at all levels. It's every Saturday from 9:00–12:00 and lasts for one year. We look at photography, how to draw and much more. Our teachers give you advice on how to get better and you can make new friends who also share your love of art.

## FILE 3    UNIT 10

### 10A EXERCISE 11, CONVERSATION PRACTICE

> **STARTERS**
> Tomato soup
> Greek salad
>
> **MAIN COURSES**
> Vegetarian pizza
> Steak and chips
> Chicken with local vegetables
> Fish with salad
>
> **DESSERTS**
> Ice cream
> Chocolate cake
> Fruit
> Cheese
>
> **DRINKS**
> Wine, Juice, Cola, Water, Tea, Coffee

## FILE 4    UNIT 10

### 10C EXERCISE 4, VOCABULARY

**Student A**

1  Ask your partner what these foods are. Listen to your partner explain. Write the word in your first language. Then, look at your partner's photos and check. Did you have the right word?

almonds   cabbage   coriander   mussels   salmon   strawberry

2  Answer your partner's questions. Use the photos to help you explain what the foods are. Use actions or draw if you need to. Don't let your partner see your photos. Use these phrases to help you.

> *It's a kind of meat / fish / seafood / etc.*
> *It's (a bit like) pasta / rice / a cow / etc.*

*A: What's a carrot?*

*B: It's a kind of vegetable. It's orange and long.*

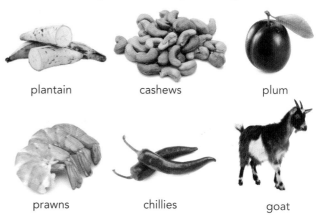

plantain          cashews          plum

prawns          chillies          goat

# FILE 5   UNIT 11

## 11A EXERCISE 13, CONVERSATION PRACTICE

**Student A**

| Trains to Liverpool | Leave | Arrive | Changes | Cost single / return | Platform |
|---|---|---|---|---|---|
| 2h 21m | 9:45 | 12:06 | none | 2nd: £54 / £122.25<br>1st: £151.30 / £251.20 | 7 |
| 2h 55m | 10:00 | 12:55 | 12:08 Chester<br>(wait 9 mins) | 2nd: £49.55 / £122.25<br>1st: £134.20 / £285.50 | 3 |
| 2h 30 | 10:30 | 13:00 | 12:15 Warrington (wait 10 mins)<br>12:31 Newton (wait 18 mins) | 2nd: £61.80 / £122.25<br>1st: £161 / £285.50 | 3 |

You'd like to buy a ticket to Oxford. Ask Student B for information.

- Say where you'd like to go to.
- Discuss the kind of ticket:
  - o Single or return?          o First or second class?
  - o Fast or regular service?    o Direct or with a change?
- Say which ticket(s) you want.

# FILE 6   UNIT 11

## 11B EXERCISE 4, READING

### Shenzen, China

Shenzen in south-east China was the first city with an electric transport **system**. As well as the metro and tram, the government helped to change all 16,000 old buses and 22,000 old taxis. They paid half the cost of the new electric buses and built places to charge batteries. Electricity is cheaper and electric buses cost less to repair. The government also gives the bus companies money to keep prices low. The city is now much less noisy and the **air** is cleaner.

### São Paulo, Brazil

The city has reduced traffic by stopping some drivers using their car for one day a week. The day of the week **depends** on the car number. São Paulo also has the highest number of helicopters in the world. There are some air 'taxi' **services** and one company, Embraer, wants to build new electric helicopters. Another company said that in one year its customers saved 10,000 hours by using its helicopter taxi service.

### Barcelona, Spain

In 2023, the city started to **charge** extra money for some companies to park their vans in the city. The city government hopes it will reduce the number of vans which deliver online shopping and also help local shops which people can walk to. Only companies that earn over €1 million a year from deliveries in the city have to pay this.

### Manchester, UK

Why don't people do more short **journeys** on foot or by bike? Maybe because it's not safe – there aren't enough street lights or places to cross busy roads. Manchester is **creating** 1,600 km of safe paths around the city. These paths are wide enough for parents to push their kids in a double pushchair and for other people to walk next to them. They're also going to improve places to cross the road and create 25 special areas with few or no cars. These areas will have places where people can stop, rest and meet others.

# FILE 7   UNIT 6

## 6C EXERCISE 12, SPEAKING TASK

**Student B**

### LEARN ITALIAN

Italian is a very useful language for anyone interested in travel, food or music. We are a college in the city centre and we have classes at five different levels. Our very popular Beginner-level course is every Thursday evening from 18:00–20:00 – and ten weeks only costs £209.

### YOGA FOR YOU                                      **£15 a week**

Our yoga classes are every Monday evening from 19:00–20:00. Come when you can and pay by the week. Everyone can get better at yoga and we give you homework after every class to help you improve at home. Just practise for fifteen minutes every day, and start to feel happier and stronger!

# FILE 8 UNIT 5

## 5C EXERCISES 11 & 12, SPEAKING TASK

### Student B: Assistant

Use your map of the shopping centre. You need to help the customer(s). You only speak your first language.

**Situation 1:** You're at the information desk. Explain to the customer(s) where to go.

**Situation 2:** You're the assistant in a shop or café / food place. Offer help to the customer(s).

**Situation 3:** You're at the cash desk. Help the customer(s) pay and explain directions.

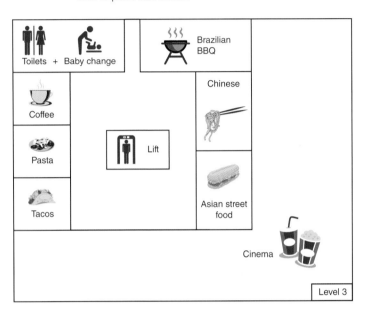

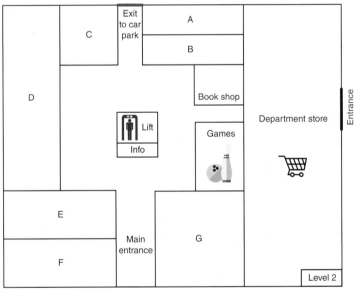

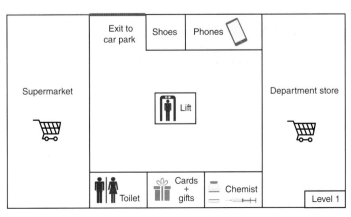

## 11A EXERCISE 13, CONVERSATION PRACTICE

**Student B**

| Trains to Oxford | Leave | Arrive | Changes | Cost single / return | Platform |
|---|---|---|---|---|---|
| 51m | 9:50 | 10:41 | none | 2nd: £30.50 / £63.50<br>1st: £68.20 / £131.70 | 3 |
| 1h 22m | 10:08 | 11:30 | none | 2nd: £9 / £23<br>1st: not available | 6 |
| 1h 3m | 10:35 | 11:38 | 10:59 Reading (wait 15 mins) | 2nd: £30.50 / £63.50<br>1st: £68.20 / £131.70 | 8 |

You'd like to buy a ticket to Liverpool. Ask Student A for information.

- Say where you'd like to go to.
- Discuss the kind of ticket:
  - Single or return?
  - Fast or regular service?
  - First or second class?
  - Direct or with a change?
- Say which ticket(s) you want.

# FILE 10   UNIT 10

## 10C EXERCISE 4, VOCABULARY

**Student B**

1 Answer your partner's questions. Use the photos to help you explain what the foods are. You can use actions or draw. Don't let your partner see your photos. Use these phrases.

> *It's a kind of meat / fish / seafood / etc.*
> *It's (a bit like) pasta / rice / a cow / etc.*

*A: What's a carrot?*

*B: It's a kind of vegetable. It's orange and long.*

| almonds | mussels | cabbage |
|---|---|---|

| strawberry | salmon | coriander |
|---|---|---|

2 Ask your partner what these foods are. Listen to your partner. Write the word in your first language. Then, look at your partner's photos and check. Did you have the right word?

cashews    chilli    goat    plum    plantain    prawns

# Audio scripts

## Lesson 1A, Exercises 6 and 7

**G = Gede, N = Nancy**

G: Let me take your bag.

N: Thank you.

G: My name is Gede.

N: I'm Nancy.

G: Hello Nancy. Welcome to Bali.

N: Good to be here.

G: Is this your first time in Bali?

N: Yeah.

G: Well, welcome! I hope you enjoy it. Are you OK? You're not tired?

N: No, thanks, I'm OK.

G: Where are you from Nancy?

N: The UK, but my parents are from Malaysia.

G: Oh, Malaysia! Where exactly? Kuala Lumpur?

N: No – Kangar. Do you know it?

G: No. Where is that?

N: It's in the north – near Thailand. We still have some family there.

G: But you live in the UK.

N: Yes, I was born there.

G: Where exactly?

N: Near Liverpool. I don't think you know it. It's a little town near the sea called Neston.

G: Living near the sea is good – clean air.

N: Yes, I'm at university in Liverpool now – it's not so good – a lot of traffic.

G: Same here in Denpasar!

N: Really?

G: Very bad.

N: So Gede, are you from Denpasar?

G: No. I live here now, but I'm from the North of Bali – a little place on the coast.

N: Is that part of the island nice?

G: Very nice but quiet. Maybe you want something more … er …

N: No. Quiet is good. My home is quiet.

## Lesson 1C, Exercises 5 & 6

### Conversation 1

A: Hello.

B: Hi. It's Jana, isn't it?

A: Yes.

B: What do you do, Jana?

A: I'm a doctor.

B: Really? Where do you work?

A: In a hospital in Warsaw.

B: Do you enjoy it?

A: I love it. But it's hard work. I work long hours.

### Conversation 2

C: So, Lewis, what do you do?

D: I'm a teacher.

C: Oh, really? Where do you work?

D: In a school in Bristol.

C: Do you enjoy it?

D: Most of the time. Sometimes the children are noisy and I get tired.

C: What do you teach?

D: French.

C: That's good. Sorry, I don't speak French!

### Conversation 3

E: And where are you from, Marta?

F: Colombia.

E: Oh, OK. Where exactly?

F: I was born in Bogotá, but I live in Cali now.

E: I don't know it.

F: Ah. It's a small city.

E: What do you do there?

F: I'm an office worker.

E: OK. Where do you work?

F: For the local government.

E: Do you enjoy it?

F: It's OK. The hours are good – not too long – and I like the other people at work.

### Conversation 4

G: What do you do, Marc?

H: I'm a guide.

G: Where do you work?

H: In a big museum in my city.

G: Interesting! Do you enjoy it?

H: Before yes, but now it's a bit boring. I need to change jobs.

G: Oh? What do you want to do?

H: I don't know … maybe work in a different museum. Or maybe do something very different – be a police officer, maybe!

G: Really? That's what I do!

## Lesson 2A, Exercise 4

A: Do you like doing sports?

B: No, not really. What about you?

A: Yeah, I do. I really enjoy playing tennis and basketball. Do you like walking?

B: No – it's boring. What about you?

A: Yeah, it's OK. I like going to the park. I sometimes walk there.

B: Do you like playing video games?

A: No, not really. How about you?

B: Oh, I love it. It's really good fun. I play every day – a lot! Do you like going to the cinema?

A: Yes, I do. It's great.

B: I love it too. Do you want to see *I Want You Back*?

A: No. I don't like films about love. I like horror films.

B: Oh.

## Lesson 2A, Exercise 10

### Conversation 1

A: Hey, Declan, do you like watching football?

B: Yeah, it's OK. Why?

A: Well, do you want to watch the match on Saturday?

B: Where?

A: In a café in town. It's on TV.

B: OK. What time does it start?

A: Five.

B: So what time do you want to meet?

A: Is four OK? We want to get a place to sit.

B: OK. Where do you want to meet?

A: Outside North Street train station?

B: That sounds good. So four o'clock outside North Street station.

A: Yes, see you there.

### Conversation 2

B: Do you like Italian food?

C: Yeah, I do. I love it.

B: Do you want to meet for lunch on Sunday? There's a really nice Italian restaurant near here.

C: Yeah, that sounds good. What time do you want to meet?

B: Is one OK?

C: Yes, sure. Where?

B: Outside the station?

C: OK, great.

## Lesson 2C, Exercises 5 & 7

**M = Matty, S = Simon, K = Kasia**

**1**

M: OK. Let's take a break! There's a café next door if you want a coffee.

S: Eh? What?

K: It's a break. He says there's a café next door.

S: Oh. OK, thanks.

K: Do you want to have a coffee?

S: Oh … yeah, but I don't have any money.

K: That's OK. I have some.

S: Are you sure?

K: Sure. You can pay another day.

S: OK, thanks. How long is the break?

K: Oh, I don't know. Teacher! Teacher!

M: Yes, Kasia?

K: How much time do we have?

M: Twenty minutes.

K: Twenty. OK. Thanks.

M: Oh, and Kasia – call me Matty, not 'teacher'!

K: Oh. OK! Sorry … Matty.

**2**

K: Er … um, teacher, er, Matty?

M: Yes, Kasia?

K: Do we have any homework?

M: Oh yes. Thanks. I forgot. OK everyone! Look on page 136. The Grammar section. OK? So do Exercise 2 on question forms and then in Revision do all three exercises.

S: All?

M: Yeah. And then try to remember the vocabulary from today's class.

S: This is a lot of homework.

M: Do you think so?

K: No, it's not much homework. I think Simon's lazy!

S: Haha. Yes, maybe a bit.

M: No, I don't think so! Simon, try to do it. Do some every day – five or ten minutes.

S: OK. Maybe.

M: OK, everyone. Thanks. See you next week.

**3**

M: OK everyone, nice to see you again. My name's Matty. Remember? Before we start, stand up everyone and try to remember each other's names.

M: OK. Stop there! Oh, hello Simon.

S: Hi … er, sorry, … I'm late.

M: That's OK. Come in and sit down. There's a place next to Kasia.

S: Er, OK.

M: OK. So everyone. Look at page 63 now. See Exercise 1. What's the answer to number 1? Anyone? Kasia?

K: Close the window.

M: Yes. That's right. OK, everyone – you find the other answers.

S: Teacher! I don't have a pen.

M: Oh, right. Does anyone have a pen? Thanks, Kasia! Oh, and Simon, call me Matty, not 'teacher'.

S: OK. OK. Er … Teacher, what does 'turn off' mean?

M: Um … er … Do you have a dictionary?

S: No. … Oh, Kasia, thanks. And I didn't bring my notebook … sorry. Kasia, do you have any paper?

## UNIT 3

## Lesson 3A, Exercises 6 & 7

### Conversation 1

A: Are you OK?

B: No. I have a headache. I need something for it.

A: Sorry. I don't have anything.

B: Is there a chemist near here?

A: Yes of course. There's one behind here, on 21st Street.

B: OK. Where's that?

A: The next street behind us. Go out of here and turn left. At the end of the road turn left and it's the first left again. There's a small food shop on the corner and the chemist is next to that.

B: OK. Thank you.

### Conversation 2

C: I need to do some exercise. I usually do something every day. Is there a pool or a gym near here?

D: There isn't really anything in this area. You need to go to Newtown – there's a sports centre there.

C: OK, nice. Where's Newtown?

D: Oh, you need to take the bus. There's a stop at the end of the road.

C: OK. What number?

D: Number 15. It's the only bus. Go to the end of the road and turn right. The stop's about 50 metres down the road but on the opposite side. You need to cross the road. The stop is in front of a school.

C: Oh, OK. Thanks.

### Conversation 3

E: Is there a bookshop near here? I forgot my book and I don't have anything to read.

F: No, sorry. But maybe try Jeffer's. It's a department store. I think they sell books – but I'm not sure.

E: OK. Where's that?

F: It's on High Street. It's the main road in the centre of town.

E: OK. Sorry, can you show me on the map?

F: Yes, sure. Look. We're here – and this is High Street. The department store's on the left. It's next to another big shop which is closed now and empty.

E: Great, thanks. I always bring a book on holiday. I hate having nothing to read.

F: Yes, me too.

## Lesson 3C, Exercises 6 & 7

### Conversation 1

A: Hey – you're back.

B: Yeah … Oh man – look at this place …

A: What?

B: It's a mess. You never keep things tidy.

A: Those are dirty clothes. I need to wash them.

B: OK, fine, so … er … so when?

A: What?

B: When are you going to wash them?

A: Later.

B: Really? But can you pick up your things from the floor?

A: Can you wait? I'm on this game.

B: I can't get to my bed without breaking something!

A: Just move everything to my side of the room. I can tidy up later.

B: OK, fine!

A: How was your trip?

B: It was good, but I'm tired.

A: What?

B: I'm tired.

### Conversation 2

C: Is the heating on?

D: Yeah, I turned it on ten minutes ago.

C: It's cold. I think it's broken.

D: Are you sure?

C: Yeah, it's not working.

D: We need to call someone to repair it. We can't stay here without heating.

C: I know. I'm cold now … Can you call?

D: Why me?

C: Your English is better than mine.

D: Really?

C: Yeah – please?

D: Sure.

### Conversation 3

A: What did he say?

B: 'It's not you, it's me.'

A: Oh … and what was that?

B: 'I don't love you anymore.'

A: Can you stop it for a second?

B: Sure.

A: Hey, you two. Can you stop talking? I can't hear the film.

C: It's boring.

D: Yeah. Can't we watch something different?

A: No, it's good!

B: Yeah – I like it.

A: If you don't want to watch it, go somewhere else to talk.

C: What do you want to do?

D: Let's go. We can sit in the kitchen.

## UNIT 4

## Lesson 4A, Exercises 4 & 5

### Conversation 1

A: Hi, Aldona. How are you?

B: OK, but very tired!

A: Oh. What did you do at the weekend?

B: We went to a music festival.

A: Yeah?

B: Yeah, it was fantastic.

A: Really? Who did you see?

B: Oh, lots of people! Um … Emily Dust, Newen Afrobeat. Who else was there? Oh, yes – I saw DJ Format on Saturday night. He was good.

A: That sounds great.

B: Yeah, it was great, but I didn't sleep much!

### Conversation 2

C: Hello.

D: Hi, how are you? Did you have a nice weekend?

C: Yes, it was OK.

D: What did you do?

C: Nothing much, really. I did some shopping on Saturday morning. I played tennis, watched TV – the usual things.

D: That sounds OK.

C: Yeah, I needed to relax.

### Conversation 3

E: Did you have a good weekend?

F: Not really.

E: Oh! That sounds bad. What did you do?

F: Nothing! I was ill. I had a bad cold. I stayed in bed all weekend.

E: Oh no! Are you OK now?

F: Yes, more or less – but I need to work today!

### Conversation 4

G: Imran! Hi! How are you?

H: Good.

G: Did you have a nice weekend?

H: Yes, it was great.

G: What did you do?

H: Well, some friends came to visit, so I showed them round the city.

G: That sounds nice. Where did you go?

H: Well, on Saturday, we went to a museum and then we had a picnic in the park, and in the evening, we went into the old town. Then on Sunday, we went to the market in the morning, and then I cooked lunch for everyone.

G: That sounds great.

H: It was. It was lovely.

## Lesson 4C, Exercises 6 & 7

**A = presenter, P = Pau, H = Hudson, G = Gabi**

A: So first, we have Pau from Barcelona who wants to tell us about a special holiday in the Catalan part of Spain – Sant Joan, or the Day of Saint John. Pau – what did you do on this day last year?

P: Well, the night before the Sant Joan holiday, we made a big fire on the beach with some friends and had a little party. We sat round the fire all night and we ate and sang songs and laughed. We had a great time. Some of my friends swam in the sea for good luck, but I didn't. The sea wasn't very warm. It usually isn't in June. Then on the 24th, I slept until four in the afternoon.

A: That sounds great. Thanks, Pau. Next, we actually have one of our teachers, Hudson, talking about Martin Luther King Jr Day, which is always on the third Monday of January. Hi Hudson. So where were you for this day this year?

H: I was back in the US visiting friends.

A: And did you do anything special?

H: We did! We went away – we went to Snowshoe Mountain in West Virginia. The snow's good in January. We left on the Saturday at three in the morning and drove to the mountains. It was good because there weren't many cars on the road. We got there at eight and spent the whole weekend skiing.

A: Wow! And was the weather OK?

H: Yeah, it was great – very clear and sunny. There wasn't a cloud in the sky. We had great views. We came home on the afternoon of the holiday Monday, but the traffic was terrible. We didn't get back home to Washington until eleven that night.

A: Oh no! But you had a good time anyway. That's what's important. Finally, today, we have Gabi. Now, I know you didn't have a great time on a special day Gabi. What happened? What went wrong?

G: Well, I wasn't in Mexico last November. I was in Toronto for work, so I missed everything because they don't really have this holiday in Canada.

A: Oh no! So what do you usually do on this day?

G: *Día de los Muertos* – or Day of the Dead – is a very old holiday – thousands of years old – and we remember and celebrate the lives of our dead. We usually prepare food and drink and activities that the dead enjoyed in life, and we paint our faces and leave flowers and gifts for them. It's a very happy, beautiful time. I'm sad I missed it.

# UNIT 5

## Lesson 5A, Exercise 6

### Conversation 1

A: Who's next?

B: Me.

A: What would you like?

B: Those things there. What do you call them in English?

A: These?

B: Yes.

A: Peaches. Do you want the yellow or the orange ones?

B: Three yellow ones.

A: Anything else? The oranges are lovely.

B: Can I have some apples?

A: These ones?

B: No, those red ones.

A: How many would you like?

B: Six.

A: OK. Anything else?

B: No, that's it thanks.

A: Do you need a bag?

B: No – can you put them in mine?

A: There you go. That's three pounds ten altogether. Who's next?

### Conversation 2

C: Those look nice.

D: Mmm. That yellow one especially.

C: Hello. Do you speak English?

E: A little.

C: You see the yellow cake? Is it lemon?

E: Yes.

C: How much is that?

E: Three euros for one piece or twenty for the whole cake.

C: Can we have half?

E: OK. That's four pieces, OK? Anything else?

C: And the brown one above it – with the orange on top? What's that?

E: That's coffee cake with orange.

D: The kids don't like coffee.

E: This cheesecake is nice. Or there's carrot cake.

C: We'll have two pieces of the cheesecake.

E: OK. Anything else?

C: No that's it.

E: That's eighteen euros.

### Conversation 3

F: English? Can I help you?

G: Yes. How much are those T-shirts?

F: Depends – seven dollars fifty, ten, fifteen dollars. Which do you like?

G: How much is that green one?

F: This one?

G: No, the other one, there at the top. With 'Türkiye' on it.

F: This one?

G: Yes.

F: Fifteen.

G: Really?

F: For you, two shirts for twenty-five.

G: You have another one like that?

F: Of course.

G: What size?

F: Any size.

G: OK. What about two for twenty dollars?

F: OK. What size do you want?

G: Can I have one in medium and a small one? Thanks.

F: Here you are.

## Lesson 5C, Exercises 6 & 8

### Conversation 1

A: Excuse me. Do you sell batteries?

B: Yes, madam. They're on the shelves by the cash desk.

A: Really? I can't see them. Do you have this kind – it's for a camera.

B: Let's see. I think so. Yes – here you are.

A: Oh, thank you.

B: Anything else?

A: Yes, I'm thinking of buying a new laptop.

B: Of course. I can show you what we have. What are you looking for?

A: I don't know. Something light. Mine is very heavy.

B: Sure. Follow me.

### Conversation 2

C: Are you going down?

D: Yes.

C: Can you move in a bit?

D: Sorry, sure.

C: I can wait for the next one.

D: No, it's OK. There's enough space.

C: Thanks.

D: Where are you going?

C: The car park. Bottom floor, please. Thanks … Wow! That's a big TV!

D: Yes – my son's 21st birthday …

C: Right … oh … Why aren't the doors opening?

D: Did you try …

C: Yes …

D: Oh, no. Can we call anyone? Is there a phone?

### Conversation 3

E: Excuse me. Do you have this in a size twelve?

F: Let's look. Hmm, I can't see any. Wait here and I can check in the back room.

G: Those jackets are nice, too. You could wear them with the dress.

E: Maybe. Are you buying anything?

G: Yeah, I'm getting this top.

E: Yeah – it looks nice on you. I like the colour.

F: Hello madam. I'm afraid that's the only size that's left.

E: That's a shame. Well, can I try these things on?

F: Of course. The changing rooms are at the back, next to the shoes.

E: Oh right. OK. Thanks.

G: I'm going downstairs to pay. I'll wait for you there.

E: OK. Then let's go for a coffee and cake. I need a rest.

**Conversation 4**

H: Hi.

I: Hi, how can I help you?

H: I need a charger for my phone. Where can I get one?

I: Well, there's a phone shop downstairs, and there's a technology shop on this floor. I think they sell chargers.

H: OK. Where is it?

I: Straight down there on the left. Can you see it – there are computers and cameras and things in the front.

H: OK, yes, OK, I see it. Oh, and another thing, is there a café or restaurant here?

I: Yes. There are a few places in the food hall on the top floor.

H: OK – thank you.

## UNIT 6

### Lesson 6A, Exercises 6 & 7

#### Conversation 1

A: So what do you do, Orla?

B: I'm a student.

A: Oh, OK. What are you studying?

B: I'm doing a degree in history.

A: Right. Interesting. And what year are you in?

B: My first. I only started this year.

A: How's the course going?

B: Really well. It's great. I'm really enjoying it. It's very interesting and the other students are very nice and friendly too, so that's good.

#### Conversation 2

C: So what do you do, Tom? Are you working?

D: No, I'm a student at university.

C: Oh, right. What are you studying?

D: Chemistry.

C: Oh, cool. And how's it going?

D: Not very well, actually. I just find it a bit boring.

C: Oh no. That sounds bad. What year are you in?

D: My second.

#### Conversation 3

E: What do you do, José? Are you working?

F: No, I'm not, actually. I'm at the local college.

E: Oh, right. What are you studying?

F: I'm doing an English course.

E: Oh, OK. How's it going?

F: OK, but it's quite difficult. It's a lot of work!

E: When do you finish?

F: I have one more term. Then after that, I have an exam in June.

E: Well, good luck with it. I hope you pass.

F: Thanks. Me too.

### Lesson 6C, Exercises 6 & 8

#### 1 Charlie

I'm doing a great course at the moment. I'm learning to make clothes. It's every Monday and Wednesday evening from 6:30 to 9. It lasts for ten weeks and we get a diploma at the end. It's quite expensive, but it's really good – and very useful. The

teachers help a lot and give us great advice. I was a beginner when I started, but I'm learning a lot and I love seeing what the other students make as well. I want to change my job and hope I can work in fashion, so doing this course is a good start.

#### 2 Ella

We had a special training course at work last week. It wasn't very long – it only lasted for about an hour – but it was awful. The boss told everyone to go, so we all went. I really didn't want to, though. It was about how to improve our emails! I didn't learn anything new. They just repeated things we already knew. It wasn't much fun!

#### 3 Kate

I'm learning to ride. I started taking classes about six months ago and I usually ride once a week – or twice, if I'm not busy. I grew up in the countryside and when I was young, I always wanted to ride and have a horse, but my parents didn't have much money so I didn't have the chance. I'm really enjoying the lessons. My teacher's wonderful and I'm getting quite good now.

#### 4 Chris

I'm doing an online course at the moment – learning how to become a better writer. My wife started it with me, but she stopped. She didn't like it because it's an open course, so she was doing it with thousands of other students. On the course, we watch lots of videos and discuss them. Then we do our own writing. I'm trying to write a book. I'm spending about ten hours a week on it. Another thing I like about the course is there's no exam at the end. I hate taking exams. I always fail.

## UNIT 7

### Lesson 7A, Exercises 7 and 8

#### Conversation 1

A: Do you have any brothers or sisters, Zoe?

B: Yes, I do. I have two brothers.

A: Oh, right. How old are they?

B: My older brother is 28 and my younger one is nineteen. So I'm in the middle.

A: What do they do?

B: Neil – my older brother – is a teacher, and my younger brother, Tim, is in his second year at university.

A: Oh, OK. What's he studying?

B: Chemistry.

#### Conversation 2

C: So, are you married, Ted?

D: Yes, I am – 30 years next year.

C: Wow! Really?

D: Yep.

C: So, what does your wife do?

D: She's a nurse.

C: And do you have any children?

D: Yeah, just one son – Ted Junior. He's finishing college this year.

C: Really? OK. What's he studying?

D: Nursing. He wants to be a nurse like his mom.

#### Conversation 3

E: Did you go out yesterday, Alain?

F: Yeah, I did. I met my cousin and her boyfriend for a coffee.

E: Oh, nice. Are they visiting from France?

F: No, they're not. They're English. They live in Brighton.

E: Oh right – you have family here. I didn't know.

F: Yes. My uncle Julien came to England to study and then he got a job in a company here, and my auntie Ruth was his colleague for a short time.

E: Oh right. So, he never went back to France?

F: No – I mean, for holidays, but not to live.

E: So how old is your cousin?

F: Twenty. She's a year younger than me.

E: Do you have any other cousins here?

F: No, I don't, but I have twelve back in France.

E: Really? How many aunts and uncles do you have?

F: Well just my dad has eight brothers and sisters and my mum has two, and I think seven of them are married, so, what, that's seventeen right?

E: Wow. I only have one uncle and he's single.

## Lesson 7C, Exercises 8 & 10

**1**

My brother and I are a similar size, so he borrows my clothes all the time. Normally it doesn't matter, but yesterday, he wanted to take my leather jacket, and I said no. My mum said it wasn't very kind, but the jacket was new and I saved to buy it. My brother can spend some of his own money!

**2**

Roisin and I met at school. We're like sisters. We grew up together and at university, we shared a flat in Dublin. She now lives in New York. I miss going out with her, but we often chat online. Unfortunately, she has to call me late, because New York is five hours behind Dublin. The last time we talked I didn't sleep till three at night.

**3**

I went out with a guy I met online. He invited me to a restaurant in town. The food was nice and he paid for the dinner, which was very kind. But I'm not sure I want to go out with him again. He thinks he's very funny and laughs a lot, but he says a lot of stupid things and he doesn't really listen to other people.

**4**

My mum and dad bought me Django because I didn't have a brother or sister. And he was a real friend. At home he followed me round the house and sat on my bed while I studied. When I took him for walks, kids often stopped us because he was quite small and funny-looking. He always played nicely with them. He died a few years ago now, but I still miss him.

**5**

Andrea and I are together because we're so similar, but sometimes people don't believe we're partners. For example, if we go to a party, we often chat to different people. Andrea usually dances, but I don't. And we don't hold hands or kiss like some couples do.

## UNIT 8

## Lesson 8A, Exercises 6 & 7

### Conversation 1

A: Hey … um … Kevin … listen, do you want … um … do you have time for a coffee?

B: No, sorry, I don't. I'm going to study in the library and do some reading for my history course.

A: Oh, OK. Well, maybe later?

B: I can't really. I'm not going to have time. I'm just going to go home because I really need to study. I have my exams next week, you know, so …

A: Oh, right. Well, good luck with them. What about after your exams? Do you want to go out somewhere then? Maybe go out for dinner one night?

B: I'm really sorry, but I can't. I … I have to work that night. Bye.

A: But I didn't say which night!

### Conversation 2

C: So what are your plans for today?

D: Oh, I need to book a hotel for next week, and the wi-fi in the hostel isn't very good, so I'm going to find a café and do that – and I have to check the details of my flight as well, so, you know … What about you? What are your plans?

C: I'm going to go running by the river later. I need to do some exercise!

D: That's a good idea! What about tonight? Are you going to be busy then?

C: No. Why? Do you want to meet somewhere?

D: Yeah. Great. Where?

C: How about in the main square at eight?

D: OK. Great.

C: Then I can show you some nice places where there aren't too many tourists.

### Conversation 3

E: Are you going to go to the meeting?

F: No, I'm not. I'm going to meet some new customers and have lunch with them.

E: Oh, right. Where are you going to eat?

F: A new French place in Harajuku.

E: Oh, that sounds good.

F: Yeah. What about you? What are your plans?

E: I've got to go to the meeting and then I need to collect someone from the station, but I'm going to go out somewhere after work. Do you want to come?

F: Yeah. Maybe. Call me later, OK?

E: OK.

F: Great. See you.

## Lesson 8A, Exercise 11

A: What are your plans for later?

B: I don't have any. Why? Do you want to meet somewhere?

A: Yes. Great. Where?

B: How about in the main square, under the big clock?

A: Yes, fine. What time?

B: Is six OK?

A: It's quite early.

B: Oh, sorry. Well, how about seven thirty?

A: Perfect! See you later. Bye.

## Lesson 8C, Exercises 2 & 4

**1**

I'm from Spain, but at the moment, I'm living in Manchester. I'm doing a degree here. I also work part-time and I'm saving money because, after university, I'd really like to go to São Paulo to study Brazilian jiu-jitsu. I can only practise three times a week at the moment, but I'd like to take it to the next level.

**2**

I work for a big design company in Gdańsk, but I'd like to leave and start my own business sometime in the next two or three years. I don't like having a boss. I'd like to work for myself. I'd also like to start a family, have children, but maybe that has to wait!

**3**

I'm going to stop working next year, after 38 years! It's going to be strange, but I'm looking forward to it. I'd like to spend more time gardening. I have a small piece of land and I'd like to grow my own fruit and vegetables. I'd also like to spend more time with my husband and children.

**4**

I'd like to be really famous. I'd like to have my own TV show and I'd like to have lots and lots of money. I'd like someone to drive me round in a big car and I'd like to eat in expensive restaurants – and I'd like everyone in the world to know my name!

# UNIT 9

## Lesson 9A, Exercises 5 & 6

A: Have you been to Istanbul before?
B: No, never. But Harry came here two or three years ago, right?
C: Yeah, but it was for work, so I didn't see much then.
A: Right. So… when did you arrive?
B: Last Friday.
C: Yeah – it was late. And we got up quite late too, so we didn't do that much on Saturday.
A: So where have you been?
B: Well, this morning we went round the Grand Bazaar. That was great. Then we went over to Galata and walked round there.
A: Did you go up the Galata Tower?
C: No. There was a long queue and we didn't want to wait.
A: Really? You get a great view from the top.
C: Yeah, I heard. Another time, maybe.
A: Have you been to Topkapı Palace?
B: Yes, we went there at the weekend. It's amazing, and it's so big!
A: I know. How long did you spend there?
B: All day! We were tired at the end.
C: Yeah, really tired!
A: I'm sure.
B: We also went to the Hagia Sophia.
A: Did you? I've never been in there.
B: But you live here!
A: I know, but sometimes you don't think about visiting places when they're near.
B: That's true. We live in London and I've never been to Buckingham Palace.
A: So, what are you doing later?
C: We'd like to go out for dinner somewhere, but we're not sure where.
A: Well, have you tried the fish here?
B: No, we haven't.
A: Oh, you should! It's very good – very fresh. There's a great place quite near here. I can take you there, if you want.
C: Oh, that sounds great. Thank you.

## Lesson 9C, Exercises 6 & 7

A: Hi there – you're listening to the five o'clock show with me, Andy Jones …
S: … and me Sabera Kapasi. Welcome back!
A: If you're just joining us, we're talking about this amazing story about an unknown woman who saved an old man's life. Bao Lam was out walking along a river near his home when he fell into the water. Bao can't swim, but he was very lucky …
S: A woman with a dog saw Mr Lam fall and she jumped in the river to save him. After she pulled him out, she called an ambulance and it took him to hospital before Mr Lam got her name. Mr Lam is now looking for the woman to give her a large gift of money to say thank you.
A: So, today we'd like to hear about people you want to thank and why. You can call us on 08117722 or email fiveoclock@radio.com.

## Lesson 9C, Exercise 10

S: So, we have our first caller. Mo, tell us your story.
C: Yeah. Last week, I was flying home from Morocco and there was a really bad storm during the flight. I was so afraid.
S: Oh, I hate flying in bad weather.
C: Yeah, I felt really bad, but the lady next to me was so kind and funny. She talked to me and helped me stay calm. So I hope she's listening, and I'd like to say thanks.

A: Thanks, Mo. So Jess. You also have a special person who helped you.
J: Yes. When I was younger my life was very difficult. I was often upset and angry, and I had a lot of problems at school. Anyway, the school had this lovely woman who talked to kids with problems. I went to see her every week for almost a year. I talked to her about everything. She helped me find a better way to live and not get angry and fight. I would like to tell her I'm at university now and that she changed my life.
A: Fantastic. And what's this woman called?
J: Miss Latif.
A: So Miss Latif – if you're listening, good job!
S: We have another caller now. Noah.
N: Yes. Last year I was on the way home from work. It was late and I was really tired and hungry, so I went into a shop to buy something for dinner. I was waiting to pay and I heard the shop assistant say that the card machine wasn't working.
A: Oh no – you didn't have cash?
N: No, and I guess I said something to myself, because the guy in front of me turned and said, 'Don't worry. I'll pay.'
A: Wow. That was kind.
N: Yeah. Anyway, he left very quickly, and I just want to thank him again.
A: OK. So the man with cash, thank you.
S: Great. We're going to take more calls in a moment, but first the news …

# UNIT 10

## Lesson 10A, Exercises 6 & 7

A: Hello. I'm sorry – do you speak English?
B: A little, yes.
A: Great. Can we have a table for two, please?
B: Have you booked?
A: No, I'm afraid we haven't.
B: Ah. We are very busy tonight. Can you wait ten minutes?
A: Yeah, sure.
…
C: Can we see the menu, please?
B: Of course.
C: Ah. You don't have English menus?
B: We don't, I'm sorry. But I can help you. This is chicken, this is fish – but I don't know the name of the fish in English – this is steak, this is soup and this is a bird – I don't know the name – it's similar to a chicken, but smaller. It's very, very good. I recommend this.
C: Oh. I'd like to try that, please.
B: Certainly, madam. And for you, sir?
A: The fish, please.
B: I'm sorry, sir, but the fish is finished. We don't have any more.
A: Oh, right. Well, can I get a steak, please? Well cooked. No blood.
B: As you prefer.
…
B: Can I take your plates?
C: Thank you. That was delicious.
B: Would you like any dessert?
A: No, I'm fine. I can't eat another thing. Can we have the bill, please?
B: Of course. One moment.
B: Here you are.
A: Thanks. Does this include service?
B: Yes, we add fifteen per cent.
C: OK. Thank you.

## Lesson 10C, Exercises 5 & 7

### Conversation 1

A: So where do you want to eat?

B: I don't mind. I eat anything.

A: Yes, me too.

C: Actually. I don't eat meat.

A: Oh, really?

C: Yeah, but if the restaurant has some fish or vegetable dishes, that's OK.

A: Have you been to the place on the corner?

C: No.

B: Me neither. What's it like?

A: It's nice. It's Italian – more or less.

B: OK. That's fine with me.

C: Me too.

### Conversation 2

D: So what are you planning to cook for this big party, then?

E: Is Kevin just going to buy lots of sausages and do a barbecue again?

F: No. No! He's a much better cook than you think, you know. I mean, he likes a good barbecue, sure, but he can do lots of other things too.

D: OK. So ….?

F: Well, we've decided we're going to do Mexican.

D: Oh wow! Save some for me. I'd really like to try that.

E: Oh, I wouldn't.

F: No? Why not?

E: It's too hot. I don't like anything with chillies in.

F: It is hot, but it's amazing. I love it. It's one of my favourite kinds of foods.

D: Mine too.

E: Hmmm.

### Conversation 3

G: What are you going to have?

H: I can't decide.

G: Me neither.

I: Hmm, it all looks delicious. What about the mussels?

G: Oh, I don't like seafood.

I: Really? I do! I love it.

H: Me too. Don't you like any seafood?

G: Not really. I've tried prawns before, but I prefer meat.

H: Oh, OK.

I: Right. I've decided. Talking of prawns, I'm going to have the prawn curry.

H: Hmm. Good choice. I saw Jamie Oliver on TV last night and he made a prawn curry.

I: Oh yeah. I saw that too. Maybe that's why I thought of it!

H: Yeah.

G: OK, I think I'll have the steak.

H: Oh, right. It's so hard to decide! OK. I'm going to have the pasta.

## UNIT 11

## Lesson 11A, Exercises 7 & 8

A Hello. I'm sorry – do you speak English?

B: Of course. How can I help?

A: Hi. We'd like two tickets to Groningen, please.

B: Groningen. No problem. There's one at five to two.

A: Yeah, that's fine.

B: A single or return?

A: Return, but we're not sure when we're coming back.

B: Ah, so it's probably best to buy a single and buy another for the return journey when you've decided.

A: Oh, OK. How much are the single tickets?

B: Second class is 29.40 euros and first class is 49.98.

A: Two second class is fine, thank you.

B: That's 58.80 euros then please. Card or cash?

A: Card.

B: OK. If you can just touch your card here. … No. Try again – just at the top here.

A: Like that?

B: Yep … no, sorry. It hasn't worked. Can you put it in the machine and use your number?

A: Oh right, sure.

B: That's done it. Thank you.

A: Great. What platform does the train leave from?

B: Five. It's the train to Enschede and you change at Amersfoort.

A: Oh, it's not direct?

B: No, there aren't any direct trains from here.

A: I see. How long does it take then?

B: About 2 hours 50 minutes. You have to wait 15 minutes when you change trains at Amersfoort and you'll arrive in Groningen around quarter to five.

A: OK. And it's platform five, yes?

B: Yes, the 13:55 train to Enschede.

A: OK. Thanks for your help.

C: Did you get the tickets OK?

A: Yes, our train's at five to two. What time is it now? Do we have time for a coffee?

C: Yeah – plenty of time. It's quarter past one.

## Lesson 11C, Exercise 4

Hello, everyone. Welcome to our bus tour of Madrid. My name is Miguel and I'm your guide today. On the tour, we'll see some of Madrid's most famous places and I'll tell you about the history of this great city. If you have any questions on the way, please ask me. Our tour today will take about 90 minutes – depending on traffic. We'll sometimes stop and get off the bus for photos. OK … is everyone comfortable? Are we ready? OK. Let's start.

## Lesson 11C, Exercises 6 & 7

### Conversation 1

M: So today we're starting the tour outside the Prado Museum. It's Spain's most important museum. The collection has 7,600 paintings and includes our greatest artists. The main building was designed in 1785 to be a science museum, but later the new king and queen decided to use it for art instead. They opened the art museum in 1819. … Sorry, you have a question?

A: Yes. How much does it cost to go in?

M: Fifteen euros, but there are discounts for students and young people.

A: Oh – I think I'm too old!

M: Don't worry. Entrance is also free after 6 p.m. Monday to Friday. It closes at 8 so you won't have time to see all the paintings, but I think you can see enough. Has anyone been there?

B: Yes – fantastic! I loved it. Fifteen euros is cheap.

### Conversation 2

M: OK …We're now driving through an area called Barrio de Salamanca. There are 21 areas in Madrid and this is one of the richest. A flat here often costs over a million euros. We're going to stop here a moment. Over there is Madrid's biggest indoor stadium. They hold big concerts there as well as basketball and handball matches. There's been … Yes?

B: What basketball team plays here?

M: It's the home of two teams – Real Madrid and my team Estudiantes. They've also had the World Cup of Basketball here.

B: Did Spain win?

M: Not that year unfortunately, but Spain has won it twice! … Anyway, there have been three stadiums here in the last 150 years. The first was a bullring. Then the second was an indoor arena like this one, but in 2001 there was a big fire that destroyed that stadium. This one opened in 2005.

### Conversation 3

M: OK, this is the last stop before we return to the Prado Museum. We're going to get off and enter the Plaza Mayor or main square. It's perhaps the loveliest square in Madrid. OK, follow me … the building on the north side is the oldest – it's from the 16th century and is called Casa de la Panadería … do you know what a *panadería* is?

C: It looks like a hotel.

M: *Pan* means bread.

C: A bakery?

M: Yes … it was a bread shop!

C: What? The whole building? That's a lot of bread!

M: Well, no. Just the ground floor was the bakery.

C: What's there now?

M: It's a tourist office. Now, if you look at the paintings on the outside …

## UNIT 12

### Lesson 12A, Exercises 6 & 8

#### Conversation 1

A: Are you OK?

B: Yeah, I'm OK. I just have a bit of a stomach ache.

A: Maybe you should lie down.

B: No, it's OK. I think I'm just hungry.

A: Are you sure?

B: Yeah. Really. I'll be fine after I have something to eat.

#### Conversation 2

C: What's the matter?

D: I slept badly last night and woke up with a terrible headache.

C: Oh no. Maybe you should phone your boss and take the day off.

D: No, it's OK. I just need to turn the lights off for a bit and maybe put some ice on my head.

C: Are you sure?

D: Yeah, really, I'll be fine. It's nothing serious.

#### Conversation 3

E: Are you OK?

F: No, I feel a bit sick.

E: Maybe you should go out and get some fresh air.

F: Yes, I think I will. I'll be back in a moment.

E: OK. Take your time. There's no need to hurry.

#### Conversation 4

G: Are you OK?

H: Yeah, yeah. I'm alright. Thank you.

G: Have you been to the doctor?

H: No. It's just a cold.

G: Are you sure? That doesn't sound good. I really think you should see someone. Maybe you need some medicine.

H: Really, it'll be fine in a couple of days.

#### Conversation 5

I: Are you alright?

J: Yeah, I'm fine. My knee just hurts a bit, that's all.

I: Maybe you shouldn't play tennis, then.

J: It's OK. I told Fabio I'm going to.

I: Yeah, but are you sure you can play?

J: Yeah, I'll be fine when I start.

### Lesson 12C, Exercises 6 & 7

I heard a story on the news this morning about the happiest countries in the world. What surprised me about the United Nations research is that my husband's country – Finland – came first – and has done for six years now. It's funny because the Finns' neighbours in Norway and Sweden think of them as quiet and a bit boring!

One interesting thing about the research is that it shows money isn't the only thing you need for a happy life. For example, Singapore is one of the richest countries in the world, but is 25th on the list – behind Costa Rica, which isn't even one of the 50 richest countries.

In one of his books, Professor Daniel Kahneman found this was also true not just for countries, but for people. He asked some women in Texas, US, to write down how they felt at different times in their day – and most of them were happy most of the time – those with a lot of money and those with less! The thing that made them happiest was spending time with friends and family. They enjoyed this more than looking after their children! They hated travelling to and from work.

I wanted to test this idea, so I decided to start recording what I do at different times of the day and then listening later to see how I feel when I'm doing different things. Here's what I did yesterday.

### Lesson 12C, Exercises 9 & 10

1 I got the bus to work. I was lucky because I got a seat. I sat and read my book. It was quite a nice journey.

2 When I got to work, we had a meeting. The boss was quite angry. She shouted a bit and told us we need to work harder. It was really horrible.

3 After the meeting finished, I sat and thought about everything I had to do. I got a headache. I sent a few emails and tried not to think about anything else.

4 I had lunch with my aunt. She lives near my office. She always makes me smile. I felt better after seeing her.

5 After lunch, I met some customers. It was a successful afternoon. I sold a few things, and it's always nice to meet people.

6 Back in the office, I had to answer about 30 emails. It was slow and not very interesting.

7 After work, I had to wait for the bus for half an hour and then when it came, it was full, so I couldn't sit and read.

8 When I got home, I went for a run with my friend, Viv. We're going to go on holiday together, so we talked about that. It was a lovely warm evening.

9 After dinner, I watched the news on TV. I wanted to watch a film as well, but I fell asleep on the sofa.

## UNIT 13

### Lesson 13A, Exercises 5 & 6

#### Conversation 1

A: What do you want to do tomorrow?

B: I don't know. What's the weather going to be like?

A: Better. It's not going to be so hot. They said it might fall to 30 degrees or less.

B: Really? Why don't we go to the swimming pool then?

A: We could do. Which one?

B: The one in the sports centre. The café there does a nice lunch which is quite cheap.

A: OK. Let's do that.

## Conversation 2

C: What do you want to do today?

D: I don't know. What's the weather going to be like? It looks a bit cloudy.

C: It said it might rain this morning, but it's going to be dry this afternoon.

D: OK. Well, why don't we relax this morning and then go for a walk this afternoon?

C: Could do. Where?

D: How about taking the car and going to the hills?

C: OK. Let's do that. We haven't been there recently.

## Conversation 3

E: Do you want to go away at the weekend?

F: I'm not sure. What's the weather going to be like?

E: I think it's going to be cold. They said it might snow.

F: Really? Why don't we just stay here? I don't want to drive if there's ice on the roads.

E: That's true. We should go shopping one day, though – we need to get some presents for the kids.

F: I guess so. When exactly?

E: Early on Saturday morning. We can take the train.

F: Can we be back before the football starts?

E: Maybe. What time?

F: It starts at three.

E: I guess – if we go early.

F: OK. Let's do that. We have to do it sometime.

## Lesson 13C, Exercises 6 & 7

### Conversation 1

A: Hey, did I tell you? I have foxes in my garden.

B: Really? Living there?

A: I think so, yes. I see them quite a lot, anyway.

B: Wow! So how long have they been there?

A: For a few months, I guess.

B: And are they OK? I mean, do they cause problems?

A: Not really, no. Well, sometimes they use the garden as a toilet … but I love having them there and watching them play.

B: Have they ever tried to come inside?

A: Once, yes. They stole one of my shoes, actually! I found it outside the next day – half-eaten.

B: Oh!

A: I haven't had any problems recently, though, because I have a cat now and I think they're a bit scared of her!

### Conversation 2

C: Look. This one's a photo of my dog. Here.

D: He's huge!

C: I know. He weighs 51 kilos.

D: Really? That's amazing. What's his name?

C: He's called Sheriff.

D: And how long have you had him?

C: Five years. I got him when we moved out of the city. We have more space now, so …

D: Mmm.

C: He's very friendly. He always jumps on you when you come home.

D: Woah! Scary!

C: No, it's fine. And he's very funny too. I mean, he plays very well with our cat, Kira. He follows her and she runs around, but they've never had any fights or anything.

### Conversation 3

E: What's that noise?

F: That? Oh, we have rats in the house. Didn't I tell you?

E: No. How annoying! How long have you had them?

F: Well, we've been here a year now and they've been here the whole time.

E: Ugh!

F: I know. They eat our food and I worry they'll bite the kids one day.

E: So what are you going to do?

F: Well, we've tried all kinds of things already, but nothing has worked, so I think we need to pay someone to come in and do something about them.

## Lesson 13C, Exercise 11

**1**

A: I have a dog.

B: How long have you had it?

A: Two years.

**2**

B: My mum works for a bank in the city.

A: How long has she worked there?

B: I don't know – a long time.

**3**

A: I heard they're going to get married.

B: Really? How long have they been together?

A: Not long. A few months.

**4**

B: We're having a party for our wedding anniversary.

A: Nice. How long have you been married?

B: Five years.

**5**

A: I'm going to visit my brother in Hong Kong.

B: That's cool. How long has he lived there?

A: Not long. About a year.

**6**

B: Who's that in the photo?

A: Oh that's my best friend, Clover.

B: Nice. How long have you known her?

A: All my life! Her dad and my dad were friends.

## UNIT 14

## Lesson 14A, Exercises 6 & 7

### Conversation 1

A: Have you ever seen a film called *The Lighthouse*?

B: No, I haven't. I've heard of it, but I've never seen it. What's it like?

A: It's brilliant. It's got one of my favourite actors, Robert Pattinson, in …

B: Oh, I know him.

A: But it's <u>very</u> strange. And for some scenes, I had to cover my eyes.

B: Yeah? It sounds terrible.

A: No. Really. It's great! It's a very clever film too. It's not all blood and killing or anything. The two main guys live away from other people, by the sea, and there's a lot about their relationship and … well, I don't want to tell you too much.

B: Don't worry. It's definitely not for me!

A: No, it's really good! Honestly!

### Conversation 2

C: Have you seen the musical *Hamilton* yet?

D: Yes, I have. I saw it last week, actually.

C: Oh really? We went to see it last night. What did you think of it?

D: It was OK. Nothing special. I enjoyed some scenes, but I just didn't think the writing was very good.

C: No? Oh, I thought the whole thing was brilliant – one of the best things I've seen in a long time.

D: Yeah? OK.

C: It had such energy. The dancing and the music were great – and I loved the way they used the stage. It was very funny too. I couldn't stop laughing!

D: What about the way it ended? I thought it was too much!

C: Not for me! I started crying it was so sad!

D: Really? Oh well. I guess we just like different kinds of things, then.

## Lesson 14C, Exercises 2 & 3

**1**

Tomorrow, people across the country will choose a new government – and at the moment, it's very hard to say what the result will be. The two main parties both say they hope to win, but most people think that they will probably have to work together and share power. We'll know the final results early on Monday morning.

**2**

One of the largest companies in the country has said that it is going to cut 5,000 jobs. The company lost 385 million dollars last year and now plans to close its two biggest factories in the north of the country.

**3**

Abroad, talks between the United Kingdom and the European Union are continuing. The two sides still can't agree on how to do business together or on how people can move between the different countries, but both say they still hope the talks will end well.

**4**

Next, music – and some news that has surprised many people. The winner of last year's TV Idol show – Myleene – is planning to get married – to her boyfriend of two months, who she met while they were both working on a new TV show.

**5**

And finally, the national Women's Team go into their important World Cup match tonight without one of their star players, Williams, who hurt herself in the gym yesterday. It's now possible that she won't play in the next two or three games.

## Lesson 14C, Exercise 5

**a**

This'll be terrible for the whole area. It'll be really bad because lots of people will have to move to find work.

**b**

It won't last. I don't think they'll be together by the end of the year.

**c**

I don't think the situation will get worse. They both have too much to lose. I'm sure they'll solve the problems they're having.

**d**

This loss won't change anything. They'll still have a very strong team tonight.

**e**

It'll be better if there's no clear winner. It'll mean they all have to talk to each other and solve problems together!

# UNIT 15

## Lesson 15A, Exercise 4

**1**

wiring.co.uk
That's wiring W-I-R-I-N-G dot co dot U-K.

**2**

teddybod98@cmail.ge
That's T-E-double D-Y-B-O-D 9-8 at cmail, C-M-A-I-L dot G-E.

**3**

The password is Bobscafe1.
*Bobscafe* is all one word with a capital B at the start and the rest in small letters, so capital B, then O-B-S-C-A-F-E, and then 1 at the end.

## Lesson 15A, Exercises 6 & 7

### Conversation 1

A: I like your phone.

B: Yeah, it's nice isn't it. I actually bought it used.

A: Really? It doesn't look used.

B: I know. It's quite a recent model, but it's so much cheaper than getting something new.

A: Right. Actually, I'm thinking of getting another phone because I dropped mine and broke the screen – so maybe I should get a used one.

B: Yeah, you should.

A: But what if it doesn't work or it breaks? Do you get your money back?

B: Yeah, yeah, I think anytime in the first year or eighteen months.

A: OK. That's good. So can you recommend anywhere good?

B: Well, I bought this from a shop near my house, but there's a website called usedtech.co.eu, which is good. I bought a laptop from there and I'm really happy with it. It's really light, lots of memory and I haven't had any problems … so …

A: Right – so what's the website again – usedtech? Is that C-H at the end?

B: Yeah, used U-S-E-D tech T-E-C-H dot co dot E-U. I'll send you a text with the link, if you like.

A: Oh great. Thanks.

### Conversation 2

C: You have an electric bike, don't you?

D: Yeah, why?

C: I'm thinking of getting one but they're quite expensive. Are you happy with yours?

D: Yeah, I love it, but I guess it depends how much you're going to use it.

C: Well, I recently got a new job …

D: Oh, congratulations!

C: Thanks, yeah – and anyway, the job isn't too far away, but I have to take two buses, so I'm thinking of cycling. But there's also a big hill on the way.

D: Yeah, well electric bikes are great for going up hills.

C: So how did you choose yours?

D: I actually have a friend who sells them. You should talk to him. He let me borrow one to try before I bought mine.

C: That would be great. Have you got a number or email?

D: Yeah, email might be best … let me see. Yeah, it's jmorgan@terri33.com.

C: OK, wait a second. Again?

D: jmorgan – that's all one word.

C: J-M-O-R-G-A-N.

D: Yep, @terri33.com, so T-E-double R-I-3-3 dot com.

C: Is that it?

D: Yeah, that's it. I'll let him know that you might contact him. He's a lovely guy.

C: Thanks.

## Lesson 15C, Exercises 6 & 7

**1**

Well, a phone – obviously. Then I nearly always wear headphones, because I love listening to music. And I also wear a smart watch, so that's three almost always with me. Then, if I'm going to university, I often take a laptop. And I have a card to pay for things – I guess that is a kind of technology. I mean I never pay in cash for anything these days.

**2**

At work, we still use it a lot. They have tried to reduce how many people send, but I recently had two weeks' holiday and when I got back to the office, I had 300 waiting for me in my inbox. But with friends and family, I usually just use an app for messages. I have a younger brother and I've stopped sending him emails because he doesn't check his account for days, or even weeks.

**3**

The short answer is too much. I actually realized how much I looked at it when I went camping with some friends a few weeks ago. There was no connection where we were, and I immediately felt strange about not being able to check my social media. But then, after a few days, we all realized we were talking more and it felt good being without our phones. When I got back, I wanted to continue, but it's actually really difficult. You can't change your behaviour easily.

**4**

This is actually terrible because I work in a tech company and I know I shouldn't open files when you don't know where they're from. Anyway, a friend sent me a text with a file and the message 'this is great'. I clicked on the link without thinking and I immediately realized it was a mistake. The phone suddenly started deleting all my messages and I couldn't do anything about it. So stupid!

# UNIT 16

## Lesson 16A, Exercises 7 and 8

**Conversation 1**

A: Did I tell you Owen's going to get married?

B: No. Really? Wow! I didn't even know he had a girlfriend! How long have they been together?

A: Two or three months, I think.

B: That's not long! What's she like?

A: She's really nice – and very clever! She's a computer engineer.

B: Oh, that's great. I'm pleased for him. Say 'congratulations' from me.

A: I will.

B: So, where are they going to live?

**Conversation 2**

C: Hey, did I tell you that my brother's wife is pregnant?

D: No. Wow! So you're going to be an uncle.

C: Yep. I'm quite excited.

D: Do they have a date yet?

C: The doctors said sometime in May.

D: OK. And do they know if it's a boy or a girl?

C: No. They said they want it to be a surprise.

**Conversation 3**

E: Did I tell you Imke and Thorsten have broken up?

F: No! Why's that?

E: I think she wanted kids, but he didn't – and they argued about it a lot.

F: Oh, that's sad! How long were they together?

E: Not that long. Four years, I think.

F: What a shame! They made such a lovely couple.

E: I know. I hope we can stay friends with them both.

**Conversation 4**

G: Did I tell you that I had a date on Friday?

H: No. Who with?

G: A guy from my French class.

H: So what's he like?

G: He seems very nice. He's quite quiet, but he's funny.

H: Is he good-looking?

G: I think so, yeah. He has lovely eyes.

H: OK. So what did you do? Something romantic?

G: Not really, no. We had a drink together and then we met some of his friends for karaoke.

## Lesson 16C, Exercises 3 & 5

**1**

My wife and I spent two years looking for the right place to live. We weren't looking very hard for the first year and a half, but then she got pregnant and we had to find somewhere fast. We saw five houses every weekend for six months, but didn't like any of them. One day, we were driving home from another appointment when we saw it – the house of our dreams! And, amazingly, it was for sale. We knocked at the door and the people that lived there let us look around. It was everything we wanted! We offered the price they were asking for it and moved in soon after that.

**2**

When I was a kid, I always loved music and musical instruments. For my twelfth birthday, my uncle gave me a guitar – and it was love at first sight. My uncle was a really important person for me then. He was playing in a band at the time and I went to see them one night. That had a big effect on me. After that, the guitar became the centre of my world. I played it 24 hours a day, seven days a week. Later, I studied music at university and now I have a job making guitars. All because of that special day!

**3**

I play online games a lot and love thinking of new characters. You design them, choose their names and the way they look and then make lives for them. Last year, I was in a relationship, but things weren't going very well. We were arguing all the time, so I started spending more and more time online. One night, I was playing one of my favourite games when I met my future husband. He was new to the game and looked lost, so I decided to help him. His name in the game was Nyxon and with his cat ears, blue skin and big eyes, he looked great. It was love at first sight. Nyxon soon asked my character to marry him and I said yes. We were married online in July. It was very romantic. He then asked me in the real world and I agreed. We haven't actually met yet, but I know that he's the one for me.

**NATIONAL GEOGRAPHIC LEARNING**

National Geographic Learning,
a Cengage Company

*Outcomes Elementary Student's Book,*
**3rd Edition**
**Hugh Dellar and Andrew Walkley**

Publisher: Rachael Gibbon

Managing Development Editor: Delia Kidd

Content Editors: Alison Sharpe and Nicole Elliott

Director of Global Marketing: Ian Martin

Senior Product Marketing Manager: Caitlin Thomas

Heads of Regional Marketing:

   Charlotte Ellis (Europe, Middle East and Africa)

   Justin Kaley (Asia and Greater China)

   Irina Pereyra (Latin America)

   Joy MacFarland (US and Canada)

Senior Production Manager: Daisy Sosa

Content Project Manager: Ruth Moore

Media Researcher: Jeff Millies

Operations Support:  Hayley Chwazik-Gee

Senior Designer: Heather Marshall

Senior Media Producer: Monica Writz

Art Director (Video): Macy Lawrence

Inventory Manager: Julie Chambers

Manufacturing Planner: Eyvett Davis

Composition: MPS North America LLC

Audio Producer: Tom Dick & Debbie Productions Ltd

Contributing Writer: Jon Hird (Endmatter)

For permission to use material from this text or product,
submit all requests online at **cengage.com/permissions**
Further permissions questions can be emailed to
**permissionrequest@cengage.com**

Outcomes Elementary Student's Book, 3e
ISBN: 978-0-357-91717-6

Outcomes Elementary Student's Book with
the Spark platform, 3e
ISBN: 978-0-357-91716-9

**National Geographic Learning**
Cheriton House, North Way,
Andover, Hampshire, SP10 5BE
United Kingdom

Locate your local office at **international.cengage.com/region**

Visit National Geographic Learning online at **ELTNGL.com**
Visit our corporate website at **www.cengage.com**

Printed in Greece by Bakis SA
Print Number: 01  Print Year: 2024

FSC
www.fsc.org
MIX
Paper | Supporting
responsible forestry
FSC™ C169932

# Credits

**Illustrations:** All illustrations are owned by © Cengage.

**Photography:**

**Cover** © Xaume Olleros

**2** (tl1) Matthew Williams-Ellis Travel Photography/Alamy Stock Photo, (tl2) Yusufozluk/iStock/Getty Images, (tl3) Alberto Bernasconi/Laif/Redux, (cl1) Marcelo Nacinovic/Moment/Getty Images, (cl2) Danny Lehman/The Image Bank/Getty Images, (bl1) © Annie Griffiths/Life as Lived, (bl2) Tang Ming Tung/Stone/Getty Images, (bl3) 10'000 Hours/DigitalVision/Getty Images; **4** (tl1) Glenn Bemont/Alamy Stock Photo, (tl2) Brostock/iStock/Getty Images, (tl3) Umomos/Shutterstock.com, (cl1) Stephen Chung/Alamy Stock Photo, (cl2) Joel Sartore/National Geographic Image Collection, (bl1) Dpa Picture Alliance/Alamy Stock Photo, (bl2) Directphoto Collection/Alamy Stock Photo, (bl3) Simonkr/E+/Getty Images; **6–7** (spread) Matthew Williams-Ellis Travel Photography/Alamy Stock Photo; **8** (cl) Viktollio/Shutterstock.com, (c) Matulee/Shutterstock.com, (cr) DianeBentleyRaymond/Getty Images, (bl1) Max shen/Moment/Getty Images, (bl2) Billion Photos/Shutterstock.com, (bc1) Felix Mizioznikov/Shutterstock.com, (bc2) Ekaterina Pokrovsky/Shutterstock.com, (br1) Dmytro Sidashev/Alamy Stock Photo, (br2) James Kirkikis/Alamy Stock Photo; **11** (tl) Christa Stroo photography/Alamy Stock Photo, (tr) NaughtyNut/Shutterstock.com, (bl) David Kleyn/Alamy Stock Photo, (br) cbfly/Getty Images; **12** Graham Prentice/Alamy stock photo; **13** Agencja Fotograficzna Caro/Alamy Stock Photo; **14–15** (spread) Yusufozluk/iStock/Getty Images; **17** Nick David/Stone/Getty Images; **19** Canbedone/Alamy Stock Photo; **21** Ammentorp Photography/Alamy Stock Photo; **22** (br1) Catarina Belova/Shutterstock.com, (br2) Sdstockphoto/iStock/Getty Images; **23** (bl1) SFL Travel/Alamy Stock Photo, (bl2) Wirestock Creators/Shutterstock.com, (bc1) V. Matthiesen/Shutterstock.com, (bc2) VDWI Automotive/Alamy Stock Photo, (br1) Irina Kvyatkovskaya/Shutterstock.com, (br2) Emme Celera/Shutterstock.com; **24** © Cengage; **26–27** (spread) Alberto Bernasconi/Laif/Redux; **31** Mohamed Abdelrazek/Alamy Stock Photo; **34–35** (spread) Marcelo Nacinovic/Moment/Getty Images; **36–37** (spread) PA Images/Alamy Stock Photo; **39** (tl) Tim Graham/Alamy Stock Photo, (cl1) GeoStock/Oxford Scientific/Getty Images, (cl2) Design Pics Inc/Alamy Stock Photo, (b) Ion Mes/Alamy Stock Photo; **40–41** (spread) Sundry Photography/Alamy Stock Photo; **42** Jose Luis Stephens/Alamy Stock Photo; **43** (tl) Krakenimages.com/Shutterstock.com, (cl) Steven690/Shutterstock.com; **44** © Cengage; **46–47** (spread) Danny Lehman/The Image Bank/Getty Images; **48** Helen King/The Image Bank/Getty Images; **49** (bl1) Westend61/Getty Images, (bl2) Sergiy Tryapitsyn/Alamy Stock Photo, (bc1) Hero Images Inc./Alamy Stock Photo, (bc2) Alvarez/E+/Getty Images; **51** PA Images/Alamy Stock Photo; **52** Dukas Presseagentur GmbH/Prisma/Alamy Stock Photo; **54–55** (spread) © Annie Griffiths/Life as Lived; **56** © Chris Frezza/Cengage; **59** John Giustina/The Image Bank/Getty Images; **60** (bl) Vladimir Vladimirov/E+/Getty Images, (br) Luis Alvarez/DigitalVision/Getty Images; **61** (bl) Monty Rakusen/Cultura/DigitalVision/Getty Images, (br) Manfred Grebler/Alamy Stock Photo; **63** Viacheslav Nikolaenko/Shutterstock.com; **64** © Cengage; **66–67** (spread) Tang Ming Tung/Stone/Getty Images; **68** © Aaron Huey/National Geographic Image Collection; **71** FatCamera/E+/Getty Images; **73** Hero Images Inc./Alamy Stock Photo; **74–75** (spread) 10'000 Hours/DigitalVision/Getty Images; **76** FilippoBacci/E+/Getty Images; **79** © Chris Hill/National Geographic Image Collection; **80** (tl) Tom Merton/OJO Images/Getty Images, (tr) Pekic/E+/Getty Images, (cl) Yuko Yamada/Moment/Getty Images, (cr) Miljko/E+/Getty Images; **83** Caia Image/Collection Mix: Subjects/Getty Images; **84** © Cengage; **86–87** (spread) Glenn Bemont/Alamy Stock Photo; **89** Ugurhan/E+/Getty Images; **91** Media Drum World/Alamy Stock Photo; **92** FG Trade/E+/Getty Images; **94–95** (spread) Brostock/iStock/Getty Images; **96–97** (spread) Cathyrose Melloan/Alamy Stock Photo; **99** (t) Miemo Penttinen - miemo.net/Moment/Getty Images, (cr) Fabrice Coffrini/AFP/Getty Images; **100** (cl) Edmund Lowe Photography/Moment/Getty Images, (c) Cavan Images/Getty Images, (cr) Oleksandra Naumenko/Shutterstock.com, (bl1) Jeffrey Isaac Greenberg 16+/Alamy Stock Photo, (bl2) New Africa/Shutterstock.com, (bc1) Epsylon_lyrae/Shutterstock.com, (bc2) Bella Falk/Alamy Stock Photo, (br) Wulingyun/Moment/Getty Images; **102** AleksandarGeorgiev/E+/Getty Images; **106–107** (spread) Umomos/Shutterstock.com; **104** © Cengage; **108** Keith Gentry/Shutterstock.com; **111** William Perugini/Shutterstock.com; **113** Sergio Azenha/Alamy Stock Photo; **114–115** (spread) Stephen Chung/Alamy Stock Photo; **117** Viacheslav Iakobchuk/Alamy Stock Photo; **119** (tc) PA Images/Alamy Stock Photo, (br) Stephen Barnes/iStock/Getty Images; **120** Silvia Otte/Stone/Getty Images; **122** (bl) Danilovi/iStock Unreleased/Getty Images, (br) AndreasF/Alamy Stock Photo; **123** (bl) Sorin Colac/Alamy Stock Photo, (br) Dutchy/E+/Getty Images; **124** © Cengage; **126–127** (spread) © Joel Sartore/National Geographic Image Collection; **128–129** (spread) Pete Leong/500px Prime/Getty Images; **131** (tr) Ingrid Pakats/Shutterstock.com, (cr) Lee Hudson/Alamy Stock Photo, (b) Crispin la valiente/Moment/Getty Images; **132–133** (spread) Giedrius Stakauskas/Alamy Stock Photo; **134–135** (spread) Dpa Picture Alliance/Alamy Stock Photo; **136–137** (spread) Directphoto Collection/Alamy Stock Photo; **139** Jaromir Chalabala/Shutterstock.com; **141** NurPhoto SRL/Alamy Stock Photo; **142** (tr) Vergani Fotografia/Shutterstock.com, (cl1) Michaeljung/Shutterstock.com, (cl2) Ostill is Franck Camhi/Shutterstock.com, (cr) Julia Zavalishina/Shutterstock.com, (bl) Mauritius Images GmbH/Alamy Stock Photo, (bc) Tom King/Alamy Stock Photo, (br) Zakaz86/iStock/Getty Images; **143** (bl) Tamara Kulikova/Alamy Stock Photo, (bc) Juniors Bildarchiv GmbH/Alamy Stock Photo, (br) Georgeclerk/E+/Getty Images; **144** © Cengage; **146–147** (spread) Directphoto Collection/Alamy Stock Photo; **149** Maskot/Getty Images; **151** (cl) © Michael Melford/National Geographic Image Collection, (cr) The Washington Post/Getty Images, (br) VCG/Visual China Group/Getty Images; **152** Lyndon Stratford/Alamy Stock Photo; **154–155** (spread) Simonkr/E+Getty Images; **156–157** (spread) Lynsey Addario/Getty Images News/Getty Images; **159** Pittawut Junmee/Alamy Stock Photo; **160** (cl) A Room With Views/Alamy Stock Photo, (cr) JuiceBros/E+/Getty Images, (b) Recep-bg/E+/Getty Images; **164** © Cengage; **191** (tl1) Miceking/Shutterstock.com, (tl2) Archivector/Shutterstock.com, (tl3) Flags Stock/Shutterstock.com, (tl4) Loveshop/Shutterstock.com, (tc1) Paul Stringer/Shutterstock.com, (tc2) Fenton/Shutterstock.com, (tc3) Loveshop/Shutterstock.com, (tc4) Alexander Ryabintsev/Shutterstock.com, (tr1) T. Lesia/Shutterstock.com, (tr2) Petch one/Shutterstock.com, (tr3) Matulee/Shutterstock.com, (tr4) Charnsitr/Shutterstock.com, (cl) Sculpies/Shutterstock.com, (c) Rido/Shutterstock.com, (cr) Krakenimages.com/Shutterstock.com, (bl1) Kzenon/Shutterstock.com, (bl2) Poppy Pix/Shutterstock.com, (bc1) Zurijeta/Shutterstock.com, (bc2) New Africa/Shutterstock.com, (br1) Melhijad/Shutterstock.com, (br2) Fizkes/Shutterstock.com; **192** (tl1) Monkey Business Images/Shutterstock.com, (tl2) J.R. Bale/Alamy Stock Photo, (tc1) StratfordProductions/Shutterstock.com, (tc2) Alexey Yudenkov/Shutterstock.com, (tr1) New Africa/Shutterstock.com, (tr2) Lzf/Shutterstock.com, (cl) SeventyFour/Shutterstock.com, (c) Xiao Yu/Shutterstock.com, (cr) LightField Studios/Shutterstock.com, (bl1) Alenacepl/Shutterstock.com, (bl2) Wavebreakmedia/Shutterstock.com, (bc1) Ipatov/Shutterstock.com, (bc2) Photoongraphy/Shutterstock.com, (br1) Suzanne Tucker/Shutterstock.com, (br2) Sergii Kumer/Shutterstock.com; (bl1) PeopleImages.com - Yuri A/

# Acknowledgements

The Outcomes publishing team and authors would like to thank EC English for their collaboration on the new videos in this edition, and all of the students and staff at EC Dublin and EC Brighton who took part in the filming.

The team would also like to thank the following teachers who provided detailed and invaluable feedback on this course.

João Rodrigo Lima Agildo, Colégio São Luis, São Luis; Verliscia Alexander, EC Malta, St Julian's; Patrick Allman, EC Bristol, Bristol; Francesc Martí Aluja, EOI Lleida, Lleida; Jose Luis Piñeira Alvarez, EOI Tolosa, Tolosa; Marcel lí Armengou, EOI Terrassa, Terrassa; Desmond Arnold, EC Cambridge, Cambridge; Holly Bailey, EC Brighton, Brighton; Elisabet Prím Bauzá, EOI Manacor, Manacor; Daniel Beus, Fukuoka Communications Center, Fukuoka; Mónica Salgado Blesa, EOI Palma, Palma de Mallorca; Frederik Bolz, University of Bochum, Bochum; Malachy Caldicott; EC Oxford, Oxford; Elisa Roca Burns, EOI Palma, Palma de Mallorca; Eva Cantuerk, University of Bochum, Bochum; Ana Belén Gracia Castejón, EOI Palma, Palma de Mallorca; Ana María Serra Comas, EOI Palma, Palma de Mallorca; Michael Crowe, EC Dublin, Dublin; Rebekah Currer-Burgess, EC Bristol, Bristol; Luca de Santis, EC Dublin, Dublin; Hilary Donraadt, EC Dublin, Dublin; Julia Drzechovskaja, EC Dublin, Dublin; Jordan Duggie, EC Brighton, Brighton; Rachel Fenech, EC Malta, St Julian's; Armando Fernández, EOI Palma, Palma de Mallorca; Fabiana Fonseca, Associação Brasil América, Recife; Bruno Franco, Luzianna Lanna, Belo Horizonte; Natalia Fritsler, University of Bochum, Bochum; Lukas Galea, EC Malta, St. Julian's; Antonio Berbel Garcia, EOI Almeria, Almeria; Maria dels Angels Grimalt, EOI Palma, Palma de Mallorca; Honorata Grodzinska, Future, Gorzów; Abigail Hackney, IH Manchester, Manchester; Alicky Hess, EC Dublin, Dublin; Silvia Milian Hita, EOI Prat, El Prat de Llobregat; Richard Hill; EC Cape Town, Cape Town; Roxana Irimieia, BBE Languages, Bogotá; Bronia Jacobs, EC Cape Town, Cape Town; Natalia Jakubczyk-Gajewska, Warsaw University of Life Sciences (SGGW), Warsaw; Georgine Kalil, Berlin; Jameelah Keane, EC Manchester, Manchester; Shelly Keen, EC Bristol, Bristol; Dariusz Ketla, Warsaw University of Life Sciences (SGGW), Warsaw; Gabriela Krajewska, University of Wrocław, Wrocław; Peter Kunzler, Gymnasium Kirchenfild, Bern; Juana Larena-Avellaneda, EOI Telde, Telde; Isabelle Le Gal-Maier, VHS Rottweil, Rottweil; Angela Lloyd, Polytech Brandenburg/Havel, Brandenburg an der Havel; Kenya Lopes, Luzianna Lanna, Belo Horizonte; Sandra López, EOI Palma, Palma de Mallorca; Lucía Marotta, EC Dublin, Dublin; Francesca Mesquida, EOI Manacor, Manacor; Nico Moramarco, EOI Santander, Santander; Sian Morrey, University of Sheffield, Sheffield; Vinicius Nobre, Toronto; Sue Nurse, University of Sheffield, Sheffield; Giuseppe Picone, Milan City Council, Milan; Maria Eugenia Perez Primicia, EOI Palma, Palma de Mallorca; Piotr Przywara, Warsaw University of Life Sciences (SGGW), Warsaw; Manlio Reina, EC Dublin, Dublin; Laura Rota i Roca, EOI Sabadell, Sabadell; Salvador Faura Sabe, EOI Sabadell, Sabadell; Justin Sales, Edinburgh College, Edinburgh; Paloma Seoane Sanchez, EOI Laredo, Laredo; Aïda Santamaria, EOI Palma, Palma de Mallorca; Sean Scurfield, EOI Santander, Santander; Pilar Riera Serra, EOI Palma, Palma de Mallorca;Tetiana Shyian, University of Bochum, Bochum; Vinicius Silva, Colégio Bandeirantes, São Paulo; Anna Soltyska, University of Bochum, Bochum; Glenn Standish, IH Torun, Torun; Andreas Tano, Makarios Christian School, Jakarta; Tran Thi Thu Giang, TEG international Education Centre, Hanoi; Sam Verdoodt, EC Malta, St Julian's; Aline Vianna, Colégio Humboldt, São Paulo; Rachael Worrall, IH Manchester, Manchester; Mehmet Yildiz, Bezmialem Vakif University, Istanbul

## Authors' acknowledgements

Thanks to Alison Sharpe, Clare Shaw, Nicole Elliott, Rachael Gibbon and Laura Brant for their meticulous reading of our work and to all at National Geographic Learning for the continued support and enthusiasm.

Thanks also to all the students we've taught over the years for providing more inspiration and insight than they ever realised. And to the colleagues we've taught alongside for their friendship, thoughts and assistance.